# First World War
## and Army of Occupation
# War Diary
## France, Belgium and Germany

66 DIVISION
198 Infantry Brigade
Lancashire Fusiliers
6th Battalion
2 March 1918 - 30 April 1919

WO95/3140/3

The Naval & Military Press Ltd
www.nmarchive.com
**Published in association with The National Archives**

Published by

The Naval & Military Press Ltd

Unit 10 Ridgewood Industrial Park,

Uckfield, East Sussex,

TN22 5QE England

Tel: +44 (0) 1825 749494

www.naval-military-press.com

www.nmarchive.com

*This diary has been reprinted in facsimile from the original. Any imperfections are inevitably reproduced and the quality may fall short of modern type and cartographic standards.*

# Contents

| Document type | Place/Title | Date From | Date To |
|---|---|---|---|
| Heading | WO95/3140/3 | | |
| Heading | 66th Division 198th Infy Bde 6th Bn Lancs Fus Mar 1918 To Apr 1919 From 42 Div 125 Bde. | | |
| Heading | 197th Brigade 66th Division 6th Battalion Lancashire Fusiliers March 1918 | | |
| Heading | War Diary of the 6th Battalion Lancashire Fusiliers Volume XIV | | |
| War Diary | Templeux-Le-Guerard (Map France 62.c 1/4000) | 02/03/1918 | 22/03/1918 |
| War Diary | Perohme (France) 62 C 1/40,000 | 22/03/1918 | 30/03/1918 |
| War Diary | Longeau (France) Sheet 62 D 1/40.000 | 30/03/1918 | 31/03/1918 |
| Miscellaneous | Strength Of Battalion At Beginning Of Month | | |
| Operation(al) Order(s) | Battalion Operations Order No.96 | | |
| Miscellaneous | Amendment No.1 To Operation Order No. 98 | | |
| Operation(al) Order(s) | Battalion Operation Order No.98 | 14/03/1918 | 14/03/1918 |
| War Diary | Seux | 01/04/1918 | 03/04/1918 |
| War Diary | Vachelles | 04/04/1918 | 04/04/1918 |
| War Diary | Les Quesnoy | 04/04/1918 | 04/04/1918 |
| War Diary | Buigny St Maclou | 05/04/1918 | 07/04/1918 |
| War Diary | Le Festel | 08/04/1918 | 13/04/1918 |
| War Diary | Ailly Le Haut Clocher | 14/04/1918 | 15/04/1918 |
| War Diary | L'Hedre | 16/04/1918 | 22/04/1918 |
| War Diary | Longuenesse | 23/04/1918 | 26/04/1918 |
| War Diary | Belle | 27/04/1918 | 30/04/1918 |
| Heading | War Diary of 6th Battalion The Lancashire Fusiliers. From 1st May 1918 To 31st May 1918 (Volume 13) | | |
| War Diary | Belle | 01/05/1918 | 02/05/1918 |
| War Diary | Lancheres | 03/05/1918 | 09/05/1918 |
| War Diary | Bourseville | 10/05/1918 | 22/05/1918 |
| War Diary | Woignarue | 23/05/1918 | 23/05/1918 |
| War Diary | Woignarue & Onival | 24/05/1918 | 31/05/1918 |
| Miscellaneous | The Following Reinforcements Arrived During The Month | | |
| Heading | War Diary of 6th Battalion The Lancashire Fusiliers From 1st June 1918 To 30th June 1918 (Volume 16) | | |
| War Diary | Woignarue | 01/06/1918 | 01/06/1918 |
| War Diary | Montieres | 02/06/1918 | 07/06/1918 |
| War Diary | Canchy | 08/06/1918 | 18/06/1918 |
| War Diary | St Blimont | 19/06/1918 | 21/06/1918 |
| War Diary | Buigny St Maclou | 22/06/1918 | 22/06/1918 |
| War Diary | Beaudricourt | 23/06/1918 | 30/06/1918 |
| Heading | War Diary of 6th Battalion Lancashire Fusiliers. From 1st July 1918 To 31st July 1918. Volume 17. | | |
| War Diary | Beaudricourt | 01/07/1918 | 03/07/1918 |
| War Diary | Sus-St-Leger | 04/07/1918 | 21/07/1918 |
| War Diary | Candas | 22/07/1918 | 22/07/1918 |
| War Diary | Haudricourt | 23/07/1918 | 31/07/1918 |
| Heading | War Diary of 6th Bn Lancashire Fusiliers From 1-8-18 To 31-8-18 (Volume 1) | | |
| War Diary | Haudricourt | 01/08/1918 | 31/08/1918 |

| | | | |
|---|---|---|---|
| Heading | War Diary of 6th Bn Lancashire Fusiliers From 1-9-18 To 30-9-18 Volume 2 | | |
| War Diary | Haudricourt | 01/09/1918 | 20/09/1918 |
| War Diary | Manin | 21/09/1918 | 22/09/1918 |
| War Diary | Lignereuil | 22/09/1918 | 28/09/1918 |
| War Diary | Corbie | 29/09/1918 | 29/09/1918 |
| War Diary | Harbonniers | 29/09/1918 | 30/09/1918 |
| Miscellaneous | 6th Bn Lancashire Fusiliers | 07/09/1918 | 07/09/1918 |
| Miscellaneous | Training | 01/09/1918 | 01/09/1918 |
| Miscellaneous | Notes on Traning | 03/09/1918 | 03/09/1918 |
| Miscellaneous | Demonstration In The Value Of Controlled As Against Uncontrolled Fire | 01/09/1918 | 01/09/1918 |
| Miscellaneous | Military Secretary to Commander in Chief G.H.Q | 26/08/1918 | 26/08/1918 |
| Miscellaneous | 6th Bn Lancashire Fusiliers | 14/09/1918 | 14/09/1918 |
| Miscellaneous | 6th Bn Lancashire Fusiliers. Notes On Training | | |
| Miscellaneous | Field Firing Practices | | |
| Miscellaneous | 6th Bn Lancashire Fusiliers. Programme of Training | 21/09/1918 | 21/09/1918 |
| Miscellaneous | 6th Lancashire Fusiliers Notes On Training | 15/09/1918 | 15/09/1918 |
| Operation(al) Order(s) | 6th Lancashire Fusiliers Order No.16 | 19/09/1918 | 19/09/1918 |
| Miscellaneous | 6th Bn Lancashire Fusiliers Training Programme | 28/09/1918 | 28/09/1918 |
| Operation(al) Order(s) | 6th Lancashire Fusiliers Order No.18 | 27/09/1918 | 27/09/1918 |
| Operation(al) Order(s) | 6th Lancashire Fusiliers Order No.19 | 29/09/1918 | 29/09/1918 |
| Heading | War Diary of 6th Bn. Lancashire Fusiliers From 1st Oct 1918 To 31st Oct 1918 (Volume 4) | | |
| Miscellaneous | Duplicate | | |
| War Diary | Cappy | 01/10/1918 | 01/10/1918 |
| War Diary | Mountaban | 02/10/1918 | 04/10/1918 |
| War Diary | Moulians | 05/10/1918 | 05/10/1918 |
| War Diary | St Emilie | 05/10/1918 | 07/10/1918 |
| War Diary | Le Catelet | 07/10/1918 | 07/10/1918 |
| War Diary | On The Move | 08/10/1918 | 13/10/1918 |
| War Diary | Maretz | 14/10/1918 | 16/10/1918 |
| War Diary | Reumont | 16/10/1918 | 16/10/1918 |
| War Diary | On The Move | 17/10/1918 | 21/10/1918 |
| War Diary | Premont | 22/10/1918 | 31/10/1918 |
| Operation(al) Order(s) | 6th Lancashire Fusiliers Order No.21 | 02/10/1918 | 02/10/1918 |
| Miscellaneous | 6th Lancashire Fusiliers Amend Order No.21 | 02/10/1918 | 02/10/1918 |
| Operation(al) Order(s) | 6th Lancashire Fusilier Order No.20 | 01/10/1918 | 01/10/1918 |
| Miscellaneous | 6th Lancs Fus | 21/10/1918 | 21/10/1918 |
| Miscellaneous | Special Order Appendix X | 24/10/1918 | 24/10/1918 |
| Miscellaneous | 6th Lancashire Fusiliers Operation Order | 13/10/1918 | 13/10/1918 |
| Miscellaneous | 198th Inf Bde No. B.M.239 | 11/10/1918 | 11/10/1918 |
| Miscellaneous | All Companies 6th Lancs Fus | 16/10/1918 | 16/10/1918 |
| Miscellaneous | Appendix VI | 19/10/1918 | 19/10/1918 |
| Miscellaneous | Appendix VII | 20/10/1918 | 20/10/1918 |
| Miscellaneous | Appendix VIII | 21/10/1918 | 21/10/1918 |
| Miscellaneous | Amendment To Movement Order Ref L.O 719 | 21/10/1918 | 21/10/1918 |
| Miscellaneous | Appendix XII | 27/10/1918 | 27/10/1918 |
| Miscellaneous | Account of Operations | | |
| Miscellaneous | The Advance To The Red Line | 18/10/1918 | 18/10/1918 |
| Miscellaneous | Part VI | 20/10/1918 | 20/10/1918 |
| Miscellaneous | 198th Infantry Brigade Report On Operations | 12/10/1918 | 12/10/1918 |
| Miscellaneous | Part II | 09/10/1918 | 09/10/1918 |
| Miscellaneous | Part III | 11/10/1918 | 11/10/1918 |
| Miscellaneous | 198th Infantry Brigade | | |
| Map | Map | | |

| | | | |
|---|---|---|---|
| Map | Map "D" | | |
| Heading | War Diary of 6th Bn Lancashire Fusiliers From 1st Nov 1918 To 30 Nov 1918 (Volume 5) | | |
| War Diary | Premont | 01/11/1918 | 01/11/1918 |
| War Diary | On The Move | 02/11/1918 | 10/11/1918 |
| War Diary | St Hilaire Sur-Helpe | 11/11/1918 | 11/11/1918 |
| War Diary | On The Move | 12/11/1918 | 12/11/1918 |
| War Diary | Beugnies | 12/11/1918 | 14/11/1918 |
| War Diary | Sars Poteries | 15/11/1918 | 15/11/1918 |
| War Diary | On The Move | 16/11/1918 | 17/11/1918 |
| War Diary | Rance | 18/11/1918 | 18/11/1918 |
| War Diary | On The Move | 19/11/1918 | 19/11/1918 |
| War Diary | Jamagne | 20/11/1918 | 22/11/1918 |
| War Diary | Morville | 23/11/1918 | 23/11/1918 |
| War Diary | On The Move | 24/11/1918 | 24/11/1918 |
| War Diary | Neffe | 25/11/1918 | 30/11/1918 |
| Operation(al) Order(s) | 6th Lancashire Fusiliers Order No.22 | 01/11/1918 | 01/11/1918 |
| Operation(al) Order(s) | 6th Lancashire Fusiliers Order No.23 | 02/11/1918 | 02/11/1918 |
| Operation(al) Order(s) | 6th Lanc Fusiliers Order No.24 | 04/11/1918 | 04/11/1918 |
| Operation(al) Order(s) | 6th Lanc Fusiliers Order No.25 | 05/11/1918 | 05/11/1918 |
| Operation(al) Order(s) | Lancashire Fusiliers Order No 26 | | |
| Miscellaneous | Battalion Report | 08/11/1918 | 08/11/1918 |
| Operation(al) Order(s) | 6th Lancashire Fusiliers Order 27 | 10/11/1918 | 10/11/1918 |
| Miscellaneous | Appendix VIII | 11/11/1918 | 11/11/1918 |
| Operation(al) Order(s) | 6th Lancs Fus Order No.28 | 12/11/1918 | 12/11/1918 |
| Miscellaneous | Appendix IX | 13/11/1918 | 13/11/1918 |
| Operation(al) Order(s) | 6th Lan Fusiliers Order No.29 | | |
| Miscellaneous | Special Orders By Lieut-General Sir T.L.N. Morland K.C.B. K.C.M.G D.S.O. Commanding XIII Corps | 14/11/1918 | 14/11/1918 |
| Operation(al) Order(s) | 6th Lan Fusiliers Order No.30 | 17/11/1918 | 17/11/1918 |
| Miscellaneous | Appendix XIII | 11/10/1918 | 11/10/1918 |
| Miscellaneous | Special Order Appendix XVII | 17/11/1918 | 17/11/1918 |
| Operation(al) Order(s) | 6th Lancashire Fusiliers Order No.31 | 18/11/1918 | 18/11/1918 |
| Operation(al) Order(s) | 6th Lancashire Fusiliers Order No.32 | 22/11/1918 | 22/11/1918 |
| Operation(al) Order(s) | 6th Bn Lancashire Fusiliers Order No.33 | 23/11/1918 | 23/11/1918 |
| Miscellaneous | Account of Operations | | |
| Miscellaneous | Part VII Reference Map Sheet 57A 1/40,000 | 11/11/1918 | 11/11/1918 |
| Miscellaneous | Total Captures 1st Nov-11th Nov 1918 | 11/11/1918 | 11/11/1918 |
| Heading | War Diary of 6th Lancashire Fusiliers Volume VI From 1-12-18 To 31-12-18 | | |
| War Diary | Neffe | 01/12/1918 | 14/12/1918 |
| War Diary | On The Move | 15/12/1918 | 31/12/1918 |
| Operation(al) Order(s) | 6th Lancashire Fusiliers Order No.34 | 13/12/1918 | 13/12/1918 |
| Operation(al) Order(s) | 6th Lancs Fusiliers Order No.35 | 15/12/1918 | 15/12/1918 |
| Miscellaneous | 6th Lancashire Fusiliers Administrative Instruction No.1 | 13/12/1918 | 13/12/1918 |
| Miscellaneous | On | 01/01/1919 | 31/01/1919 |
| Heading | 6th Lancashire Fusiliers War Diary February 1919 | | |
| War Diary | On | 01/02/1919 | 28/02/1919 |
| Miscellaneous | 66th Divn No. 8722/A | 09/02/1919 | 09/02/1919 |
| Miscellaneous | Madame La Directrice De l'Ecole des Reliegieuses on | | |
| Miscellaneous | History of Regimental Flag 6th (T.) Bn. Lancashire Fusiliers | | |
| Miscellaneous | Duty Order | | |
| Miscellaneous | Duties Of A Conducting Officer | | |
| Heading | War Diary 6th Bn Lancas Fusiliers From 1st March 1919 To 31st March 1919 | | |

| War Diary | On | 01/03/1919 | 04/03/1919 |
|---|---|---|---|
| War Diary | Fays | 05/03/1919 | 31/03/1919 |
| Heading | War Diary 6th Lancs Fusiliers From 1st April 1919 To 30th April 1919 | | |
| War Diary | Fays Belgium | 01/04/1919 | 30/04/1919 |

66TH DIVISION
198TH INFY BDE

6TH BN LANCS FUS.

~~JULY 1918~~ - APR 1919
MAR 1918 TO

FROM 42 DIV
125 Bde

---

ABSORBED 12 BN 1918 JULY

---

197th Brigade.
66th Division.

------------

6th BATTALION

LANCASHIRE FUSILIERS

MARCH 1918

Instructions regarding War Diaries and Intelligence Summaries are contained in F. S. Regs., Part II. and the Staff Manual respectively. Title pages will be prepared in manuscript.

# WAR DIARY
*or*
# INTELLIGENCE SUMMARY.
*(Erase heading not required.)*

Army Form C. 2118.



| Hour, Date, Place | Summary of Events and Information | Remarks and references to Appendices |
|---|---|---|
| | Confidential<br>War Diary<br>of the<br>6th Battalion<br>Lancashire Fusiliers.<br><br>Volume XIV<br><br>197/66 | Vol 14<br>March 18 |

S. P. Pollitt. Major
Commanding 6th Bn. Lancashire Fusiliers

Instructions regarding War Diaries and Intelligence Summaries are contained in F. S. Regs., Part II. and the Staff Manual respectively. Title pages will be prepared in manuscript.

# WAR DIARY ~~or INTELLIGENCE SUMMARY.~~

(*Erase heading not required.*)

6TH BATT LANCASHIRE FUSILIERS.

Army Form C. 2118.

W. H.

| Place | Date | Hour | Summary of Events and Information | Remarks and references to Appendices |
|---|---|---|---|---|
| | 1918 | | | |
| TEMPLEUX | March | | On the 1st the Batt. left VILLERS-CARBONNEL and proceeded by march route | |
| -le-Guérard | 2nd | | to BERNES (Q4d52) and went into huts for the night, leaving early next | |
| (Map FRANCE) | | | morning for TEMPLEUX QUARRIES (L3 central) here relieving the 9th Batt. | |
| 62c | | | ROYAL SUSSEX REGT. (73rd Bde 24th Division) - Major BANHAM a/commanding | |
| 1/40 000 | | | The Brigade had 2/7th Lan Fus holding the Front Line consisting of | |
| | | | several posts and strong points. The 6th Lan Fus: in Support having | |
| | | | 'A' Coy holding 3 posts. 'B' & 'C' Coys in the Quarries in tunnels with | |
| | | | trenches wired and dug ready to be held in front of the Quarries | |
| | | | and 'D' Coy back at ROISEL (K16 central). The 2/8th Lan Fus were | |
| | | | in Reserve also in ROISEL. | |
| | 6th | | TEMPLEUX QUARRIES and immediate surroundings heavily | |
| | | | shelled from 1-0pm to 6-0pm with 5.9 guns. Approx: 300 | |
| | | | shells. Casualties 4 slightly wounded. | |
| | 8th | | Relieved 2/7th Lan. Fus in the front line 3 Coys 'A' 'B' & 'C' holding | |
| | | | the front line posts. 'D' Coy being in support. [illegible] Appendix No. 0 attached | No. 0 |
| | 10th | | At 5-30 a.m (Summer time) a party of 1 Off. and 25 O.R. from the 2/7 Lan Fus: | |

D. D. & L., London, E.C.
(A7883) Wt W809-M1672 350,000 4/17 Sch 52a Forms/C/2118/14

Instructions regarding War Diaries and Intelligence Summaries are contained in F. S. Regs., Part II. and the Staff Manual respectively. Title pages will be prepared in manuscript.

# WAR DIARY of 6TH BATTN LANCASHIRE FUSRS
or
INTELLIGENCE SUMMARY.

(Erase heading not required.)

W.D. Army Form C. 2118.

| Place | Date | Hour | Summary of Events and Information | Remarks and references to Appendices |
|---|---|---|---|---|
| TEMPLEUX | March | | raided the German line on the sector front. Two prisoners | |
| le-Gerard | 10th | | were taken. Our casualties were nil. Lt Col BUNBURY | |
| (FRANCE) | | | having gone to hospital - sick Major T J BIDDOLPH 2/8th | |
| 62c | | | LAN: FUS. took over the temporary Command of the Battalion. | |
| 1/40 000 | | | on the 8th of March. Capt F.A.H. BEALEY also on this day | |
| | | | reported for duty from the Divl Reinforcement Wing, where he | |
| | | | had been in command with the temporary rank of Major. | |
| | 14th | | Wire received from Brigade of an impending German attack the | |
| | | | Battn manned battle positions from 12.45 am. to 6-30 am. No | |
| | | | enemy attack took place. Battn was relieved by the 2/7th | |
| | 15th | | LAN: FUS. as attached Appendix marked No 1 and attached | No 1 |
| | 16th | | At 7-0 am the Battalion "stood to" on receiving the warning | |
| | | | order "Prepare to Attack". Normal Conditions were resumed | |
| | | | at 8-10 am. Battalion finding working parties | |
| | 17th | | Battn in reserve at ROISEL working parties found | |
| | 18th | | Battn in reserve at ROISEL working parties found Capt J. L. LEE M.C. reported from Course of instruction | |
| | | | 2nd Army Central School WISQUES | |

D. D. & L., London, E.C. (A7283) Wt W809/M1672 50,000 4/17 Sch 52a Forms/C/2118/14

Instructions regarding War Diaries and Intelligence Summaries are contained in F. S. Regs., Part II. and the Staff Manual respectively. Title pages will be prepared in manuscript.

# WAR DIARY ~~or INTELLIGENCE SUMMARY.~~ of 6TH BATTN LANCASHIRE FUSLRS

(Erase heading not required.)

Army Form C. 2118.

| Place | Date | Hour | Summary of Events and Information | Remarks and references to Appendices |
|---|---|---|---|---|
| TEMPLEUX | MARCH | | Battn in reserve at ROISEL working parties found | |
| le Gerrard | 19th | | | |
| (FRANCE) | 20th | | Battn in reserve at ROISEL working parties found Lt. a/CAPT. BARKER J. S reported from | |
| 62C | | | Course of Instruction 1st ARMY SCHOOL - LIEUT V. H. LEVI reported from XI Corps School | |
| 1/40.000 | | | where he had been acting as instructor LIEUT. E ORMEROD returned from Hospital | |
| | | | CAPT. C. H. POTTER M.C. evacuated to Field Ambulance | |
| | | P.M. 10.0 | Order received to 'Stand by' ready to move to battle positions at 10 minutes notice | |
| | 21st | ~~P.M.~~ 4.0 A.M. | Order received to move to positions in 'BROWN LINE' battle positions from L.1 central | |
| | | | to L.1.d 0.5 were manned by 6 0 A.M. The Battn being heavily shelled whilst | |
| | | | getting into position with H.E and Gas - weather fine but thick mist. | |
| | | 10.0 A.M. ~~[illegible]~~ | (approx) Information received that enemy had attacked the Front Line ~~about 11 0 A.M.~~ | |
| | | 11.0 A.M. | (approx) Enemy reported in TEMPLEUX le Gerrard - Order received to counter attack | |
| | | | Counter attack launched by A and D Coys under MAJOR WIKE which cleared | |
| | | | the village but was subsequently forced to retire onto the Sunken Road L.2.c 0.9 | |
| | | | to L. 2. c central | |
| | 22nd | 2.0 A.M. | Verbal instructions received from BDE to hold on to this position and only retire fighting | |

D. D. & L., London, E.C. (A7883) Wt W809/M1672 750,000 4/17 Sch 52a Forms/C/2118/14

Instructions regarding War Diaries and Intelligence Summaries are contained in F. S. Regs., Part II, and the Staff Manual respectively. Title pages will be prepared in manuscript.

# WAR DIARY ~~or~~ of 6TH BATT^LN^
# ~~INTELLIGENCE SUMMARY.~~ LANCASHIRE - FUS^LRS^

(Erase heading not required.)

Army Form C. 2118.

| Place | Date | Hour | Summary of Events and Information | Remarks and references to Appendices |
|---|---|---|---|---|
| TEMPLEUX le Gerrard | MARCH 22nd | | Under orders from Batt^ln^ H.Q. (BROWN LINE) MAJOR WIKE left Sunken road and | |
| FRANCE 62c | | | returned to Batt^ln^ H.Q leaving A and D Coys in charge of Lt/Col NORTON. D.S.O | |
| 1/40,000 | | | O.C TEMPLEUX defences who with his force had retired into that position | |
| | | | After about one hours heavy shelling the enemy attacked about dawn overwhelmed | |
| | | | the Sunken road position and penetrated the 'BROWN LINE' and surrounded | |
| | | | and captured Batt^ln^ H.Q only two officers Capt DINGLEY. R.A.M.C. | |
| | | | and 2/Lt SUTHERLAND Assistant Adj^t^ succeeding in escaping | |
| | | | 2/Lt SUTHERLAND collected stragglers and formed a defensive post about | |
| | | | 70 yards behind the 'BROWN LINE' where he was killed shortly afterwards | |
| | | | The Batt^ln^ then fell back upon a defensive line held by a dismounted | |
| | | | Cavalry Regiment EAST of ROISEL. — The Batt^ln^ then fell back fighting | |
| | | | in isolated parties through the 50th DIV who were holding the 'GREEN LINE' | |
| | | | to a point near CARTIGNY where they re-organised under Lt. a/CAPT. | |
| | | | BARKER | |
| | | 8.0 P.M | Orders received ~~from the~~ for the Batt^ln^ to march through DOINGT. and through | |
| | | | PERONNE to a point O.3.c.3.6 and orders were there received to | |

D. D. & L., London, E.C. (A7883) Wt W809/M1672 50,000 3/17 Sch 52a Forms/C/2118/14

Instructions regarding War Diaries and Intelligence Summaries are contained in F. S. Regs., Part II. and the Staff Manual respectively. Title pages will be prepared in manuscript.

# WAR DIARY or ~~INTELLIGENCE SUMMARY.~~

(Erase heading not required.)

6TH BATTN LANCASHIRE FUSLRS

Army Form C. 2118.

| Place | Date | Hour | Summary of Events and Information | Remarks and references to Appendices |
|---|---|---|---|---|
| PERONNE | MARCH | | place 3 posts on the WEST bank of the SOMME and to cover a front | |
| (FRANCE) | 22ND | | roughly from O.36 c.0.6 to and including the Railway bridge at I.33.a.6.2 | |
| 62 C | | | This position was taken up by midnight | 6th Lancashire Fusiliers<br>War Diary 24th March 1918<br>In column for date opposite 3rd line from bottom insert "25th"<br>In same column at top of next page for "24th" read "25th".<br>H.M. Davies<br>14.10.26. |
| 1/40,000 | 23RD | 10.0 AM | (approx) Information received that enemy were advancing on PER[ONNE] the bridges over the river would be blown up by noon. | |
| | | 4.0 PM | (approx) Orders received from O.C. Bde in Reserve to send [one Coy] (C. Coy) to reinforce the 2/5th Battn MANCHESTER REG[T] flank | |
| | 24TH | | This position was held for 24 hours under heavy Shell and M.[G fire during] which time repeated efforts made by the enemy to cross the [river were] repulsed — During this period also a wooden bridge o[ver the river] which had been partially destroyed by the R. Es. was soaked and burnt by the Battn | |
| X | X | | Somewhere between 4 and 5 P.M. the Battn on our left was [driven from its] ground enabling the enemy to turn our position — The Battn thereupon (under very heavy Artillery and M.G fire fought its way back for a distance of | |

D. D. & L., London, E.C. (A7883) Wt W309/M1672 50,000 4/17 Sch 52a Forms/C/2118/14

Instructions regarding War Diaries and Intelligence Summaries are contained in F. S. Regs., Part II. and the Staff Manual respectively. Title pages will be prepared in manuscript.

# WAR DIARY or ~~INTELLIGENCE SUMMARY.~~

(Erase heading not required.)

6th BATTn LANCASHIRE FUSrs

Army Form C. 2118.

| Place | Date | Hour | Summary of Events and Information | Remarks and references to Appendices |
|---|---|---|---|---|
| PERONNE (FRANCE) 62 C | MARCH 22nd | | place 3 posts on the WEST bank of the SOMME and to cover a front roughly from O.36.c.6. to and including the Railway bridge at I.33.a.6.2 This position was taken up by midnight | |
| 1/40,000 | 23rd | 10.0 AM | (approx) Information received that enemy were advancing on PERONNE and that the bridges over the river would be blown up by noon. | |
| | | 4.0 PM | (approx) Orders received from O.C Bde in Reserve to send the Battn reserve (C. Coy) to reinforce the 2/5th Battn MANCHESTER REGT on our left flank | |
| | 24th | | This position was held for 24 hours under heavy shell and M.G fire during which time repeated efforts made by the enemy to cross the river were repulsed — During this period also a wooden bridge over the river which had been partially destroyed by the R. Es. was soaked in petrol and burnt by the Battn | |
| X | X | | Somewhere between 4 and 5 P.M. the Battn on our left was obliged to give ground enabling the enemy to turn our position — The Battn thereupon (under very heavy Artillery and M.G fire fought its way back for a distance of | |

D. D. & L., London, E.C. (A7853) Wt W809/M1672 350,000 4/17 Sch 52a Forms/C/2118/14

Instructions regarding War Diaries and Intelligence Summaries are contained in F. S. Regs., Part II. and the Staff Manual respectively. Title pages will be prepared in manuscript.

Army Form C. 2118.

# WAR DIARY ~~or~~ ~~INTELLIGENCE SUMMARY.~~ of 6TH BATTN LANCASHIRE - FUSLRS

(Erase heading not required.)

| Place | Date | Hour | Summary of Events and Information | Remarks and references to Appendices |
|---|---|---|---|---|
| PERONNE (FRANCE) 62 C 1/40,000 | MARCH 24th | | about a mile to a position held by troops of 50TH DIV. which was reached about dusk | |
| | | | From this time onward owing to its very heavy Casualties (all officers except two and 60 per cent of O.R) the Battn ceased to exist as a separate unit. | |
| | | | On the evening of this day. 2/Lt (a/Capt) D GRAY 2/LT A DOWSON 2/LT J H ROBINSON 2/LT D.R McKAY rejoined the unit from 66TH DIVL WING REINFORCEMENT CAMP from Course of Instruction | |
| | 25th to 30th | | During this period Small parties of the Battalion with similar Small parties from the 2 other Battns in the BDE fought a Continuous rear guard action under orders from the G.O.C BDE | |
| | | | On March 26th CAPT C.H POTTER M.C who had reported from hospital 2/LT F HEYDON who reported with draft from ENGLAND 2/LT J.B McCABE and 2/LT C.H VIMET who had reported from Courses of Instruction ~~[illegible]~~ to 66TH DIVL WING REINFORCEMENT CAMP proceeded up the line | |
| LONGUEAU (FRANCE) Sheet 62 D 1/40,000 | | | 2/LT. SNOWDON B. reported to transport lines at BOVES on return from leave and proceeded up to the line | |
| | | | On night 30/31st Orders were received that the Division was to be relieved and all parties to collect at LONGUEAU M. 28 C | |

D. D. & L., London, E.C. (A7839) Wt W809/M1672 350,000 4/17 Sch 52a Forms/C/2118/12

Army Form C. 2118.

Instructions regarding War Diaries and Intelligence Summaries are contained in F. S. Regs., Part II, and the Staff Manual respectively. Title pages will be prepared in manuscript.

# WAR DIARY ~~or~~ ~~INTELLIGENCE~~ SUMMARY. of 6TH BATTN LANCASHIRE FUSRS

(Erase heading not required.)

| Place | Date | Hour | Summary of Events and Information | Remarks and references to Appendices |
|---|---|---|---|---|
| LONGUEAU | MARCH | | Battn collected at LONGUEAU and on roll call was found to number | |
| (FRANCE) | 31st | | 1 officer and 80 O.R. | |
| Sheet 62D | | | Orders were received to march to SEUX on the following day | |
| 1/40,000 | | | | |

D. D. & L., London, E.C.
(A7853) Wt W809/M1672 350,000 4/17 Sch 52a Forms/C/2118/14

Instructions regarding War Diaries and Intelligence Summaries are contained in F. S. Regs., Part II. and the Staff Manual respectively. Title pages will be prepared in manuscript.

# WAR DIARY
or
~~INTELLIGENCE SUMMARY.~~
(Erase heading not required.)

6th Battalion. Lancashire Fusiliers

Army Form C. 2118.

| Hour, Date, Place | Summary of Events and Information | Remarks and references to Appendices |
|---|---|---|
| Strength of Battalion at | beginning of month - 52 Officers | 961 Other Ranks. |
| -do- | -do- end of month - 12 -do- | 363 -do- -do- |
| Reinforcements during month:— | | |
| Officers:— Nil. | | |
| Other Ranks:— | 144. | |
| Casualties:— Officers— | | |

Major (A/Lt-Col) C H de St. F. Bunbury (A.P.W.O. Yorks. Regt) to U.K. Sick 16. 3. 18.
Capt (A/Lt. Col) E. S. Hurlbatt M.C. (7th Manchester Regt) Killed in Action 27. 3. 18.

Major W. Wike (5th Lan. Fus) missing 21. 3. 18
Capt F A H Bealey. Wounded & Missing 21. 3. 18
Capt L M Robinson M.C. Missing 21. 3. 18
Capt F Chesnutt-Chesney Wounded 30. 3. 18
Capt J. L. Lee M.C. Wounded & Missing 21. 3. 18
Capt H C Gill. Wounded 21. 3. 18
Lieut (A/Capt) J. R. Cameron. Killed in Action 21. 3. 18
2/Lt (A/Capt) D. Gray (22nd London Regt) wounded 27. 3. 18
Lt (A/Capt) J. S. Barker Wounded 27 3 18
Lt C. Gray (6th Lan. Fus) Missing 21 3 18
Lt W. H Prince Wounded 21 3 18
Lt V N Lee (1st Royal Fus) Wounded 21 3 18
Lt C W Morrow Wounded 21 3 18
2/Lt F Haydon Wounded 27 3 18
2/Lt H Hewitt ~~[illegible]~~ (8th Lan. Fus) Missing 21. 3. 18

2/Lt E Bowden Wounded 27. 3 18
2/Lt J B Garside (4th Lan. Fus) Wounded 21 3 18
2/Lt J W Clough to U.K. Sick 1. 3 18
2/Lt E Mead Wounded 28 3 18
2/Lt R Truesdale Wounded 21 3 18
2/Lt V. B. Delaney Missing 21 3 18
2/Lt D R Mackay. Missing 27 3 18
2/Lt J Sutherland Killed in action 21 3 18
2/Lt A. Dowson Wounded 28 3 18
2/Lt C H Vines Missing 27 3 18
2/Lt A L Clarke (3rd Res. Lan. Fus) Wounded 27 3 18
2/Lt T P Miller (1st & 2nd Lan. Fus) Killed in Action 28 3 18
2/Lt A Wilson Wounded & Missing 27 3 18
2/Lt J B McCabe Missing 28 3 18

(73989) W4141—463. 400,000. 9/14. H.&J.Ltd. Forms/C. 2118/10.

Instructions regarding War Diaries and Intelligence Summaries are contained in F. S. Regs., Part II. and the Staff Manual respectively. Title pages will be prepared in manuscript.

# WAR DIARY
*or*
~~INTELLIGENCE SUMMARY.~~
*(Erase heading not required.)*

6th Battalion Lancashire Fusiliers

Army Form C. 2118.

| Hour, Date, Place | Summary of Events and Information | | Remarks and references to Appendices |
|---|---|---|---|
| | Casualties. Officers:- (Continued) | | |
| | 2/Lt A. F. Stoker wounded | 25. 3. 18. | |
| | 2/Lt H T Smith missing | 21. 3. 18. | |
| | 2/Lt J D A Bell missing | 21. 3. 18. | |
| | 2/Lt A. Inglis wounded | 21. 3. 18. | |
| | 2/Lt C R Curtis (1st & 2nd Lan. Fus) Missing | 21. 3. 18. | |
| | 2/Lt J N Robinson (1st & 2nd Lan. Fus) wounded | 27. 3. 18. | |
| | 2/Lt I Skene wounded & Missing | 21. 3. 18. | |
| | 2/Lt W A Benson wounded | 21. 3. 18. | |
| | 2/Lt J E F Stanley To U K Sick | 9. 3. 18. | |
| | Casualties - Other Ranks — | | |
| | Killed in action 20 | | |
| | missing 436. | | |
| | wounded & Missing 27. | | |
| | wounded 145. | | |
| | Died of wounds 1 | | |
| | Total 629 | | |

Copy [illegible]

SECRET

# BATTALION OPERATION ORDER No. 96

1. The 6th Lon. Fus. will relieve the 2/7th Lon Fus in the front line [illegible] 6th March 1918.

2. Companies will be relieved as follows :-
[illegible] Coy 2/7th L.F. by B. Coy 6th L.F. on the left.
[illegible] " " " [illegible] " " " in the centre.
[illegible] " " " [illegible] " " " on the right.
[illegible] " " " [illegible] " " " in support.

3. (a) Platoon guides for B,C and D Companies will be at the junction of [illegible] near 2/7th L.F. H.Q. at [illegible] in the above order, [illegible] Coy arriving [illegible] p.m. Companies will march there in the above order at intervals of [illegible] minutes. Companies at [illegible] p.m. and the other companies [illegible] will march via the valley running from [illegible] to [illegible]
(b) Platoon guides for [illegible] Coy will be at entrance to [illegible] at 5.30 p.m.
All movement [illegible] of [illegible] to be by sections in artillery formation.
Guides for posts will meet [illegible] the Companies they are relieving.

4. The 2/8th Lon Fus will take over the support area from the 6th L.F. on 6th March 1918 as follows:-
[illegible] Coy 2/8th L.F. area occupied by [illegible] Coy 6th L.F.
[illegible] " " " " " " [illegible] " " "
C " " " " " " [illegible] " " "
[illegible] " " " " " " [illegible] " " "

(a) Representative N.C.Os of B,C and D Companies will remain behind to show the incoming units where the accommodation for the Coy is, Guides will not be sent from these Companies.
(b) 2 Guides for each post and 1 for Coy H.Q. occupied by [illegible] Coy ([illegible] POINT, and [illegible]) will be at [illegible] ([illegible]) at [illegible] p.m. [illegible] Coy will detail an officer to go with the party. The Company of the 2/8th L.F. relieving [illegible] Coy will be in the posts before [illegible] Coy leaves.

5. All maps, defence schemes and other documents relating to the sector will be taken over. Lists of Trench Stores taken over to be forwarded to Orderly Room by 10.0 a.m. 9th March 1918.

6. Completion of relief to be wired to Battalion H.Q. by code word "[illegible]".

7. Instruction as to working parties will be issued separately.

8. [illegible]

## ADMINISTRATIVE INSTRUCTIONS.

1. Transport Officer and Quartermaster will ensure that water and rations are brought up at the same hours and in the same way as for the 2/7th Lon Fus.

2. Mess Cart, [illegible] Cart and [illegible] for officers' kit will be at [illegible]

P.T.O

2. (Contd.) TEMPLEUX QUARRIES by 11.0 a.m. 8th.March.1918.

F.W.Robinson
Captain.
Adjt.6th. Bn.Lan.Fus.



DISTRIBUTION.

Copy No.1. O.C."A" Coy.
" " 2. " "B" "
" " 3. " "C" "
" " 4. " "D" "
" " 5. " H.Q. "
" " 6. Quartermaster.
" " 7. Transport Officer.
" " 8. Medical Officer.
" " 9. 2/7th. Lan. Fus.
" "10. 2/8th. " "
" "11. W.D.
" "12. W.D.

S E C R E T.

Amendment No.1. to OPERATION ORDER NO.96. Copy No. 12

1. Owing to working parties, times of relief have been put back. Para. 3. of above order is therefore amended as follows:-
   (a). "A", "B", & "C" Coys. will be relieved about 8.0.p.m.
   (b). No change.

2. Para. 2 of administrative instructions is amended as follows:-
   (a). L.G. Limbers for B & C Coys. & Maltese Cart at HUZZAR RD at 3.30.p.m.
   (b). -do- "A" Coy. -do- 3.30.p.m.
   (c). -do- "D" " at "D" Coy. H. . at 8.0.p.m.
   (d). No changes.
   (e). Charger for 2nd.in Command to come up with Mess Cart.
   " " C.O. & Adjt. to be on road at F.27.a.6.0. at 8.30.p.m.
   " " Medical Officer. to come up with Maltese Cart.

[illegible]

Captain.
Adjt. 8th. Bn. Lan. Fus.

[illegible]
Issued to recipients of O.O. No. 96.

8th BATTALION,
LANCASHIRE FUSILIERS.
No. 11/390

------

SECRET. Copy No. 12

BATTALION OPERATION ORDER No.98.

Reference MARGICOURT Special Sheet 1/10,000.

1. Owing to an inter-Battn. relief taking place in the 198th.Inf.Bde. on night 16/17th.March. The reliefs mentioned oin Battn.Warning Order No.97. will take place to-morrow 15th.March. and not as stated.

2. Reliefs. will take place as follows:-

| | | | | |
|---|---|---|---|---|
| "C" Coy. 2/8th L.F. | will relieve | "D" | Coy.6th.L.F. | on the Right. |
| "A" " | -do- | "B" | -do- | in the Centre. |
| "D" " | -do- | "C" | -do- | on the Left. |
| "B" " | -do- | "A" | -do- | in Support. |

3. (a)."B" & "C" Coys. will be relieved at about 10.0.a.m.
"A" Coy. at about 2.0.p.m.
Guides for posts will be at Coy. H.Q. at above hours.
(b). "D" Coy. will be relieved at about 7.0.p.m.
Guides for posts will be at PIMPLE POST at 7.0.p.m.

4. "B", "C", &"D" Coys. will each supply one night picquet of 1 N.C.O. and 3 men (minimum) which will stay out until dawn in accordance with Bde. letter S.354 issued 13.3.18.

5. Companies on relief will move back to ROISEL.
Movement E. of Templeux Quarries to be by sections in artillery formations.
Movement W. of -do- by Platoons at 200x distance.

6. (a). All maps, diagrams, defence schemes and documents relating to the sector will be handed over.
(b). All trench Stores will be handed over. The Bn.Advanced dump will be handed over by O.C."A" Coy.
Receipts for all the above will be obtained and forward to Battn. H.Q. by 10.0.a.m. on the 16th.March. together with certificates of cleanliness from the incoming unit.

7. Relief complete to be wired by Code word "THANGOD".

8. ACKNOWLEDGE.

Issued at 2.15 p.m.
14.3.18.

A.C. Robinson
Captain.
Adjt.6th.Bn.Lan.Fus.

ADMINISTRATIVE INSTRUCTIONS.

1. Baths at ROISEL are being arranged by the Q.M.

2. Transport arrangements are as follows:-
(a).L.G.Limbers for B. & C. Coys.& Maltese Cart at HUZZAR RD. at 10.30.a.m.
(b). -do- "A" Coy. " " " 2.30.p.m.
(c) -do- "D" " " PIMPLE RD " 8.0.p.m.
(d). Officers Mess Cart & H.Q. Limber at Bn.H.Q. at 2.30.p.m.

3. New area will be taken over by Q.M. & C.Q.M.S. C.Q.M.S's. will be prepared to conduct Coys to billets on arrival.

A.C. Robinson
Captain.
Adjt.6th.Bn.Lan.Fus

14.3.18.

DISTRIBUTION.

| | |
|---|---|
| Copy.No.1.O.C."A" Coy. | Copy.No.2.O.C."B" Coy. |
| " " 3. " "C" " | " " 4. " "D" " |
| " " 5. " H.Q." " | " " 6. Quartermaster. |
| " " 7. Transport Officer. | " " 8. Medical Officer. |
| " " 9. Bn.on Left. | " " 10. Bn.On Right. |
| " " 11. W.D. | " " 12. W.D. |
| " " 13. File. | " " 14. Spare. |

6th Bn. Lan. Fus.

# WAR DIARY
or
~~INTELLIGENCE~~ SUMMARY.

(Erase heading not required.)

Army Form C. 2118.

Instructions regarding War Diaries and Intelligence Summaries are contained in F. S. Regs., Part II, and the Staff Manual respectively. Title pages will be prepared in manuscript.

197/66

| Place | Date | Hour | Summary of Events and Information | Remarks and references to Appendices |
|---|---|---|---|---|
| SEUX | 1.4.18 | | The Battalion were at rest | |
| SEUX | 2.4.18 | | The Battalion were still at rest time being occupied in cleaning equipment etc | |
| SEUX | 3.4.18 | | Marched to VACHELLES LES QUESNOY do | |
| VACHELLES | 4.4.18 | | MAJOR G.P. POLLITT DSO RE joined the Battalion, 2nd Lt SOMERVILLE rejoined Battalion from L.G. course | |
| LES QUESNOY | | | at G.H.Q small arm school. Battalion marched to BUIGNY ST MACLOU. | |
| BUIGNY ST MACLOU | 5.4.18 | | Battalion Training | |
| " | 6.4.18 | | Battalion Training | |
| " | 7.4.18 | | MAJOR G.P. POLLITT DSO RE was cross posted as 2nd in Command of 5TH BORDER REGT. CAPT G.H. POTTER MC assumed Command | |
| LE FESTEL | 8.4.18 | | Battalion left BUIGNY ST MACLOU and marched to LE FESTEL | |
| " | 9.4.18 | | Battalion Training | |
| " | 10.4.18 | | Battalion Training | |
| " | 11.4.18 | | MAJOR G.P. POLLITT DSO RE was cross posted to COMMAND the Battalion from 5TH BORDER REGT | |
| " | 12.4.18 | | Battalion Training | |
| " | 13.4.18 | | Battalion marched from LE FESTEL VIA BUSSUS BUSSUE to billets in AILLY LE HAUT CLOCHER | |
| AILLY LE HAUT | 14.4.18 | | Battalion Training Cadre marched to L'HEURE. remaining personnel remained with Brigade | |
| CLOCHER | 15.4.18 | | composite Battalion under Capt G.H. Potter MC | |

D. D. & L., London, E.C. (A7883) Wt W3o9/M1672 350,000 4/17 Sch 52a Forms/C/2118/14

Instructions regarding War Diaries and Intelligence Summaries are contained in F. S. Regs., Part II, and the Staff Manual respectively. Title pages will be prepared in manuscript.

# WAR DIARY

*or*

~~INTELLIGENCE SUMMARY~~.

*(Erase heading not required.)*

Army Form C. 2118.

| Place | Date | Hour | Summary of Events and Information | Remarks and references to Appendices |
|---|---|---|---|---|
| L'HEURE | 16-4-18 | | Battalion Cadre Training | |
| L'HEURE | 17-4-18 | | do | |
| L'HEURE | 18-4-18 | | do | |
| L'HEURE | 19-4-18 | | do | |
| L'HEURE | 20-4-18 | | do 2/Lt. F.J. CLEMENTS joined for Duty | |
| L'HEURE | 21-4-18 | | do CAPT. T. McCARA joined for Duty | |
| L'HEURE | 22-4-18 | | Battalion entrained at LONGPRÉ, detrained at WIZERNES and marched to billets at LONGUENESSE | |
| LONGUENESSE | 23-4-18 | | Battalion Cadre Training CAPT. A.S.C. FOTHERGILL joined for duty | |
| LONGUENESSE | 24-4-18 | | Battalion Cadre Training | |
| LONGUENESSE | 25-4-18 | | do | |
| LONGUENESSE | 26-4-18 | | Battalion marched VIA LUMBRES to BELLE | |
| BELLE | 27-4-18 | | Battalion Cadre Training | |
| BELLE | 28-4-18 | | LIEUT COL B P POLLITT DSO RE and 2/Lt. B. SNOWDON left the Battalion on detachment and reported to HQrs 40th Division at RUYELD to supervise Chinese constructing a line of trenches between HERZEELE and WINNEZEELE. HON LIEUT and QUARTERMASTER H. WOOD in command of the Battalion | |

D. D. & L., London, E.C. (A7283) Wt W809/M1672 350,000 4/17 Sch 52a Forms/C2118/14

Instructions regarding War Diaries and Intelligence Summaries are contained in F. S. Regs., Part II. and the Staff Manual respectively. Title pages will be prepared in manuscript.

# WAR DIARY
or
~~INTELLIGENCE SUMMARY.~~
(Erase heading not required.)

Army Form C. 2118.

| Place | Date | Hour | Summary of Events and Information | Remarks and references to Appendices |
|---|---|---|---|---|
| BELLE | 29.4.18 | | Battalion Cadre Training | |
| BELLE | 30.4.18 | | Battalion Cadre Training | |
| | | | The following reinforcements arrived during the month | |
| | | | LIEUT COLONEL G.P. POLLITT DSO RE | |
| | | | CAPT A.S.C. FOTHERGILL | |
| | | | LIEUT ACT/CAPT T. McCARA  OTHER RANKS 92 | |
| | | | 2/LIEUT F.J. CLEMENTS | |
| | | | The following were transferred during the month | |
| | | | HON. LIEUT and QUARTERMASTER C.W. JAMES to BASE LABOUR CORPS | |
| | | | 2/LIEUT G CHATFIELD ordered medical Board | |
| | | | LIEUT H.C.B. GOLDSMITH crossposted to 2/6 BN MANCHESTER REGT | |
| | | | OTHER RANKS transferred to BASE 298. | |
| | | | G.P.Pollitt. LIEUT COLONEL COMMANDING 6TH BN LANCS FUSTRS | |

(A7883) Wt W809/M1672 350,000 4/17 Sch 52a Forms/C/2118/14
D. D. & L., London, E.C.

33 J.
7 sheets

Vol

# C O N F I D E N T I A L

W A R  D I A R Y

O F

6th. BATTALION THE LANCASHIRE FUSILIERS.

From :- 1st. May 1918.  To :- 31st. May 1918.

( VOLUME 13. )

9/1/16

6TH BN LANCASHIRE FUSILIERS

Instructions regarding War Diaries and Intelligence Summaries are contained in F. S. Regs., Part II. and the Staff Manual respectively. Title pages will be prepared in manuscript.

# WAR DIARY
or
~~INTELLIGENCE SUMMARY.~~
(Erase heading not required.)

Army Form C. 2118.

| Place | Date | Hour | Summary of Events and Information | Remarks and references to Appendices |
|---|---|---|---|---|
| BELLE | 1·5·18 | | Battalion Cadre Training. LIEUT COLONEL POLLITT D.S.O. R.E. and 2/LIEUT B. SNOWDON rejoined the Battalion from the 40TH Division | |
| BELLE | 2·5·18 | | On receipt of 197TH Brigade Operation Order No 85, the Battalion Instructional Cadre proceeded by march route, and entrained at DESVRES, detraining at NOYELLES-SUR-SOMME and marched to billets at LANCHERÈS | |
| LANCHERÈS | 3·5·18 | | Battalion Cadre Training. | |
| LANCHERÈS | 4·5·18 | | Do | |
| LANCHERÈS | 5·5·18 | | Do | |
| LANCHERÈS | 6·5·18 | | Do | |
| LANCHERÈS | 7·5·18 | | Do | |
| LANCHERÈS | 8·5·18 | | Do | |
| LANCHERÈS | 9·5·18 | | On receipt ~~of~~ of 197TH Brigade Operation Order No 86, the Battalion Instructional Cadre proceeded by march route to Billets in BOURSEVILLE. LIEUT D.Y. McLACHLAN 6TH LANCS FUS?RS and 2/LT W.R. BRADBERRY 15TH LONDON REGT joined the Battalion as reinforcements | |
| BOURSEVILLE | 10·5·18 | | Battalion Cadre Training | |

D. D. & L., London, E.C. (A7283) Wt W809/M1672 350,000 4/17 Sch 52a Forms/C/2118/14

Instructions regarding War Diaries and Intelligence Summaries are contained in F. S. Regs., Part II, and the Staff Manual respectively. Title pages will be prepared in manuscript.

6th Lancashire Fusiliers

# WAR DIARY
or
# ~~INTELLIGENCE SUMMARY.~~

(Erase heading not required.)

Army Form C. 2118.

| Place | Date | Hour | Summary of Events and Information | Remarks and references to Appendices |
|---|---|---|---|---|
| BOURSEVILLE | 11.5.18 | | Battalion Cadre Training | |
| BOURSEVILLE | 12.5.18 | | Battalion Cadre Training Lieut Colonel G. P. Pollitt DSO RE proceeded to the 25th Division to take command of 11th Bn Lancashire Fusiliers | |
| BOURSEVILLE | 13.5.18 | | Capt C H Potter MC assumed command of the Battalion<br>Battalion Cadre Training | |
| BOURSEVILLE | 14.5.18 | | Do | |
| BOURSEVILLE | 15.5.18 | | Do | |
| BOURSEVILLE | 16.5.18 | | Capt. C H Potter MC met the 2nd Bn 325 Infantry Regt American E. F. which detrained at EU at 6AM, and proceeded by march route to Billets in BOURSEVILLE, one Company of the American Battn being billeted in MARTAINEVILLE. Company Commanders of the Battalion Cadre met the corresponding Coy. of the American Battn, & conducted them to billets. Being the first long march which the American Battn had done, a great number of the American troops were exhausted on arrival in BOURSEVILLE. All officers of the American Battn were entertained to luncheon at the Battalion Cadre H.Qrs. | |

D. D. & L., London, E.C. (A7583) Wt W809/M1672 59,000 4/17 Sch 52a Forms/C/2118/14

Instructions regarding War Diaries and Intelligence Summaries are contained in F. S. Regs., Part II and the Staff Manual respectively. Title pages will be prepared in manuscript.

6th Lancashire Fusiliers

# WAR DIARY

or

~~INTELLIGENCE~~ ~~SUMMARY~~.

(Erase heading not required.)

Army Form C. 2118.

| Place | Date | Hour | Summary of Events and Information | Remarks and references to Appendices |
|---|---|---|---|---|
| BOURSEVILLE | 17.5.18 | | Baths no parades | |
| BOURSEVILLE | 18.5.18 | | Do | |
| BOURSEVILLE | 19.5.18 | | Battalion Church Parade, American Battn resting | |
| BOURSEVILLE | 20.5.18 | | Lieut Colonel E P NARES M.C. The Cheshire Regiment joined the Battalion to take command. Coy Comdrs, C.S.M's, Musketry, and Gas instructors paraded with the corresponding Coy of the American Battn. for training. The Battn Lewis Gun Officer started a class of American N.C.O's on instruction on the Lewis Gun. The Battn Bombing N.C.O supervised the construction of a Bombing Pit at MARTAIGNEVILLE. The Battn P.T. & B.F. instructors supervised the construction of an Assault Course. | |
| BOURSEVILLE | 21.5.18 | | American Battn Training with Battn Cadre attached. | |
| BOURSEVILLE | 22.5.18 | | On receipt of 197 Brigade Operation Order No 89 the Battalion Instructional Cadre proceeded by march route to billets in WOIGNARUE vacated by the 2/7 Bn Lancs Fusilrs, and were attached to the 3rd Bn 325 Inf Regt American E F as Instructional Cadre. | |
| WOIGNARUE | 22.5.18 | | American Battn Training with the Battn Instructional Cadre attached. | |

D. D. & L., London, E.C. (A7883) Wt W809/M1672 350,000 4/17 Sch 52a Forms/C/2118/14

6th Lancashire Fusiliers

Instructions regarding War Diaries and Intelligence Summaries are contained in F. S. Regs., Part II. and the Staff Manual respectively. Title pages will be prepared in manuscript.

# WAR DIARY
or
INTELLIGENCE SUMMARY.
(Erase heading not required.)

Army Form C. 2118.

| Place | Date | Hour | Summary of Events and Information | Remarks and references to Appendices |
|---|---|---|---|---|
| WOIGNARUE | 23.5.18 | | The following courses of instruction commenced | |
| | | | Lewis Gun course of 40 NCO's of the 3rd Battn 325 Inf Regt American E.F. under the Battn cadre Lewis Gun Officer | |
| | | | Gas course of 16 American NCO. under Capt C H Potter MC | |
| | | | SOS course under Capt A S C Fothergill | |
| | | | Musketry course of 16 American NCO's under the 4 Battn cadre Musketry Instructors | |
| | | | PT & BF course of 16 American NCO's under the Battn cadre PT & BF instructors | |
| | | | The 2nd Bn 325 Inf Regt moved to camp at ONIVAL near AULT. The Coy Cadre of Nos 2 and 4 Coys were attached to them, and continued similar training & courses of instruction as given to the 3rd Bn 325 Regt A.E.F. Each Battn was allotted a 30x range. The 300x range being allotted by the 197 Infy Brigade. Musketry was carried out daily, including night firing with the aid of Verey lights | |
| WOIGNARUE ONIVAL | 24-5-18 | | American Battns training & courses of instruction with Battn cadre attached | |
| WOIGNARUE ONIVAL | 25.5.18 | | No training. Brigade Church Parade at HAUTEBUT | |
| DO. | 26.5.18 | | American Battns training & courses of instruction with Battn cadre attached | |

D. D. & L., London, E.C. (A 8153) Wt W859/M1672 350,000 4/17 Sch 52a Forms/C2118/4

6th Lancashire Fusiliers

Instructions regarding War Diaries and Intelligence Summaries are contained in F. S. Regs., Part II, and the Staff Manual respectively. Title pages will be prepared in manuscript.

# WAR DIARY
or
# ~~INTELLIGENCE~~ ~~SUMMARY.~~
(Erase heading not required.)

Army Form C. 2118.

| Place | Date | Hour | Summary of Events and Information | Remarks and references to Appendices |
|---|---|---|---|---|
| WOIGNARUE & ONIVAL | 27.5.18 | | American Battns training & courses of Instruction with Battn Instructional Cadre attached | |
| DO | 28.5.18 | | DO | |
| DO | 29.5.18 | | DO | |
| DO | 30.5.18 | | American Battns training. Between 9 PM and 10.30 PM at a system of trenches on the coast between CAYEAU-SUR-MER and AULT the Divisional Gas Officer assisted by the Brigade Gas N.C.O's gave a demonstration of a Gas Attack to the 2nd & 3rd Bns 325 Inf Regt with the Battn Instructional Cadre attached. | |
| WOIGNARUE & ONIVAL | 31.5.18 | | American Battalions training & courses of Instruction with the Battn Cadre | |

[illegible signature]
Comdg [illegible] Lancashire Fusiliers

D. D. & L., London, E.C. (A7283) Wt W8c3/M1672 750,000 4/17 Sch 52a Forms/C/2118/14.

Army Form C. 2118.

Instructions regarding War Diaries and Intelligence Summaries are contained in F. S. Regs., Part II. and the Staff Manual respectively. Title pages will be prepared in manuscript.

6th Lancashire Fusiliers

**WAR DIARY**

*or*

**~~INTELLIGENCE SUMMARY~~.**

*(Erase heading not required.)*

| Place | Date | Hour | Summary of Events and Information | Remarks and references to Appendices |
|---|---|---|---|---|
| | | | The following reinforcements arrived during the month | |
| | | | LIEUT COLONEL E P WARES M.C. THE CHESHIRE REGT | |
| | | | LIEUT D.Y. McLACHLIN 6TH LANCS FUS | |
| | | | LIEUT H.C.B. GOLDSMITH. 10TH LONDON REGT | |
| | | | LIEUT F.A RIDLER M.C 4TH GLOUCESTER REGT | |
| | | | 2/LIEUT W.R BRADBURY 15TH LONDON REGT | |
| | | | 6. O.R's | |
| | | | | |
| | | | The following were transferred. | |
| | | | LIEUT COLONEL G.P. POLLITT D.S.O. to command 11TH BN LANCS FUSRS | |
| | | | 2/LIEUT F.J. CLEMENTS 6TH LANS FUSRS to BASE | |
| | | | 2/LIEUT W.R BRADBURY 15TH LONDON REGT. to BASE | |
| | | | 77 O.R's transferred to BASE | |

D. D. & L., London, E.C.
(A7853) Wt W809/M1672 350,000 4/17 Sch 52a Forms/C/2118/14

34J.
10 sheets

C O N F I D E N T I A L.

W A R D I A R Y

O F

6th. BATTALION THE LANCASHIRE FUSILIERS.

From :- 1st. June 1918. To:- 30th. June 1918.

( VOLUME 16. )

;-;-;-;-;-;-;-;-;-;-;-;-;-;-;-;-;-;-;-;-;-;-;-;-;

6th Lancashire Fusiliers

Instructions regarding War Diaries and Intelligence Summaries are contained in F. S. Regs., Part II, and the Staff Manual respectively. Title pages will be prepared in manuscript.

# WAR DIARY
*or*
# INTELLIGENCE SUMMARY.
*(Erase heading not required.)*

Army Form C. 2118.

| Place | Date | Hour | Summary of Events and Information | Remarks and references to Appendices |
|---|---|---|---|---|
| WOIGNARUE | 1-6-18 | | On receipt of 197th Brigade operation order No 90 the Batt: Instructional Cadre, in conjunction with 3rd Batt 325 Inf Regt, moved by route march from WOIGNARUE via ALLENAY – DETHENCOURT – YZENGREMER – DARGNIES – BEAUCHAMPS – GAMACHES to billets in MONTIERES (distance 13½ miles) and relieved the 4th East Lancs Regt. The 3rd Batt 325th Regt AEF going under canvas near MONTIERES. Batt came under orders of 199th Inf Bde. | |
| | | | No 2 & 4 Coy Cadre moved independently with the 2nd Batt 325th Inf Regt by route march to billets in TILLOY-FLORIVILLE | |
| MONTIERES | 2-6-18 | | Battalion at rest. LIEUT F A RIDLER MC 4th GLOUCESTER REGT joined the Batt. | |
| MONTIERES | 3-6-18 | | Training commenced Lewis Gun, Musketry, PT & BF, SOS with Batt Instructional Cadre attached. | |
| | | | The G O C 66th Division gave a lecture to 325th Infantry Regt and instructional cadre. | |
| | | | On receipt of 199th Brigade Operation Orders No 99 No 2 & 4 Coy Cadres together with 2nd Batt 325th Inf Regt moved to camp on GAMACHES – | |

D. D. & L., London, E.C. (A7883) Wt W809/M1672 50,000 4/17 Sch 52a Forms/C/2118/14

6th Lancashire Fusiliers.

Army Form C. 2118.

Instructions regarding War Diaries and Intelligence Summaries are contained in F. S. Regs., Part II. and the Staff Manual respectively. Title pages will be prepared in manuscript.

# WAR DIARY
or
# ~~INTELLIGENCE SUMMARY.~~

*(Erase heading not required.)*

| Hour, Date, Place | Summary of Events and Information | Remarks and references to Appendices |
|---|---|---|
| MONTIÈRES 3/6/18 | – MONTIÈRES. 3/4 mile SE of GAMACHES. | |
| MONTIÈRES 4/6/18 | American Battalions training, & Courses of instruction with Battn instructional Cadre attached | |
| MONTIÈRES 5/6/18 | American Battn training, courses of instruction with Battn instructional Cadre attached. | |
| MONTIÈRES 6/6/18 | American Battn training, courses of instruction with Battn instructional Cadre attached. | |
| MONTIÈRES 7/6/18 | On receipt of 199 Infantry Bde operation order No 100, the Batt Instructional Cadre moved by lorry from MONTIÈRES via BOUTTENCOURT – ABBEVILLE to billets in CANCHY and district, relieved the 5/6th N Staffs Regt and were attached to the 108th Inf Regt A.E.F.<br>The Batt Instructional Cadre were disposed as follows –<br>Batt H.Q. & No 2 Coy Cadre – CANCHY with 108th Inf Regt HQ & 3rd Bn<br>No 1 Coy Cadre – FROYELLES-FONTAINE with 1st Batt, 108 I R<br>No 3 do – MACHY with 102nd Engineers Regt. 108 I R<br>No 4 do – DOMVAST with 2nd Batt 108 I R | |
| CANCHY 8/6/18 | Battn Cadre at rest. 2/Lieut B SNOWDON was transferred to the Base as surplus to establishment. | |

(73989) W4141—463. 400,000. 9/14. H.&J.Ltd. Forms/C. 2118/10.

6th Lancashire Fusiliers.

Instructions regarding War Diaries and Intelligence Summaries are contained in F. S. Regs., Part II. and the Staff Manual respectively. Title pages will be prepared in manuscript.

# WAR DIARY
*or*
# ~~INTELLIGENCE~~ SUMMARY.
*(Erase heading not required.)*

Army Form C. 2118.

| Hour, Date, Place | Summary of Events and Information | Remarks and references to Appendices |
|---|---|---|
| CANCHY 9/6/18 | The 2nd & 3rd Battalions, 108th Inf Regt AEF arrived by route march from NOYELLES. The Coy Cadre commanders attached to these Batts assisting in their billeting etc. The 1st Batt, & 102nd Engineer Regt had already arrived in their respective areas. | |
| CANCHY 10/6/18 | The following courses of instruction commenced. | |
| | (a) Lewis Gun Course of 4 officers each from 2nd & 3rd Batts under the Batt Cadre LGO, duration 6 days. | |
| | Lewis Gun Course of 9 NCOs each from 1st, 2nd & 3rd Batts under the Batt Cadre LG NCO instructors, duration 6 days | |
| | (b) Musketry Course of 4 officers & 12 NCOs each from 1st, 2nd & 3rd Batts, and 102nd Engineer Regt under the Batt Cadre Musketry instructors, duration 6 days | |
| | (c) PT & BF Course of 4 officers & 16 NCOs each from 1st, 2nd & 3rd Batts, and 102nd Engineer Regt under the Batt Cadre PT & BF instructors, duration 3 days. | |
| | (d) Cooking Course of 4 Mess Sgts & 4 O.R. each from 1st, 2nd & 3rd Batts and 102nd Engineer Regt under the 4 Coy Cadre QM Sgts supervised by the Batt Cadre Quartermaster, duration 2 days. | |

(73989) W4141—453. 400,000. 9/14. H.&J.Ltd. Forms/C. 2118/10.

6th Lancashire Fusiliers.

# WAR DIARY
*or*
# INTELLIGENCE SUMMARY.
*(Erase heading not required.)*

Army Form C. 2118.

Instructions regarding War Diaries and Intelligence Summaries are contained in F. S. Regs., Part II. and the Staff Manual respectively. Title pages will be prepared in manuscript.

| Hour, Date, Place | Summary of Events and Information | Remarks and references to Appendices |
| --- | --- | --- |
| CANCHY 10/6/18 | (e) Scouting Course of 1 officer & 16 OR. from 3rd Batt under Capt A S C Fothergill.<br>Scouting Course of 1 officer & 16 OR from 2nd Batt under Lieut H C D Goldsmith. duration 12 days<br>(f) Bombing of 16 O.R. for the 1st Batt under the Batt Cadre Bombing instructor. | |
| CANCHY 11/6/18 | American Battalions training & courses of instruction with Batt Cadre attached. | |
| CANCHY 12/6/18 | American Battalions training & courses of instruction with Batt Cadre attached. | |
| CANCHY 13/6/18 | Lt Col Campbell D.S.O. gives a lecture on PT & B.F. to the 108th Inf Regt Complete and instructional cadres.<br>American Batts training with Batt Cadre attached. | |
| CANCHY 14/6/18 | American Batts training & fitting of Small box Respirators under supervision of Div Gas Officer & Batt Cadre Gas N.C.O.s. | |
| CANCHY 15/6/18 | American Batts training with Batt Cadre attached. | |
| CANCHY 16/6/18 | Batt Cadre Church Parade with 108th Inf Regt.<br>American Batts resting. | |

(73989) W4141—463. 400,000. 9/14. H.&J.Ltd. Forms/C. 2118/10.

6th Lancashire Fusiliers.

# WAR DIARY
*or*
# INTELLIGENCE ~~SUMMARY~~.

*(Erase heading not required.)*

Army Form C. 2118.

Instructions regarding War Diaries and Intelligence Summaries are contained in F. S. Regs., Part II. and the Staff Manual respectively. Title pages will be prepared in manuscript.

| Hour, Date, Place | Summary of Events and Information | Remarks and references to Appendices |
|---|---|---|
| CANCHY 17-6-18. | American Batt training & courses of instruction with Batt Instructional Cadre attached. | |
| CANCHY 18-6-18. | On receipt of 198th Infantry Bde operation order No 96, the Batt Instructional Cadre, in conjunction with the 108th Inf Regt AEF complete, moved by route march from CANCHY via LAMOTTE-BULEUX – HAUTVILLERS – BUIGNY-ST MACLOU – Gd LAVIERS – CAMBRON – LAMBERCOURT – BOUBERT – ARREST to billets in ST BLIMONT, and were attached to the 108th Inf Regt H.Q. and 3rd Batt. The Batt Instructional Cadre came under the orders of the 197th Infantry Bde. No 3 Coy Cadre moved independently from MACHY and joined the Batt Instructional Cadre at ST BLIMONT. LIEUT A.M. COWAN evacuated to U.K wounded whilst attached on probation to the R.G.A. | |
| ST BLIMONT 19-6-18 | The following Courses of instruction commenced. Lewis Gun Course of 2 NCO's + 8 first privates from each Coy under the Batt Lewis Gun instructors, duration 6 days also 2 teams per Coy under American instructors just trained. Supervised by the L.G.O. Duration 12 days. | |

(73989) W4141—463. 400,000. 9/14. H.&J.Ltd. Forms/C. 2118/10.

6th Lancashire Fusiliers

# WAR DIARY
*or*
# INTELLIGENCE SUMMARY.
(*Erase heading not required.*)

Army Form C. 2118.

Instructions regarding War Diaries and Intelligence Summaries are contained in F. S. Regs., Part II. and the Staff Manual respectively. Title pages will be prepared in manuscript.

| Hour, Date, Place | Summary of Events and Information | Remarks and references to Appendices |
|---|---|---|
| St BLIMONT 19-6-18 | (b) Bombing course of 1 bombing section per platoon under American instructors just trained. Supervised by the Batt Instructional Cadre Bombing Sgt. Duration 4 days.<br>(c) Musketry course of 5 NCOs per Coy under the Batt Inst Cadre musketry instructors. Duration 4 days.<br>The Scouting class under Capt A S C Fothergill continued.<br>The Batt Cadre Pl Sgt instructors supervised the training of affiliated Coys.<br>The Batt Cadre Coy QM Sgts gave all possible assistance to the American Mess Sgts, Supply Sgts Cooks. Lt. QM Harwood supervised. | |
| St BLIMONT 19/6/18 2pm | The Batt Instructional Cadre came under the orders of the 199th Inf Bde. | |
| St BLIMONT 20-6-18 | American Battalion training. Courses of instruction with Batt Inst Cadre attached. | |
| St BLIMONT 21-6-18 | On receipt of 199th Infantry Brigade operation order No 102, the Batt Instructional Cadre in conjunction with 3rd Batt 108th Inf Regt moved by route march from St BLIMONT | |

(73989) W4141—463. 400,000. 9/14. H.&J.Ltd. Forms/C. 2118/10.

6th Lancashire Fusiliers

# WAR DIARY
*or*
# INTELLIGENCE SUMMARY.

(*Erase heading not required.*)

Instructions regarding War Diaries and Intelligence Summaries are contained in F. S. Regs., Part II. and the Staff Manual respectively. Title pages will be prepared in manuscript.

Army Form C. 2118.

| Hour, Date, Place | Summary of Events and Information | Remarks and references to Appendices |
|---|---|---|
| ST BLIMONT 21/6/18 | via ARREST – LAMBERCOURT – CAMBRON – GRAND LAVIERS to billets in BUIGNY ST MACLOU. | |
| BUIGNY ST MACLOU 22-6-18 | Pursuant to 66th Division Order No 79, Addenda No 3 and 197th Infantry Brigade letter G451/1 the Batt Instructional Cadre in conjunction with 3rd Batt 108th Inf Regt moved by Bus from BUIGNY ST MACLOU via ABBEVILLE – ST RIQUIER – AUXI-LE-CHATEAU – DOULLENS – BOUQUEMAISON – SUS-ST LEGER to billets in BEAUDRICOURT. The Batt Cadre embussed on main ABBEVILLE – MONTREUIL Road by B of BRICKWORKS, one mile N of ABBEVILLE. | |
| BEAUDRICOURT 23-6-18 | Battalion Cadre & American Battalion at rest. | |
| BEAUDRICOURT 24-6-18 | Training commenced and Instructional classes as detailed on 19/6/18 at ST BLIMONT were continued. Batt Instructional Cadre attached. | |
| BEAUDRICOURT 25-6-18 | American Batt training & courses of instruction with Batt Inst Cadre attached | |
| BEAUDRICOURT 26-6-18 | American Batt: training & courses of instruction with Batt. Inst Cadre attached. LIEUT (A/CAPT) T. McARA, LIEUT D Y McLACHAN and 2/LT J G ROBERTSON were crossposted to the 2/7th Lancs Fus & left the Batt | |

6th Lancashire Fusiliers.

# WAR DIARY

*or*

# INTELLIGENCE SUMMARY.

*(Erase heading not required.)*

Instructions regarding War Diaries and Intelligence Summaries are contained in F. S. Regs., Part II. and the Staff Manual respectively. Title pages will be prepared in manuscript.

Army Form C. 2118.

| Hour, Date, Place | Summary of Events and Information | Remarks and references to Appendices |
|---|---|---|
| BEAUDRICOURT 27-6-18 | American Batt training courses of instruction with Batt Inst Cadre attached | |
| | Capt L.B.L. SECKHAM M.C., LIEUT (A/CAPT) G.S. TURNER M.C. and | |
| | 2/LT D. McK CHRISTELOW were transported from 2/1st Lancs Fus | |
| | and joined the Batt. 2/Lt D McK CHRISTELOW remaining | |
| | at 197th Brigade Headquarters. | |
| 12 noon | The Batt came under the orders of the 197th Infantry Brigade | |
| BEAUDRICOURT 28-6-18 | The Batt Instructional Cadre was re-adjusted, as follows: | |
| | Batt Headquarters to 108th Inf Regt Headquarters | |
| | No 1 Coy attached to 1st Battalion, 108th Inf Regt | |
| | No 2 Coy do to 3rd do do do | |
| | No 3 Coy do to 2nd do do do | |
| | No 4 Coy do to H.Q. Coy 108th Inf Regt | |
| | No 1 & 4 Coys moved to SUS ST LEGER | |
| | No 3 Coy moved to IVERGNY | |
| | H.Q. & No 2 Coy remained at BEAUDRICOURT. | |
| | The American 108th Inf Regt carried out a tactical scheme with the Batt inst. cadre attached. | |

(73989) W4141—463. 400,000. 9/14. H.&J.Ltd. Forms/C. 2118/10.

6th Lancashire Fusiliers

Instructions regarding War Diaries and Intelligence Summaries are contained in F. S. Regs., Part II. and the Staff Manual respectively. Title pages will be prepared in manuscript.

# WAR DIARY
*or*
# INTELLIGENCE SUMMARY.
(*Erase heading not required.*)

Army Form C. 2118.

| Hour, Date, Place | Summary of Events and Information | Remarks and references to Appendices |
|---|---|---|
| BEAUDRICOURT 29-6-18 | American Battalions training with Batt Inst Cadre attached | |
| BEAUDRICOURT 30-6-18 | American Batts & Batt Inst Cadre at rest<br>Batt Cadre Church parade | |
| | The following reinforcements arrived during the month<br>3 OR<br>The following were transferred<br>4 OR to Base<br>1 OR to RE. | |
| | [signature] LIEUT-COLONEL<br>COMMANDING 6th BATT LANCASHIRE FUSILIERS | |

(73989) W4141—463. 400,000. 9/14. H.&J.Ltd. Forms/C. 2118/10.

35 J
5 sheets

# C O N F I D E N T I A L.

W A R   D I A R Y

O F.

6 th. B A T T A L I O N

L A N C A S H I R E   F U S I L I E R S.

From :- 1st. July 1918.          To :- 31st. July 1918.

V O L U M E 17.

9/18

Instructions regarding War Diaries and Intelligence Summaries are contained in F. S. Regs., Part II, and the Staff Manual respectively. Title pages will be prepared in manuscript.

6th Lancashire Fusiliers

# WAR DIARY
or
~~INTELLIGENCE SUMMARY.~~
(Erase heading not required.)

Army Form C. 2118.

| Place | Date | Hour | Summary of Events and Information | Remarks and references to Appendices |
|---|---|---|---|---|
| BEAUDRICOURT | 1-7-18 | | American Batt. training with Batt Inst Cadre attached. | |
| BEAUDRICOURT | 2-7-18 | | 27th American Division left the present area & 3rd Batt. 108th Inf Regt left BEAUDRICOURT at 11 Am & route marched to BOUQUEMAISON to entrain; the Coy officers accompanying them to assist in the entraining. | |
| BEAUDRICOURT | 3-7-18 | | On receipt of 197th Inf Bde operation order No 96 the Batt Inst Cadre moved by route march from BEAUDRICOURT to billets in SUS-ST-LEGER. | |
| SUS-ST-LEGER | 4-7-18 | | Batt Cadre parade & firing on long range at LUCHEUX | |
| do | 5-7-18 | | Batt Cadre parade & firing on long range at LUCHEUX. | |
| SUS ST LEGER | 6-7-18 | | The 320th American Inf Regt HQs (80th Div) and 1st Batt. 320th Inf Regt detrained at BOUQUEMAISON & were met by representatives of the Batt: Cadre. They marched to SUS-ST-LEGER, arriving at 11³⁰pm. | |
| SUS-ST-LEGER | 7/7/18 | | American Batt at rest. Batt: Inst Cadre church parade. | |
| SUS-ST-LEGER | 8-7-18 | | The following courses of instruction commenced. | |
| | | | ① Lewis Gun. 8 teams per Coy under American Instructors supervised by British LG NCOs. | |
| | | | In addition 1 hours instruction per day to above American instructors by Batt Cadre Lewis Gun NCOs. | |

(A9173) Wt W2338/P360 600,000 12/17 D. D. & L. Sch. 52a. Forms/C2118/15.

Instructions regarding War Diaries and Intelligence Summaries are contained in F. S. Regs., Part II. and the Staff Manual respectively. Title pages will be prepared in manuscript.

# WAR DIARY
*or*
# ~~INTELLIGENCE SUMMARY.~~
*(Erase heading not required.)*

Army Form C. 2118.

| Place | Date | Hour | Summary of Events and Information | Remarks and references to Appendices |
|---|---|---|---|---|
| SUS-ST-LEGER | 8-7-18 | | (b) Rifle Grenade course of 4 NCO's per Coy under Batt: Cadre Bombing instructor. for 2 days. | |
| | | | after above course R.G. teams to be trained by the American instructors under the | |
| | | | supervision of Batt: bombing instructor. | |
| | | | (c) P.T. & B.T. course of 4 NCO's per Coy under Batt P.T. instructor | |
| | | | (d) Musketry course of 5 NCO's per Coy under the Batt. musketry instructors | |
| | | | (e) Mechanics Class of 2 ORo's per Coy | |
| | | | The Batt Cadre Coy Q.M. Sgts gave all possible help & assistance to the American | |
| | | | Mess Sgts, Cooks etc. Lt. Q.M. Atwood supervised | |
| SUS: ST. LEGER | 9-7-18 | | American Battalion training & courses of instruction with Batt: Inst Cadre attached. | |
| do | 10-7-18 | | do do do do do | |
| do | 11-7-18 | | do do do do do | |
| do | 12-7-18 | | do do do do do | |
| do | 13-7-18 | | American Batt: practising for Div. platoon competition. The Batt: Inst: Cadre fired | |
| | | | on the long range. | |
| do | 14-7-18 | | Batt: Cadre Church Parade | |
| do | 15-7-18 | | American Batt: training & courses of instruction, with Batt: Inst: Cadre attached. | |

(A9175) Wt W2358/P560 600,000 12/17 D. D. & L. Sch. 52a. Forms/C2118/15.

Instructions regarding War Diaries and Intelligence Summaries are contained in F. S. Regs., Part II, and the Staff Manual respectively. Title pages will be prepared in manuscript.

6th Lancashire Fusiliers

# WAR DIARY
or
~~INTELLIGENCE SUMMARY.~~
(Erase heading not required.)

Army Form C. 2118.

| Place | Date | Hour | Summary of Events and Information | Remarks and references to Appendices |
|---|---|---|---|---|
| SUS-ST. LEGER | 16.7.18 | | American Batt: training, & courses of instruction, with Batt Inst: Cadre attached. | |
| do | 17-7-18 | | do do do do do | |
| do | 18-7-18 | | do do do do do | |
| do | 19-7-18 | | American Batt practising for Div. platoon competition. The Batt: Inst Cadre fired on the long range | |
| do | 20-7-18 | | American Divisional platoon etc competition Batt Cadre at rest. | |
| do | 21-7-18 | | On receipt of 197th Inf Bde wire The Batt: Inst: Cadre moved by route march from SUS-ST. LEGER via LUCHEUX-DOULLENS to billets at CANDAS | |
| CANDAS | 22-7-18 | | On receipt of 197th Inf. Bde operation order No 97 the Batt: Inst: Cadre moved by train to the ABANCOURT - SERQUEUX area (Sheet DIEPPE 16) and detrained at SERQUEUX. They then moved by route march from SERQUEUX via GAILLEFONTAINE - CONTEVILLE - BEAUFRESNE to HAUDRICOURT and went under canvas. The Batt: came under the orders of the 199th Inf: Bde. | |
| HAUDRICOURT | 23-7-18 | | Batt Cadre at rest. | |
| do | 24-7-18 | | Batt Cadre Parade and Kit inspection | |
| do | 25-7-18 | | Batt Cadre Parade | |

(A9475) Wt W2358/P360 600,000 12/17 D. D. & L. Sch. 52a. Forms/C2118/15

Instructions regarding War Diaries and Intelligence Summaries are contained in F. S. Regs., Part II. and the Staff Manual respectively. Title pages will be prepared in manuscript.

6th Lancashire Fusiliers

# WAR DIARY
or
~~INTELLIGENCE SUMMARY.~~
(Erase heading not required.)

Army Form C. 2118.

| Place | Date | Hour | Summary of Events and Information | Remarks and references to Appendices |
|---|---|---|---|---|
| HAUDRICOURT | 26-7-18 | | Batt Cadre Parade | |
| do | 27-7-18 | | Batt Cadre Parade | |
| do | 28-7-18 | | Batt Cadre Church Parade | |
| do | 29-7-18 | | Batt Cadre Parade | |
| do | 30-7-18 | | Batt Cadre Parade | |
| do | 31-7-18 | | Batt Cadre Parade | |
| | | | The following reinforcements arrived during the month | |
| | | | 2/LIEUT. B. SNOWDON | |
| | | | LIEUT. H.W. WALTON | |
| | | | The following were transferred | |
| | | | 2 O.R to Base | |
| | | | 2 O.R to R.E | |
| | | | 2/LIEUT T SOMERVILLE evacuated to U.K., sick | |
| | | | [signature] LIEUT. COLONEL | |
| | | | COMMANDING. 6th BATT. LANCASHIRE FUSILIERS. | |

(A9475) W: W2358/F360 600,000 12/17 D. D. & L. Sch. 52a. Forms C2118/13.

36 J.
13 sheets

19866

WO 95/2919

(6339) Wt. W160/M3016 1,500,000 10/17 McA & W Ltd (E 1898) Forms W3091.

Army Form W.3091.

# Cover for Documents.

Nature of Enclosures.

CONFIDENTIAL

WAR DIARY

OF

6th Bn LANCASHIRE FUSILIERS

FROM 1-8-18 TO 31-8-18

(VOLUME 1)

Notes, or Letters written.

Instructions regarding War Diaries and Intelligence Summaries are contained in F. S. Regs., Part II. and the Staff Manual respectively. Title pages will be prepared in manuscript.

# WAR DIARY
*or*
# INTELLIGENCE SUMMARY.
*(Erase heading not required.)*

Army Form C. 2118.

| Place | Date | Hour | Summary of Events and Information | Remarks and references to Appendices |
|---|---|---|---|---|
| HAUDRICOURT | 1/8/18 | | Weather, fine, bright sunshine all day. To celebrate the 159th anniversary of the Battle of MINDEN. The Battalion were given a General Holiday. Sports of all kind were arranged & the Officers & men had an enjoyable day. The Earl of Denbigh lectured to Officers & N.C.O.s at 1800 hours. Subject "German War Aims". 7 O.R. proceeded on leave to U.K. | J.F. |
| – " – | 2/8/18 | | Weather, intermittent rainfall through day. The Battalion carried out Gas training & work on the Ranges during the afternoon. A Tactical Scheme for Officers was carried out during the evening. 5 O.R. proceeded on leave to U.K. | J.F. |
| – " – | 3/8/18 | | Weather, stormy during morning, fine & bright during afternoon. Owing to the rain it was found impossible to carry out parades during the morning but Gas training was continued under | |

A7092). Wt. W12839/M1293 750,000. 1/17. D. D & L., Ltd. Forms/C2113/14.

Instructions regarding War Diaries and Intelligence Summaries are contained in F. S. Regs., Part II. and the Staff Manual respectively. Title pages will be prepared in manuscript.

# WAR DIARY
*or*
# INTELLIGENCE SUMMARY.
*(Erase heading not required.)*

Army Form C. 2118.

| Place | Date | Hour | Summary of Events and Information | Remarks and references to Appendices |
|---|---|---|---|---|
| HAVRINCOURT | 3/8/18 | | the Brigade Gas Officer. Work was continued during the afternoon. 4 O.R. proceeded on leave to U.K. & 1 O.R. rejoined from leave, two others who should have rejoined today were absent. | JF |
| " | 4/8/18 | | Weather fine. Battalion resting. The Battalion attended Divine Service at 1000 hours. Weekly Training Programme for week ending 10/8/18 was issued to all concerned at 1700 hrs for details see APPENDIX I attached. Capt. I.S. Rutherford & 1 O.R. rejoined from leave, two others were absent | JF |
| " | 5/8/18 | | Weather intermittent rainfall throughout the day. The Divisional Commander (Maj Gen H K BETHELL CMG DSO) inspected the Battalion in Marching Order at 0900 hours. Training work was carried out afterwards status until 1330 hours. Lt. R.F. Hinson & 5 O.R. proceeded on leave to U.K. | JF |

A7092). Wt. W12839/M1293. 750,000. 1/17. D. D & L., Ltd. Forms/C2118/14.

Instructions regarding War Diaries and Intelligence Summaries are contained in F. S. Regs., Part II. and the Staff Manual respectively. Title pages will be prepared in manuscript.

# WAR DIARY
*or*
# INTELLIGENCE SUMMARY.
*(Erase heading not required.)*

Army Form C. 2118.

| Place | Date | Hour | Summary of Events and Information | Remarks and references to Appendices |
|---|---|---|---|---|
| HAVERSKERQUE | 6/8/18 | | Weather intermittent rainfall throughout day. A & D Coys working on Rifle Range, Assault Course etc. B & C Coys Platoon Training. Tactical Scheme for all N.C.O.s was carried out at 1800 hours. 5. O.R. proceeded on leave to U.K. | JF |
| -"- | 7/8/18 | | Weather fine, sunshine during afternoon. A & D Coys working as yesterday. B & C carried out Range practices. 5. O.R. proceeded on leave to U.K. 2 O.R. rejoined. | JF |
| -"- | 8/8/18 | | Weather fine sunshine all day. Companies carried out training in accordance with weekly programme. 4. O.R. proceeded to U.K. on leave | JF |
| -"- | 9/8/18 | | Weather fine bright sunshine all day. Companies continued training in accordance with programme, see appendix I attached. 27. O.R. & Capt Pennington proceeded on leave to U.K. | JF |

A7092). Wt. W12839/M1293 750,000. 1/17. D D & L., Ltd. Forms/C2118/14.

Army Form C. 2118.

# WAR DIARY
*or*
# INTELLIGENCE SUMMARY.
*(Erase heading not required.)*

Instructions regarding War Diaries and Intelligence Summaries are contained in F. S. Regs., Part II. and the Staff Manual respectively. Title pages will be prepared in manuscript.

| Place | Date | Hour | Summary of Events and Information | Remarks and references to Appendices |
|---|---|---|---|---|
| HAUDRICOURT | 10/8/18 | | Weather fine bright sunshine all day. Companies continued training. The Divisional Commander inspected the transport at 0900 hours. The Battalion carried out a short Ceremonial Parade at 1130 hours & finished with a "March Past". The movements & handling of arms were quite good. | J.F. |
| " | 11/8/18 | | Weather fine with bright sunshine all day. Battalion resting. The Bde baths were allotted to the Battalion & full use was made of same. Weekly Training Programme issued. | J.F. |
| " | 12/8/18 | | Weather fine bright sunshine very hot. The Battalion carried out training in accordance with Weekly Programme see APPENDIX II attached. Bathing was carried out during the afternoon. 2/Lt P.F. Sarrant, 2/Lt H.E. Atkins and 132. O.R. proceeded on leave to U.K. Divisional | |

A7092). Wt. W12839/M1293. 750,000. 1/17. D. D & L., Ltd. Forms/C2118/14.

Instructions regarding War Diaries and Intelligence Summaries are contained in F. S. Regs., Part II, and the Staff Manual respectively. Title pages will be prepared in manuscript.

# WAR DIARY
*or*
# INTELLIGENCE SUMMARY.
*(Erase heading not required.)*

Army Form C. 2118.

| Place | Date | Hour | Summary of Events and Information | Remarks and references to Appendices |
|---|---|---|---|---|
| HAVRINCOURT | 12/8/18 | | Letter A.G.'s No. A.G. 4210 (O) H.Q. L. of C. No W.A. 640//1 received. This letter states that it has been decided to adopt the following organisation forthwith:- 6th Bn (TERRITORIAL) Lancashire Fusiliers to absorb the 12th (SERVICE) Bn Lancashire Fusiliers, the Bn so formed to be designated "6th Bn Lancashire Fusiliers". Brigade A.248 orders the amalgamation to take place early as possible & nominal rolls of Officers and N.C.O's surplus to establishment to be forwarded by the 15th August. | JF |
| —do— | 13/8/18 | | Weather fine with bright sunshine all day. The Battalion carried out training in accordance with Training Programme (see appendix II) 199th Bde letter A.248/2 dated 12/8/18 reads as follows:- "The 13th August 1918 will be the date taken as the date | |

A7092). Wt. W12839/M1293. 750,000. 1/17. D. D & L., Ltd. Forms/C2118 14.

Instructions regarding War Diaries and Intelligence Summaries are contained in F. S. Regs., Part II. and the Staff Manual respectively. Title pages will be prepared in manuscript.

# WAR DIARY
*or*
# INTELLIGENCE SUMMARY.
*(Erase heading not required.)*

Army Form C. 2118.

| Place | Date | Hour | Summary of Events and Information | Remarks and references to Appendices |
|---|---|---|---|---|
| HAIDRICOURT | 13/6/18 | | of Disbandment of the Battalion to be absorbed" The Battalion adopts its new designation (6th Bn Lancashire Fusiliers) from today. Capt A.O. BISSON R.A.M.C. 2/Lt C.W. CAVE and 235 O.R. proceeded to U.K. on leave for 14 days. Capt L.B.L. SECKHAM, M.C., Lieut A/Capt & Adjutant F.A. RIDLER M.C. & Lieut H.W. WALTON joined the battalion for duty on amalgamation of the two Battalions. Capt C.H. POTTER M.C. is posted to the Battalion, but is at present on leave to U.K. | JF |
| — " — | 14/6/18 | | Weather fine. Battalion training in accordance with weekly Programme. Copy of a letter sent to Lieut-Gen Sir J.J. ASSER K.C.M.G. K.C.V.O. C.B. Commanding L. of C. area, by the C in C B.E.F. was received today see Appendix III attached. This letter has been read at the head of each Platoon on parade. | JF |

A7092). Wt. W12839/M1293. 750,000. 1/17. D. D & L., Ltd. Forms/C2118/14.

Instructions regarding War Diaries and Intelligence Summaries are contained in F. S. Regs., Part II. and the Staff Manual respectively. Title pages will be prepared in manuscript.

# WAR DIARY
*or*
# INTELLIGENCE SUMMARY.
*(Erase heading not required.)*

Army Form C. 2118.

| Place | Date | Hour | Summary of Events and Information | Remarks and references to Appendices |
|---|---|---|---|---|
| HAUDRICOURT | 15/8/18 | | Weather fine with bright sunshine all day. Battalion training as usual. Information received from Bde that No 33079 Private A DAVIES was killed in a train accident whilst proceeding on leave to UK. A firing party consisting of 20 OR under Lieut C.G.E. HELDER attended the interment which took place at ABANCOURT at 1530 hours. | |
| | 16/8/18 | | Weather fine. Battalion training as usual. 2/Lt H.H. SMITH 4th EAST LANCS joined for duty & was posted to D Company. | |
| | 17/8/18 | | Weather fine. Battalion training as usual. | |
| | 18/8/18 | | Weather fine, dull during morning but bright sunshine during the afternoon. Battalion resting. Weekly Training Programme was issued to all concerned at 1400 hours see Appendix IV | |

A7092). Wt. W12839/M1293 750,000. 1/17. D. D & L., Ltd. Forms/C2118/14.

Instructions regarding War Diaries and Intelligence Summaries are contained in F. S. Regs., Part II. and the Staff Manual respectively. Title pages will be prepared in manuscript.

# WAR DIARY
*or*
# INTELLIGENCE SUMMARY.
(*Erase heading not required.*)

Army Form C. 2118.

| Place | Date | Hour | Summary of Events and Information | Remarks and references to Appendices |
|---|---|---|---|---|
| HAUDRICOURT | 19/8/18 | | Weather fine but dull. Battalion training in accordance with weekly programme see appendix I attached. | JF |
| " " | 20/8/18 | | Weather, fine with bright sunshine most of the day. Battalion training as usual. 2/Lt J.R. SMITH-SAVILLE joined for duty & posted to B Coy | JF |
| " " | 21/8/18 | | Weather fine, exceedingly hot today. Battalion training as usual. Lieut H.N. Walton & 5 OR joined the Bde L.T.M. Bty today. 31 OR proceeded to Div H.Q. to prepare Div Signal School. | JF |
| " | 22/8/18 | | Weather fine & warm. Battalion training as usual. The Brigade baths were allotted to the Battalion & all men bathed. | JF |
| " " | 23/8/18 | | Weather fine with bright sunshine all day. The Battalion carried out a Route March to-day. Route via VILLIERS-LA COUTURE-MORIENNE-AUMALE-HAUDRICOURT. Approximate distance | |

A7092). Wt. W12839/M1293 750,000. 1/17. D. D & L., Ltd. Forms/C2118/14.

Army Form C. 2118.

Instructions regarding War Diaries and Intelligence Summaries are contained in F. S. Regs., Part II. and the Staff Manual respectively. Title pages will be prepared in manuscript.

# WAR DIARY
*or*
# INTELLIGENCE SUMMARY.
*(Erase heading not required.)*

| Place | Date | Hour | Summary of Events and Information | Remarks and references to Appendices |
|---|---|---|---|---|
| HAUDRICOURT | 23/8/18 | | 10 miles. The men marched exceedingly well and the march was accomplished without casualties. | J.F. |
| — " — | 24/8/18 | | Weather fine. Battalion training. 2/Lt W.J. MOORE joined for duty & was posted to "A" Company. 2/Lt F.C. MARRIOTT joined for duty & was posted to "B" Company. 3 O.R. proceeded to U.K. on leave | J.F. |
| — " — | 25/8/18 | | Weather dull & changeable, light rainfall during evening. Battalion resting. 2/Lt R.A.T. CAVE-MATHIESON joined for duty and was posted to "B" Company. Capt A. PENNINGTON & 23 O.R. rejoined from leave to U.K. Weekly Training Programme issued to all concerned at 1400 hours. For details see APPENDIX V attached | [illegible] |
| — " — | 26/8/18 | | Weather showery with spells of sunshine. Battalion training in accordance with Weekly Programme see APPENDIX V | |

Instructions regarding War Diaries and Intelligence Summaries are contained in F. S. Regs., Part II. and the Staff Manual respectively. Title pages will be prepared in manuscript.

# WAR DIARY
*or*
# INTELLIGENCE SUMMARY.
*(Erase heading not required.)*

Army Form C. 2118.

| Place | Date | Hour | Summary of Events and Information | Remarks and references to Appendices |
|---|---|---|---|---|
| HAUDRICOURT | 26/8/18 | | The Comdg Officer inspected the transport personnel vehicles at 0930 hrs & the animals at 1700 hours. Also Bn HQ in marching Order at 1400 hours. 3 OR proceeded to UK on leave | JF |
| — " — | 27/8/18 | | Weather intermittent rainfall throughout day. Battalion training according to programme. 2nd Lt W. VALCANS joined for duty and was posted to "A" Company. 2nd Lt A.F. STOKER joined for duty and was posted to "C" Company. | JF |
| — " — | 28/8/18 | | Weather showery with spells of bright sunshine. Battalion training according to programme. 2nd Lt C. CHENEY joined for duty and was posted to "D" Company. 8 OR proceeded to UK on leave. Lt P. TARRANT 2/Lt H.E. ATKINS and 75 OR rejoined from leave | JF |

A7092). Wt. W12839/M1297 750,000. 1/17. D. D & L., Ltd. Forms/C2118/14.

# WAR DIARY
*or*
# INTELLIGENCE SUMMARY.
*(Erase heading not required.)*

Army Form C. 2118.

Instructions regarding War Diaries and Intelligence Summaries are contained in F. S. Regs., Part II and the Staff Manual respectively. Title pages will be prepared in manuscript.

| Place | Date | Hour | Summary of Events and Information | Remarks and references to Appendices |
|---|---|---|---|---|
| HAVRINCOURT | 29/8/18 | | Weather fine with bright sunshine all day. Battalion training according to programme. Lieut G.H. Smith and Lieut F.A. Shipp rejoined from hospital for duty. | |
| — " — | 30/8/18 | | Weather fine with occasional spells of sunshine. Battalion training according to programme. Capt C.H. POTTER M.C. 2/Lt W.H. CAVE and 202 O.R. rejoined from leave to U.K. Capt & Adj F. FRANKS 2/Lt J.N. CAMPBELL and 100 O.R. proceeded to U.K. on leave. | |
| — " — | 31/8/18 | | Weather fine Battalion training as per programme. 13 O.R. rejoined from leave. | |

[illegible signature] Lt Colonel
Comdg [illegible] Bn Lanc Fusiliers

A7092). Wt. W12839/M1293 750,000. 1/17. D. D & L., Ltd. Forms/C2118/14.

87 J.
Stewart

(6339) Wt. W160/M3016 1,500,000 10/17 McA & W Ltd (E 1898) Forms W3091. Army Form W.3091.

4/R 2

# Cover for Documents.

**Nature of Enclosures.**

CONFIDENTIAL

WAR DIARY

OF

6th Bn LANCASHIRE FUSILIERS

FROM 1·9·18 TO 30·9·18.

VOLUME 2.

**Notes, or Letters written.**

9

Instructions regarding War Diaries and Intelligence Summaries are contained in F. S. Regs., Part II. and the Staff Manual respectively. Title pages will be prepared in manuscript.

# WAR DIARY
*or*
~~INTELLIGENCE~~ SUMMARY.
*(Erase heading not required.)*

Army Form C. 2118.

| Place | Date | Hour | Summary of Events and Information | Remarks and references to Appendices |
|---|---|---|---|---|
| HAUDRICOURT | 1-9-18 | | Weather fine. Battalion at rest. Voluntary Church Services. LIEUT. A.B.G. MANSON, 2/LT H.E. ATKINS and 2 ORs proceeded to the Divisional Lewis Gun Course, and 2/LT W.J. MOORE, 2/LT R.A.T. CAVE-MATHIESON and 3 ORs proceeded to the Divisional P+B.T. course. LIEUT G.H. RIMELL, 2/LT C.W. JONES and 11 O.R proceeded on leave to UK for 14 days. | FaR |
| HAUDRICOURT | 2-9-18 | | Weather fine, occasional showers. Battalion training as per programme issued to company commanders on 1/9/18, see APPENDIX I. The Commanding Officer gave a lecture to all officers at 5 pm, subject "The writing of messages and orders". The Divisional Band played in the camp from 3pm to 4pm | FaR |
| HAUDRICOURT | 3-9-18 | | Weather fine. "C" Coy, "D" Coy, H.Q, & Transport bathed. Batt training as per programme. The I.G.C. gave a lecture to all officers at 5pm, subject "Allotment of Tasks" | FaR |
| ~~HAUDRICOURT~~ | 4-9-18 | | Weather fine. Batt training as per programme. "A" & "B" Coys bathed. | FaR |
| HAUDRICOURT | 5-9-18 | | Weather fine. The Batt. carried out a route march under Capt L.B.L. SECKHAM M.C. Route:- HAUDRICOURT - COUPIGNY - PT RONCHOIS - LA HALLE GOUCHE - BEAUFRESNE - HAUDRICOURT. A+B Coys fired on the range in the afternoon. The Commanding Officer held a tactical scheme with all officers. | FaR |

A7092). Wt. W12839/M1293 750,000. 1/17. D. D & L., Ltd. Forms/C2118/14.

# WAR DIARY

*or*

~~INTELLIGENCE SUMMARY.~~

*(Erase heading not required.)*

Army Form C. 2118.

Instructions regarding War Diaries and Intelligence Summaries are contained in F. S. Regs., Part II. and the Staff Manual respectively. Title pages will be prepared in manuscript.

| Place | Date | Hour | Summary of Events and Information | Remarks and references to Appendices |
|---|---|---|---|---|
| HAUDRICOURT | 6-9-18 | | Weather fine. Batt training as per programme. The staff Captain 199th Inf Bde gave a lecture to all officers & N.C.O's at 18.00 hours, on "The supply of ammunition in the field" | |
| ~~HAUT~~ | | | A composite platoon of "C" Coy under 2/Lt C A BATHAM. DCM gave a demonstration to the Officers and NCO's of the Bde. in the value of Controlled as against uncontrolled fire. Tracer ammunition was used and the demonstration was a great success and also very instructive. | JaR<br>APPENDIX II |
| | | | A draft of 2 officers and 55 other ranks arrived and were taken on strength | |
| HAUDRICOURT | 7-9-18 | | Weather fine. Batt: training as per programme, the commanding officer inspected the draft at 9 am and the transport at 9.30 am | |
| | | | A draft of 11. O.R arrived and were taken on strength. | JaR |
| | | | A copy of a letter from the MS to C in C was received from Bde stating that the Battn formed by the amalgamation of the 6th (T) Bn Lanc: Fus and 12th Bn (S) Lanc Fus was the 6th (T) Battn Lancs Fus and that the 12th Bth Lanc Fus had ceased to exist. See APPENDIX III | |
| HAUDRICOURT | 8-9-18 | | Weather wet, heavy rain. Voluntary Church Services. The Transport and "C" Coy bathed in the afternoon. Training programme issued to Coys. See APPENDIX IV | JaR |

A7092). Wt. W12839/M1293 750,000. 1/17. D. D & L., Ltd. Forms/C2118/14.

Instructions regarding War Diaries and Intelligence Summaries are contained in F. S. Regs., Part II. and the Staff Manual respectively. Title pages will be prepared in manuscript.

# WAR DIARY
*or*
# ~~INTELLIGENCE SUMMARY.~~
*(Erase heading not required.)*

Army Form C. 2118.

| Place | Date | Hour | Summary of Events and Information | Remarks and references to Appendices |
|---|---|---|---|---|
| HAUDRICOURT | 9-9-18 | | Weather fine Training as per Programme. HQ "A", "B" & "D" Coys bathed. The commanding officer inspected the transport personnel at 09.00 hours | |
| HAUDRICOURT | 10-9-18 | | Weather stormy. Owing to rain, training was carried on in the afternoon instead of the morning. The B.G.C. lectured to all officers and N.C.O.s at 5 pm in the Y.M.C.A. tent. Subject of lecture "Attack in mobile warfare" | |
| HAUDRICOURT | 11/9/18 | | Weather still unsettled, with frequent storms. Training as per Programme. The B.G.C inspected the transport at 10.30 am & remarked on the good turn out. A lecture was given to all ranks at 5 pm by Dr IRVINE entitled the "HISTORY OF THE AMERICAN ARMY" which was greatly appreciated. | |
| HAUDRICOURT | 12/9/18 | | Weather wet. Batt. Route march via BEAUFRESNE, LA HALLEGOUCHE, Pt RONCHOIS, SOUS LES QUESNES, HAUDRICOURT. Rain was continuous practically during the whole march. An interesting lecture on Machine Guns was given by Col. Charteris at 6 pm, which all officers and N.C.O.s attended. | |
| HAUDRICOURT | 13/9/18 | | Weather unsettled. Batt. training as per Programme | |

A7092). Wt. W12839/M1293 750,000. 1/17. D. D & L., Ltd. Forms/C2118/14.

Instructions regarding War Diaries and Intelligence Summaries are contained in F. S. Regs., Part II. and the Staff Manual respectively. Title pages will be prepared in manuscript.

# WAR DIARY
*or*
# INTELLIGENCE SUMMARY.
*(Erase heading not required.)*

Army Form C. 2118.

| Place | Date | Hour | Summary of Events and Information | Remarks and references to Appendices |
|---|---|---|---|---|
| HAUDRICOURT | 14-9-18 | | Weather still unsettled, training as per Programme. "C" D HQ Coy and the Transport bathed during the day. A Brigade cross country run was held during the afternoon, distance 3 miles. | |
| | | | LIEUT. A.B.G. MANSON, 2/LT H.E. ATKINS, 2/LT W.J. MOORE, 2/LT R.A.T. CAVE-MATHIESON and 5 o.Rs returned from the Divisional PT & LG School. | |
| HAUDRICOURT | 15-9-18 | | Weather fine. Voluntary Church Services. Programme of training for week ending 21st was issued to Coy Commanders. See APPENDIX V | |
| | | | Major J.S. TOWNSEND. M.C. joined for duty & assumed the duties of 2nd in Command of the Battalion. Capt F Franks 2/Lt C.W. Campbell + 57 O.R. rejoined from leave to U.K. | |
| — " — | 16/9/18 | | Weather fine, bright sunshine all day. Companies training in accordance with programme see appendix V. The Battalion Sports were held during the afternoon the events were keenly contested & proved of great interest to all ranks. The following are the results:– 100x 2/Lt T.C. MARRIOTT 2/Lt A.F. STOKER 1st Heat Pte ASHWORTH | |

Instructions regarding War Diaries and Intelligence Summaries are contained in F. S. Regs., Part II. and the Staff Manual respectively. Title pages will be prepared in manuscript.

# WAR DIARY
*or*
# INTELLIGENCE SUMMARY.
(*Erase heading not required.*)

Army Form C. 2118.

| Place | Date | Hour | Summary of Events and Information | Remarks and references to Appendices |
|---|---|---|---|---|
| HAUDRICOURT | 16/9/18 | | Sergt BROMLEY 2nd Heat. Sergt SMALLWOOD Pte FISH 3rd Heat. Sgt Webster Pte Osborne 4th Heat. The semi final & finals will be run off later. 440x 2/Lt A.F. STOKER 2/Lt W.J. MOORE. 220x Sergt DELANEY Sergt BRERETON 1st Heat Pte ELLIS Sgt BROMLEY 2nd Heat. High Jump Pte BROOKS 4' 3". Long Jump Pte HOWARTH 17'. 880x Pte ELLIS. Kicking the football Pte TODD. Throwing the Cricket Ball Pte BADEMAN. One mile 2/Lt A.F. STOKER. Tug of War B Company D Company. Hurdle Race Corpl DELANEY. Relay Race B Company C Company. | FF |
| " | 17/9/18 | | Weather fine, bright sunshine all day. Battalion training according to weekly programme. | FF |
| " | 18/9/18 | | Weather fine, rather warm. The Battalion carried out a Route March; distance 8 miles. The men marched very well | |

A7092). Wt. W12839/M1293 750,000. 1/17. D. D & L., Ltd. Forms/C2118/14.

Instructions regarding War Diaries and Intelligence Summaries are contained in F. S. Regs., Part II, and the Staff Manual respectively. Title pages will be prepared in manuscript.

# WAR DIARY
*or*
# INTELLIGENCE SUMMARY.
(*Erase heading not required.*)

Army Form C. 2118.

| Place | Date | Hour | Summary of Events and Information | Remarks and references to Appendices |
|---|---|---|---|---|
| HAUDRICOURT | 15/9/18 | | The finals for the Bde & Bn competitions were held at 1730 hours with the following results:- C Company were defeated by the 5th Connaught Rangers & B Company were defeated by the Bde H.Q. Staff in the Tug of War. The 100x was won by 2/Lt T.C. MARRIOTT Pte ASHWORTH taking 2nd place. The 220x was won by Sergt DELANEY Pte Ellis taking 2nd place. | JF |
| — " — | 19/9/18 | | Weather fine, with bright sunshine all day. Verbal orders received that the Battalion will move to FOMERIE STn and entrain, enroute to First Army area on the 20th Sept 1918. All Training cancelled in order to give companies time to prepare for move. The C.O. inspected the Battalion in Marching Order at 1100 hours. 199th Bde Order 107 received at 1400 hours which states that the Battalion will join the 198th Bde on arrival | |

A7092). Wt. W12839/M1293 750,000. 1/17. D, D & L., Ltd. Forms/C2118/14.

Instructions regarding War Diaries and Intelligence Summaries are contained in F. S. Regs., Part II. and the Staff Manual respectively. Title pages will be prepared in manuscript.

# WAR DIARY
*or*
# INTELLIGENCE SUMMARY.
*(Erase heading not required.)*

Army Form C. 2118.

| Place | Date | Hour | Summary of Events and Information | Remarks and references to Appendices |
|---|---|---|---|---|
| HAUDRICOURT | 19/9/18 | | in new area. Bde Operation Order No 108 received at 2230 hours. 5th Lancashire Fusiliers Order No 16 issued to all concerned at 2100 hours see APPENDIX VI attached | |
| " | 20/9/18 | | Weather showery. The Battalion marched out at 0510 in accordance with Order No 16 see APPENDIX VI attached entrained at FORMERIE Station at 1235 hours (Bn HQ A & C Coys) B & D Companies entrained at 1515 hours. The first half Battalion arrived at TINCQUES at 2400 hours and marched into Billets at MANIN arriving at 0200 hours 21/9/18. B & D Companies arrived in Billets at 0600 hours. 'C' Company were detailed for detraining duty & did not arrive in Billets until 1200 hours. The Billets are exceptionally good & the men are quite comfortable. | |
| MANIN | 21/9/18 | | Weather showery during the morning, bright sunshine during afternoon | |

A7092). Wt. W12839/M1293. 750,000. 1/17. D D & L., Ltd. Forms/C2118/14.

Army Form C. 2118.

# WAR DIARY
*or*
# INTELLIGENCE SUMMARY.
*(Erase heading not required.)*

Instructions regarding War Diaries and Intelligence Summaries are contained in F. S. Regs., Part II. and the Staff Manual respectively. Title pages will be prepared in manuscript.

| Place | Date | Hour | Summary of Events and Information | Remarks and references to Appendices |
|---|---|---|---|---|
| MANIN | 21/9/18 | | The Comdg Officer inspected all the Battalion billets during the day. Following wire received from 199th Bde:- Acting appointment of Capt J.S. TOWNSHEND 6th Dorset Regt as 2nd in Command 6th Lan F was approved aaa Authy Mil Secy wire F21 of 19/9/18 199th Bde | JF |
| MANIN / LIGNEREUIL | 22/9/18 | | Weather showery. Battalion resting. Bde wire BM148 received at 0800 hours ordering Bn to move to LIGNEREUIL today, move to be completed by 1700 hours. The Battalion marched off at 1400 hours arrived in billets at LIGNEREUIL at 1530 hours. The Comdg Officer visited Bde H.Q (198th) From today the Battalion are under the orders of the 198th Bde. | |
| LIGNEREUIL | 23/9/18 | | Weather showery with spells of sunshine. The Comdg Officer inspected the Battalion's billets at 0930 hours & attended at Bde Conference | |

Instructions regarding War Diaries and Intelligence Summaries are contained in F. S. Regs., Part II. and the Staff Manual respectively. Title pages will be prepared in manuscript.

# WAR DIARY
*or*
# INTELLIGENCE SUMMARY.
*(Erase heading not required.)*

Army Form C. 2118.

| Place | Date | Hour | Summary of Events and Information | Remarks and references to Appendices |
|---|---|---|---|---|
| LIGNEREUIL | 23/9/18 | | at 1230 hours. Companies carried out Platoon training during the afternoon. Training Programme for week ending 28th inst was issued to all concerned at 1200 hours. see APPENDIX VII attached. Conference for Coy Comdrs was held in Bn H.Q. Mess at 2030 hours subject training. | JF |
| " " | 24/9/18 | | Weather showery. Companies carried out training in accordance with weekly training programme. 12 O.R. rejoined from leave to U.K. | JF |
| " " | 25/9/18 | | Weather showery. Companies training as yesterday. Warning Order received from Bde that Brigade will be prepared to move from present area on or about 27th Sept. | JF |
| " " | 26/9/18 | | Weather fine but rather cold. Brigade Route march at 0900 hours distance approx 11 miles Drum Marching Order. The Battalion returned to billets at 1250 hours. Lunch | |

A7092). Wt. W12839/M1293 750,000. 1/17. D D & L., Ltd. Forms/C2118/14.

Instructions regarding War Diaries and Intelligence Summaries are contained in F. S. Regs., Part II. and the Staff Manual respectively. Title pages will be prepared in manuscript.

# WAR DIARY
*or*
# INTELLIGENCE SUMMARY.
*(Erase heading not required.)*

Army Form C. 2118.

| Place | Date | Hour | Summary of Events and Information | Remarks and references to Appendices |
|---|---|---|---|---|
| LIGNEREUIL | 26/9/18 | | CGE HELDER proceeded to 198th Bde H.Q as Bde Gas Officer. | J.F. |
| – " – | 27/9/18 | | Weather fine & warm. Brigade Route march at 0815 hours. Battalion returned to billets at 1150 hours. 25 O.R. fell out from the line of march. At 1430 hours an aeroplane gave a demonstration in Height & Communication with aeroplanes, which all Officers & N.C.O.s attended. Rev C.F. WHITING C.F. was admitted to hospital. | J.F. |
| – " – | 28/9/18 | | Weather stormy. The Battalion moved to CORBIE in accordance with Bn Order No 18 attached, see APPENDIX VIII and arrived at 0230 hours 29/9/18 where we were accommodated in billets. Lieut J.W. DEANE was admitted to hospital. Lieut & Q.M O'BRIEN proceeded to UK on leave. Major J.S. TOWNSHEND M.C. proceeded to BOULOGNE on a Cooking Course. | J.F. |

A7092). Wt. W12839/M1293 750,000. 1/17. D. D & L., Ltd. Forms/C2118/14.

Army Form C. 2118.

# WAR DIARY
*or*
# INTELLIGENCE SUMMARY.
*(Erase heading not required.)*

Instructions regarding War Diaries and Intelligence Summaries are contained in F. S. Regs., Part II. and the Staff Manual respectively. Title pages will be prepared in manuscript.

| Place | Date | Hour | Summary of Events and Information | Remarks and references to Appendices |
|---|---|---|---|---|
| CORBIE HARBONNIERS | 29/9/18 | | Weather showery. The Battalion moved to HARBONNIERS in accordance with Bn Order No 19 see APPENDIX IX attached and arrived at 1700 hours. The billets are fairly good considering that the enemy were in occupation only three months ago | [illegible] |
| HARBONNIERS | 30/9/18 | | Weather showery. Battalion resting & cleaning up. The Brigadier lectured to all officers & N.C.O.s at 1700 hours. Subject Notes on Recent Fighting. The Battalion sick rate during the past month has been extremely low. Admissions to hospital during the month 2 Officers 42. O.R. | [illegible] |

R. [illegible] Lt Colonel
Comdg 6th Bn Lancashire Fusiliers

D. D. & L., London, E.C. (A8094) Wt. W2771/M2031 750,000 5/17 Sch. 52 Forms/C2118/14

APPENDIX I

## 6th BN LANCASHIRE FUSILIERS.

**PROGRAMME OF TRAINING FOR WEEK ENDING 7th SEPTEMBER 1918.**

| Coy. | Date. | Hours of Training | Training Area. | Nature of Training. | Lectures. | Tactical Exercise | Remarks. |
|---|---|---|---|---|---|---|---|
| A. | 2nd Sept. | 08.00 to 12.00 hours. | A2 | Individual | Lecture by C.O. 18.00 hours. | —— | A & B Coys will make full use of bombing pit by mutual arrangement. |
| B. | | | A2 | „ | | | |
| C. | | | A1 | Musketry. | | | B. Range. C Coy Tgts 1-8 |
| D. | | | A1 | „ | | | D. " " 9-16 |
| A. | 3rd Sept. | | A1. | Musketry. | Lecture B.G.C. to all Officers, 17.00 hours. | —— | B. Range. A Coy Tgts 1-8 |
| B. | | | A1. | „ | | | B " " 9-16 |
| C. | | | A2. | Individual. | | | C & D Coys will make full use of bombing pit by mutual arrangement. |
| D. | | | A2. | „ | | | |
| A. | 4th Sept. | | B3. | Individual. | Company Lecture to N.C.Os. | —— | B2 Range C Coy Tgts 1-8 |
| B. | | | B3. | „ | | | D " " 9-16. from 0800 to 12.00 hours. |
| C. | | | B2. | Musketry. | | | |
| D. | | | B2. | „ | | | |
| A. | 5th Sept. | | | Route March. | | Batt. Tactical Exercise. | B. Range A Coy Tgts 1-8 |
| B. | | | | | | | B Coy " 9-16 from 1400 to 1600 hours. |
| C. | | | | | | | |
| D. | | | | | | | |
| A. | 6th Sept. | | C1. | Route march combined with Indvd Instruction. | Brigade Lecture "Supply of Ammunition" 18.00 hours. | | |
| B. | | | C2. | | | | |
| C. | | | A1 | Musketry. | | | A. Range C Coy Tgts 1-8 |
| D. | | | A1 | „ | | | D. " " 9-16. |
| A. | 7th Sept. | | A1 | Musketry | | Company Tactical Exercise. | A. Range A. Coy Tgts 1-8 |
| B. | | | A1. | „ | | | B Coy 9-16. |
| C. | | | C2. | Route march combined with Indvd Instruction. | | | |
| D. | | | C1. | | | | |

2. TRAINING

TRAINING will be carried out as for week ending Sept.7th1918. O.C.Coys will pay special attention to the training of men in the Mills No.36.

During Gas training Officers and NCOs will wear their Box Respirators with the men.

CLASSES OF INSTRUCTION. A Musketry Class under C.S.M.Whittam, for backward men, will start on Sept.2nd at 0800 hours. O.C.Coys will forward a nominal roll to this Office of men attending above.

The Riding Class for Officers will be held on Sept.~~2nd, 4th~~ 3rd & 6th.

INSPECTIONS- MARCHING ORDER.

| | | | |
|---|---|---|---|
| Transport. | Sept.2nd. | 0930 hours. | Personnel & Vehicles Horses will be hooked in. |
| " | " 3rd. | " " | Animals. |
| Batt. H.Q Drums. | " 2nd. | 1400 " | |
| A & D Coys. | " 3rd. | 1400 " | |
| B & C Coys. | " 4th. | 1400 " | |
| Harness | 5th | 1100 " | |
| Transport. | 7th | 0930 " | |

[signature] Capt,

1.9.18. Adjt. 6th Bn.Lancashire Fusiliers

## NOTES ON TRAINING.

1. Night firing will not take place this week. O.C.Companies will endeavour to complete the 300 yards practices during the week.

2. A Demonstration of Controlled and Uncontrolled Fire will take place at 3 p.m. 6th inst. on "A" ranges. All available Officers and N.C.Os. will attend.
Particulars are being issued to Companies.

3. During Platoon Training, Companies will carry out platoon competitions. The 2 best platoons in the Battalion, will represent the Battalion in the Brigade Competitions on the 24th inst.
The Platoon Competition will consist of

(a) Turnout, (Marching Order).
Drill, close order.
Handling of Arms.

(b) Assault Course Training.
Physical Training.

(c) Field Practices with ball ammunition.

(d) Tactical Handling Scheme.
The platoon will be composed as follows:-
(a) Platoon H.Q.
1. Subaltern.
1. Batman.
1. Runner.
1. Platoon Sgt.
(b) 1. Lewis Gun Section, (1. N.C.O. & 10. O.R.)
(c) 2 Rifle Sections (7. O.R. each)

Making a minimum of 29.

4. It has been decided that steel helmets shall be painted with service paint throughout the Brigade. Companies will be notified when the paint is available.

5. On Sunday 8th inst, a Rifle Meeting will be held. Further information will be issued later.

6. The cloth for the Brigade sign is being issued to the Battalion to-day 3rd inst. O.C.Companies, etc., will make arrangements with Quarter-master for sewing on above.

(Signed) F.A.Ridler, Captain,

3.9.18. Adjutant, 6th Lancashire Fusiliers.

APPENDIX II

# DEMONSTRATION

## in the value of

## CONTROLLED AS AGAINST UNCONTROLLED FIRE.

1. A platoon of 3 sections holding a defensive position. The L.G. magazines are filled with one "tracer" round to every five ordinary rounds.

2. FIRST DEMONSTRATION - UNCONTROLLED FIRE.

(a) The sentry on duty discovers the enemy and shouts "Stand to", whereupon the men of the platoon open fire without orders from platoon or section commanders, each rifleman and Lewis Gunner selecting his own target. The N.C.O's instead of controlling the fire of their commands, open fire themselves.

(b) Points to be noticed.
1. No fire control.
2. Fire erratic and not properly concentrated or distributed.
3. Fire discipline bad - men do not adjust their sights or aim correctly.
4. Waste of ammunition.
5. Both Lewis Guns fire together, and are out of action at the same time, hence loss of fire power.

3. SECOND DEMONSTRATION -CONTROLLED FIRE.

(a) The sentry on duty discovers the enemy and shouts "Stand to", whereupon the men of the platoon "Stand to" and await the orders of platoon and section commanders.
The platoon commander then gives the correct fire orders, which are repeated by section commanders. Fire is opened by riflemen and Lewis Gunners.

(b) Points to be noticed.

Increased fire effect due to good fire discipline and fire control, which permits of the fire being distributed or concentrated according to the demands of the tactical situation.
Note especially the tactics of the Lewis Gun sections. The Guns firing in alternate bursts prevent both Guns being out of action simultaneously from stoppages or other causes.
Note too, the action of the riflemen of the Lewis Gun Section when the Gun is out of action.

1.9.18.
6th Bn.Lancs.Fusiliers. SIGNED.

COPY

M.S. to C. in C.
6306

66th Divn.
6683/17/A

APPENDIX III

Military Secretary,
to Commander in Chief,
G. H. Q.

The attached A.F.W.3025 for grant of Temporary rank of Major to Captain R.M.L Scott, Cheshire Regt. attached 9th Manchester Regt. is forwarded.

The 9th (Territorial) Bn Manchester Regt. absorbed the 13th (Service) Bn. Manchester Regt, which has previously absorbed the 17t (Service) Bn. and it is not quite clear whether the present 9th Bn. is to be considered a T.T. os Service Bn. or what may be regarded as the establishment of the amalgamated Bn.

The same points arise in connection with the 6th Bn Lancashire Fusiliers.

Will you please give a ruling.

(Sgd) D.V.M.BALDERS.
Major,
for Brigadier General,
Commanding 66th Division.

26.8.18.

\- 2 -

Headquarters
66th Division.

M.S. to C.in C.
6306

6683/17/A.

With reference to the attached, the 9th Bn. Manchester Regt. and the 6th Bn Lancashire Fusiliers are Territorial Battalions; and the 13th Manchester Regt, and 12th Lancashire Fusiliers, have ceased to exist.

Sgd------------------Lt-Col.
A.M.S.
for Major General.
Military Secretary.
to Commander-in-Chief

G.H.Q.
3.9.18.

\-3 -

Headquarters,
199th Infantry Brigade.

For information with reference to your A.206 dated 12.8.18.
In view of the preceding minute the instructions given in O.D.S. 384, Section "E" will therefore not apply to the two Territorial Battalions referred to.

Sgd. D.V.M.BALDERS, Major.
D.A.A.G.
66th Division.

6.9.18.

\- 4 -

6th Lancashire Fusiliers,
9th Bn. Manchester Regt.

Forwarded for information.

Sgd J.T.Fox. Captain.
Staff Captain.
199th Inf. Brigade.

7th Sept 1918.

APPENDIX IV

# 6th Bn. LANCASHIRE FUSILIERS.

## PROGRAMME OF TRAINING FOR WEEK ENDING 14th Sept. 1918.

| Coy. | Date. | Hours of Training. | Training Area. | Nature of Training. | Lectures. | Tactical Exercise. | Remarks. |
|---|---|---|---|---|---|---|---|
| A. | 9th Sept. | 0800 to 1200 hours. | A2. | Individual & Platoon Training. | Bde Discussion. 14.30 hours. | | A & B Coys will, by mutual arrangement, make full use of bombing pit. |
| B. | | | A2. | | | | |
| C. | | | A1. | Musketry. | | | B.Range. C.Coy Tgts 1-8 |
| D. | | | A1. | | | | D. " " 9-16. |
| A. | 10th Sept. | | A1. | Musketry. | Lecture by B.G.C. to all Officers & N.C.Os. 1800 hours. | Bde Riding Class. 3 1600 to 1800 hours. | B.Range. A.Coy Tgts 1-8 |
| B. | | | A1. | | | | B " " 9-16 |
| C. | | | A2. | Individual & Platoon Training. | | | C & D Coys will, by mutual arrangement, make full use of bombing pit |
| D. | | | A2. | | | | |
| A. | 11th Sept. | | B3. | Individual & Platoon Training. | Lecture by C.O. at 1800 hours. | | |
| B. | | | B3. | | | | |
| C. | | | B2. | Musketry. | | | B2.Range. C.Coy Tgts 1-8, D " " 9-16. 0800 to 1200 hrs. |
| D. | | | B2. | | | | 1400 to 1600 hrs, Backward Musketry Class, Tgts 1-16. |
| A. | 12th Sept. | | B2 | | Lecture by Col.Charteris. on M.Gs. All Officers & NCOs. 1800 hrs | | B2 Range A.Coy Tgts 1-6 |
| B. | | | B2. | | | | B " " 7-12 |
| C. | | | | ROUTE MARCH | | | 1400 to 1600 hrs |
| D. | | | | | | | Backward Musketry Class, Tgts 13-16 1400 to 1600 hrs |
| A. | 13th Sept. | | C2. | Route March combined with Individual & Platoon Trng. | | | RIFLE MEETING. |
| B. | | | C1. | | | | |
| C. | | | A1. | Musketry. | | | A.Range. C.Coy. Tgts 1-8 |
| D. | | | A1. | | | | D " " 9-16. |
| A. | 14th Sept. | | A1. | Musketry. | | BATT. Tactical. Exercise. | A.Range. A.Coy Tgts 1-8 |
| B. | | | A1. | | | | B." " 9-16. |
| C. | | | C1. | Route march combined with Individual & Platoon Trng. | | | |
| D. | | | C2. | | | | |

6th Bn. Lancashire Fusiliers.

NOTES ON TRAINING.

1. CLASSES OF INSTRUCTION.

As last week, and in addition a class of instruction for Junior N.C.O's (Cpls & L/Cpls) under the Regimental Sergeant Major will commence at 0900 hours 9th inst. Companys will each detail 6 N.C.O's to attend.

The Riding Class for Officers will be held on Sept.10 & 13th.

2. INSPECTIONS - MARCHING ORDER.

| | | | |
|---|---|---|---|
| Transport, | Sept. 9th. | 0900 hours. | Personnel only. |
| do | " 10th. | 0930 " | by B.G.C. Personnel & Vehicles. Horses to be hooked in etc |
| do | " 13th. | 0915 " | Animals. |
| Batt.H.Q. Drums. | " 10th | 1400 " | |
| A & B.Coys. | " 11th | 1400 " | |
| C & D " | " 14th | 1400 " | |

3. The fighting kit as laid down by the G.O.C. is as follows :-

Two water bottles.

Pack containing.
Ground sheet,
Mess tin,
2 days rations,
1 pair socks,
Holdall.
Towel.
70 rds S.A.A.
150 rds S.A.A in pouches

This order will be worn on the route march 12th inst.
A & B Coys will wear fighting kit on 13th and C & D Coys on 14th inst, during their training, in order to test if same is satisfactory.
O.C.Coys will report by the end of the week whether they consider the manner of carrying the articles enumerated is satisfactory, and if not, suggestions for improving same.
To make up for the two days rations the equivalent weight will be made up with ammunition.

4. On all route marches, dismounted officers will be dressed like the men, ie; either F.M.O or Fighting Kit, as ordered. The Quartermaster is arranging to supply officers with equipment this week.

5. The Backward Musketry Squads will fire on B2 Range on 11th & 12th insts from 1400 hours to 1600 hours. See Training Programme for allocation of targets.

6. Sgt.Miles, A.G.S, will be available on the 11th & 12th insts on the Assault Course "B.3" Area. Coys will make full use of above instructor.

6th Bn.Lancashire Fusiliers.

NOTES ON TRAINING.
(2)

7. In order to practise men in the use of ground and cover Platoon training should be started.
Owing to the low strength of Companies, composite Platoons should be formed for this purpose.
Special attention to be paid to L.G.tactics.

8. BOMBING. Together with the training in the Mills No.36 H.G., hand bombing should also be practised.

9. ENTRENCHING TOOLS. In order to give men practice in the use of the entrenching tool for improving cover etc, O.C.Coys will carry out this training on A2. B3. and C2 Areas.

10. MUSKETRY. As soon as Coys are sufficiently far advanced in individual practices they should start elementary field practices. Before this is done, this Office should be notified so that arrangements etc may be made.
Appended are some suggested practices.

11. SCOUTS. The Scouts Classes under Lt.F.TYSON and 2nd Lt.SMITH-SAVILLE are allotted "B" Range A1.Area from 1400 hours to 1600 hours 9th and 10th insts.

12. LECTURES. The subject of the B.G.C's lecture on the 10th inst is "ATTACK IN MOBILE WARFARE" and that of Col.Charteris on 13th inst "MACHINE GUNS".

(signed) F.A.RIDLER, Capt,

Adjt, 6th Lancashire Fusiliers.

FIELD FIRING PRACTICES

| COMPETITION | RANGE | CONDITIONS AND SCORING |
|---|---|---|
| 1. Patrols (Teams of 6). | Unknown range (up to 350 yds) | (a) Tiles, falling plates or bottles, worked on the "knock-out" prciple. - ie; as a target is struck opposing firer ceases fire. Smart umpires required. OR (b) "Knock-out" principle, Patrols not individuals, ie; two patrols. Best patrol the one which knocks down all Tgts first. One umpire only required. |

---

2. THE PILL BOX (3rd Army Musketry Sch.)

OBJECT:- To practise men in applying fire at a Pill box.
Number:- 1 NCO and 6 - 8 men.
Method of conducting :- The section extended to one pace lies down 50 yds from the firing point, rifles loaded with 5 rounds, bayonets fixed. When ready the section Commander gives the order "Advance" and leads his men at the double to the firing point. He orders fire to be opened at the pill box. One minute after the order "Advance" the superintending officer will give the order "Cease fire".
Target:- 4' x 4' (2nd Class figure tgt) coloured grey or white, with a black band 8" wide across the tgt, the top of the band being 1' from the top of the tgt.
Range:- 200 yds.
Rounds:- 15 per man
Marking:- one point per hit on the black band deduct 3 points if fire is opened before the Sect.Commander gives the order "fire" Deduct 1 point for each shot fired after the order "Cease fire"

---

3. THE ELUSIVE HUN (3rd Army Musketry Sch)

Object:- To practise men in quick alteration of their point of aim and to demonstrate the importance of watching the front, and of re-charging magazine at the first favorable opportunity.
Numbers: 1 NCO and 6-8 men.
Method of conducting; The section assumes a firing position on the firing point. The use of cover is optional to the firers. The superintending officer gives the caution "Watch your front" and signals to the butts. A target will be exposed five times, each time in a different place for 6 seconds; 8 seconds interval between exposures. Unlimited rounds may be fired at each exposure.
Target: A figure three or four (silhouette)
Range: 200 yds.
Rounds: 15 per man.
Marking: 1 point per hit.

---

| COMPETITION | RANGE | CONDITIONS & SCORING |
|---|---|---|
| 4. Superiority of fire. | | Object:- To emphasise the importance of reaching the objective quickly, and of obtaining superiority of fire when counter-attacked.<br>Numbers: 1 NCO and 8-10 men.<br>Method of conducting: The section will be extended to 2 paces 20 yds in rear of the firing point where there will be a sack filled with straw representing a Boche opposite each man. Rifles to be loaded with 5 rounds and held at high port. Bayonets fixed. When ready the Sect.Commander will give the order "Advance"; 8-10 figure 3 silhouette tgts (according to the number of firers) will appear at the butts. The section will open fire by order of the Commander. 10 seconds after the first tgts appear 2 more will come up and similarly after every 10 seconds 2 additional tgts will appear. Tgts will disappear when hit. If at any time the number of tgts exceeds the number of firers the order "Cease fire" will be given.<br>Time limit:- One minute from the first appearance of the tgts. The section which has the fewest targets up at the end of the minute wins.<br>Range & Targets:- 200 yds. Figure 4 or 300 yds Figure 3.<br>Rounds :- 10 per firer. |
| 5. The Boche Patrol. (1 NCO and 6 Men) | | Object:- To train men to watch the front & develop tactical sense.<br>Range:- 250 -350 yds (for gallery range)<br>Rounds:- 5 per man.<br>Targets:- Six figure 3 on poles.<br>Method of conducting:- Section Commander is informed that a Boche Patrol of 6 men has been seen by a brown screen erected on butt gallery. His orders are to watch for them and try to bag the lot. When the Section takes up a fire position the following exposure of tgts are made:-<br>1. A Figure slowly looks out from behind the screen for 6 seconds and withdraws.<br>2. A Figure looks out from the opposite side for a similar period.<br>3. Three targets look out for 6 seconds, one on either side, one over the top of the screen.<br>If fire is opened no further exposures take place, and the practice is finished.<br>If no shots are fired the whole Boche patrol- Six Figures- move out from cover and proceed at a walk along the gallery, traversing a distance of 30 yds to a second screen representing cover.<br>Scoring: Two points per hit; 5 points extra if all the tgts are hit. |

| COMPETITION | RANGE | CONDITIONS AND SCORING |
|---|---|---|
| 6. The disabled Boche Machine Gun.<br>(1 NCO and 6 men) | | Object:- To train men to watch for, and prevent, removal of enemy guns.<br>Range : 250 -300 yds.<br>Rounds: 10 per man<br>Targets: Screen 4' x 3', torepresent Machine Gun, four figure 3 tgts.<br>Method of conducting: Section Commander is informed that the screen represents a Boche Machine Gun out of action and his orders are to prevent it being taken away by the enemy.<br>20 seconds after the section has taken up position two Fig.3 Tgts will stealthily appear ( one on each side of the screen) and will slowly move gun to a flank. Fig.3 Tgt will disappear if hit and movement of gun ceases for 5 seconds, after which 4 casualties will be replaced in a similar manner and the gun movement resumed. The practice ceases one ~~m~~ minute after the firing of the first shot. |
| | Marking. | Hits on the Fig.3 Tgts only to count.<br>Scoring: 2 points per hit. |
| 7. SECTION RUSHES.<br>Separate Targets for each Section. | 350 to 150 yds. | Ammunition ten rounds per man.<br>Method of conducting. 5 Fire Positions 50 yds apart to be marked by posts. Firers extended at 350 yds opposite Tgts. Sights normal. Rifle empty. Safety catches back.<br>Superintending Officer gives order ("At your tgts 2 rds fire") . Firers lie down and fire 2 rounds. 20 seconds after the order "Fire", Supervising Officer will blow whistle to "Cease fire", and after 10 seconds interval will give the order "Advance". Safety catches must be back before the firers advance. Firers must advance to the next fire position, fire 2 rounds at their tgts without further orders. 20 seconds after the order "Advance" the superin--tending officer will blow his whistle to "Cease fire" and after another interval of 10 seconds will again give the order "Advance" and so on, 20 seconds being allowed for each advance of 50 yds. and firing 2 rounds, with 10 seconds interval after firing before commencing the next advance.<br>NOTE: The second charges may be inserted any time after the first advance<br>Scoring: 4, 3, 2, 1. |

8. Platoon attack with Lewis Guns.

The following takes place:-

1. Platoon advances in artillery formation.
2. Deploys 700 yds from Target.
3. Attacks, captures and consolidates position 200 yds from target.
4. Pursuit by fire of retreating enemy.
5. Repels counter)attack.

## FIELD FIRING PRACTICES

| COMPETITION | RANGE | CONDITIONS AND SCORING |
| --- | --- | --- |
| 1. Patrols<br>(Teams of 6). | Unknown range<br>(up to 300 yds) | (a) Tiles, falling plates or bottles, worked on the "knock-out" principle. - ie; as a target is struck opposing firer ceases fire. Smart umpires required.<br>OR<br>(b) "Knock-out" principle, Patrols not individuals, ie; two patrols. Best patrol the one which knocks down all tgts first. One umpire only required. |
| 2. THE PILL BOX<br>(3rd Army Musketry Sch.) | | OBJECT:- To practise men in applying fire at a Pill box.<br>Number:- 1 NCO and 6 - 8 men.<br>Method of conducting :- The section extended to one pace lies down 50 yds from the firing point, rifles loaded with 5 rounds, bayonets fixed. When ready the section Commander gives the order "Advance" and leads his men at the double to the firing point. He orders fire to be opened at the pill box. One minute after the order "Advance" the superintending officer will give the order "Cease fire".<br>Target:- 4' x 4' (2nd Class figure tgt) coloured grey or white, with a black band 6" wide across the tgt, the top of the band being 1' from the top of the tgt.<br>Range:- 300 yds.<br>Rounds:- 15 per man<br>Marking:- One point per hit on the black band deduct 3 points if fire is opened before the Sect.Commander gives the order "fire" Deduct 1 point for each shot fired after the order "Cease fire" |
| 3. THE ELUSIVE GUN<br>(3rd Army Musketry Sch) | | Object:- To practice men in quick alteration of their point of aim and to demonstrate the importance of watching the front, and of re-charging magazine at the first favorable opportunity.<br>Numbers: 1 NCO and 6-8 men.<br>Method of conducting: The section assumes a firing position on the firing point. The use of cover is optional to the firers. The superintending officer gives the caution "Watch your front" and signals to the butts. A target will be exposed five times, each time in a different place for 6 seconds; 5 seconds interval between exposures. Unlimited rounds may be fired at each exposure.<br>Target: A figure three or four (silhouette)<br>Range: 300 yds.<br>Rounds: 15 per man.<br>Marking: 1 point per hit. |

| COMPETITION | RANGE | CONDITIONS & SCORING |
|---|---|---|
| 4. Superiority of fire. | | Object:- To emphasise the importance of reaching the objective quickly, and of obtaining superiority of fire when counter-attacked.<br>Numbers: 1 NCO and 8-10 men.<br>Method of conducting. The section will be extended to 2 paces 20 yds in rear of the firing point where there will be a sack filled with straw representing a Boche opposite each man. Rifles to be loaded with 5 rounds and held at high port. Bayonets fixed. When ready the Sect.Commander will give the order "Advance": 8-10 figure 3 silhouette tgts (according to the number of firers will appear at the butts. The section will open fire by order of the Commander. 10 seconds after the first tgts appear 2 more will come up and similarly after every 10 seconds 2 additional tgts will appear. Tgts will disappear when hit. If at any time the number of tgts exceeds the number of firers the order "Cease fire" will be given.<br>Time Limit:- One minute from the first appearance of the tgts. The section which has the fewest targets up at the end of the minute wins.<br>Range & Targets:- 200 yds. Figure 4 or 300 yds Figure 3.<br>Rounds :- 10 per firer. |
| 5. The Boche Patrol. (1 NCO and 6 Men) | | Object:- To train men to watch the front & develop tactical sense.<br>Range:- 250 -350 yds (for gallery range)<br>Rounds:- 5 per man.<br>Targets:- Six figure 3 on poles.<br>Method of conducting:- Section Commander is informed that a Boche Patrol of 6 men has been seen by a brown screen erected on butt gallery. His orders are to watch for them and try to bag the lot. When the section takes up a fire position the following exposure of tgts are made:-<br>1. A Figure slowly looks out from behind the screen for 6 seconds and withdraws.<br>2. A Figure looks out from the opposite side for a similar period.<br>3. Three targets look out for 6 seconds, one on either side, one over the top of the screen.<br>If fire is opened no further exposures take place, and the practice is finished.<br>If no shots are fired the whole Boche patrol- Six Figures- move out from cover and proceed at a walk along the gallery, traversing a distance of 30 yds to a second screen representing cover.<br>Scoring: Two points per hit; 5 points extra if all the tgts are hit. |

| COMPETITION | RANGE | CONDITIONS AND SCORING |
|---|---|---|
| 6. The disabled Boche Machine gun.<br>(1 NCO and 6 men) | | Object:- To train men to watch for, and prevent, removal of enemy guns.<br>Range : 200 -300 yds.<br>Rounds: 10 per man<br>Targets: Screen 4' x 3', torepresent Machine Gun, four figure 3 tgts.<br>Method of conducting: Section Commander is informed that the screen represents a Boche Machine Gun out of action and his orders are to prevent it being taken away by the enemy. 20 seconds after the section has taken up position two Fig.3 Tgts will stealthily appear ( one on each side of the screen) and will slowly move gun to a flank. Fig.3 Tgt will disappear if hit and movement of gun ceases for 5 seconds, after which 4 casualties will be replaced in a similar manner and the gun movement resumed. The practice ceases one minute after the firing of the first shot. |
| | Marking. | Hits on the Fig.3 Tgts only to count.<br>Scoring: 2 points per hit. |
| 7. SECTION RUSHES.<br>Separate Targets for each Section. | 350 to 150 yds. | Ammunition ten rounds per man.<br>Method of conducting. 5 Fire Positions 50 yds apart to be marked by posts. Firers extended at 350 yds opposite tgts. Sights normal. Rifle empty. Safety catches back.<br>Superintending Officer gives order ("at your tgts 2 rds fire") . Firers lie down and fire 2 rounds. 20 seconds after the order "Fire", Supervising Officer will blow whistle to "Cease fire", and after 10 seconds interval will give the order "Advance". Safety catches must be back before the firers advance. Firers must advance to the next fire position, fire 2 rounds at their tgts without further orders. 20 seconds after the order "Advance" the superin-tending officer will blow his whistle to "Cease fire" and after another interval of 10 seconds will again give the order "Advance" and so on, 20 seconds being allowed for each advance of 50 yds. and firing 2 rounds, with 10 seconds interval after firing before commencing the next advance.<br>NOTE: The second charges may be inserted any time after the firstadvance<br>Scoring: 4. 3. 2. 1. |
| 8. Platoon attack with Lewis Guns. | | The following takes place:-<br>1. Platoon advances in artillery formation.<br>2. Deploys 700 yds from Target.<br>3. Attacks, captures and consolidates position 200 yds from target.<br>4. Pursuit by fire of retreating enemy.<br>5. Repels counter)attack. |

APPENDIX V

# 6th Bn. LANCASHIRE FUSILIERS.

Programme of Training, for week ending 21st Sept. 1918.

| Coy. | Date. | Hours of Training. | Training Area. | Nature of Training. | Lectures. | Tactical Exercises. | Remarks. |
|---|---|---|---|---|---|---|---|
| A. | 16th Sept. | 0800 to 1200 hours. | C1. | Route March combined with Individual & Platoon Trng. | | Battalion Engineering Scheme for Officers + N.C.O.s will be continued during the week | Battle Order. |
| B. | | | C1. | | | | |
| C. | | | C2. | | | | |
| D. | | | C2. | | | | |
| A. | 17th. | " | C2 | ditto | | | |
| B. | | | C2. | | | | |
| C. | | | C1. | | | | |
| D. | | | C1. | | | | |
| A. | 18th | " | B. | ROUTE MARCH. | | | B.2 Range<br>Range to be used by backward Musketry Class. |
| B. | | | B. | | | | |
| C. | | | B. | | | | |
| D. | | | B. | | | | |
| A. | 19th | " | B3. | Individual and Platoon Training. | | | ditto |
| B. | | | B3. | | | | |
| C. | | | B1. | | | | |
| D. | | | B2. | | | | |
| A. | 20th | 0800 to 1200 hours. | A1. | Range practices and Individual field firing. | | | A.Coy, A.Range |
| B. | | | A1. | | | | B " B " |
| C. | | 1300 to 1700 hours. | A1. | | | | C Coy, A Range |
| D. | | | A1. | | | | D " B " |
| A. | 21st | | A. | BRIGADE SPORTS | | | |
| B. | | | A. | | | | |
| C. | | | A. | | | | |
| D. | | | A. | | | | |

6th LANCASHIRE FUSILIERS.

NOTES ON TRAINING

1. CLASSES OF INSTRUCTION. Classes of Instruction will be continued as for last week.
The Officers Riding Class will be held on Sept.16th and 20th.

2. INSPECTIONS-MARCHING ORDER.

| Unit. | Date. | Time. |
|---|---|---|
| H.Q. and Drums, | 17th Sept. | 1400 hours. |
| A, B, C and D Coys. | 19th " | 1400 " |
| Transport, | 20th " | 0915 " (Animals) |

3. P.T and B.F. Sgt.Miles, A.G.S. will be available on the Assault Course on B3 Area on Sept.19th.

4. ENTRENCHING TOOLS. Instruction in the use of entrenching tools will be continued this week.

5. GAS TRAINING. Gas training will be continued, and in addition the Box Respirator will be worn by all ranks in Camp daily from 1000 to 1100 hours.

6. STEEL HELMETS. Steel helmets will be worn both at training in the Field and at Musketry, the S.D.Cap being left in Camp.

7. DUTIES & FATIGUES. Inorder that Companies may be as strong as possible for training, all duties and fatigues will be detailed daily in each week from Companies as follows:-

| | |
|---|---|
| Monday, | A.Coy. |
| Tuesday, | B " |
| Wednesday, | C " |
| Thursday, | D " |
| Friday, | A " |
| Saturday, | B " |

8. PLATOON COMPETITIONS. The Brigade Platoon Competition will take place on Sept.30th.

9. BATTLE ORDER. In order that a decision may be arrived at as to a suitable form of Battle Order, each Battalion will detail two men for inspection by the Brigadier at 0900 hours on Thursday 19th.
The 6th Lancashire Fusiliers will show,
1 man with leather equipment, with pack,
1 " " web " " "
These two men will be found from D.Coy, and will be inspected outside the Orderly Room at 0815 hours on Thursday 19th Sept. by the Officer Commanding.
Suggestions are invited for the best method of carrying the Cardigan Jacket in Battle Order.

10. LEWIS GUN CLASS. Should the Officer in charge of the Lewis Gun Class wish to fire on the A.Ranges he will do so on the 20th, making use of B.Range.

11. REVOLVER PRACTICE. Revolver practice will be carried out.

(signed) P.Tyson, Lieut,
for Adjt, 6th Lancashire Fusiliers.

15.9.18.

APPENDIX VI

6th LANCASHIRE FUSILIERS. ORDER No.16.

Copy No 2

19th Sept.1918

1. The Battalion will move to FORMERIE STATION on the 20th September 1918, in accordance with following time table :-

TIME TABLE.

| Date. | Companies & Order of March. | Hour of start. | Starting Point. | Route via. | Remarks. |
|---|---|---|---|---|---|
| 20th | B.<br>Bn H.Q.<br>Drums.<br>"C",<br>"D",<br>"A". | 0810 hours | Guard Tent. | LES DEFEND'S<br>BOIS des PUITS<br>OBLUIERS<br>FORMERIE Stn. | DRESS: Marching order. The unexpended portion of the days rations, less meat, will be carried on the man. |
| 20th | Transport. | 06.00 | " | " | |

2. ROUTINE. Reveille 20th September 1918, ... 0500 hours
Blankets will be neatly rolled in bundles of ten, and stacked near Q.M.Stores at ... 0530 "
Breakfast ... 0600 "
Camp to be cleaned up at ... 0700 "
Officers' kits will be stacked near to the Q.M.Stores at ... 0700 "
The Battalion Orderly Officer will inspect the Camp area at ... 0730 "
Dinners will be served on arrival at FORMERIE Stn.

3. BAGGAGE PARTIES. Officer Commanding "A" Coy will detail one officer and 50 Other Ranks to load baggage on to the Motor Lorries at 06.30 hours.
O.C. "B" Coy will detail one officer and 50 Other Ranks to load baggage on the train at FORMERIE Station.

Issued at:- 2130 hours

J. Franks
Capt,
Adjt, 6th Lancs.Fusiliers.

Copies to:-
No. 1 File,
2 War Diary.
3 Major J.S.Townshend,
4 A.Coy.
5 B. "
6 C. "
7 D. "
No. 8 Transport Officer.
9 Quarter Master.
10 Spare.

APPENDIX VII

6th Bn. LANCASHIRE FUSILIERS.

TRAINING PROGRAMME FOR WEEK ENDING 28th Sept. 1918

| Date. | Coy. | Area. | Training. | Remarks. |
|---|---|---|---|---|
| Tuesday 24th Sept. | A.<br>B.<br>C.<br>D. | 1.N.E. LIGNEREUIL.<br>2.S.E. "<br>3.S.W. "<br>4.N.W. " | PLATOON. | Four hours training. |
| Wednesday 25th. | A.<br>B.<br>C.<br>D. | 2.N.of GRAND RULLECOURT.<br>3. "<br>4.E.of LIENCOURT.<br>1.W.of AVERT. | Owing to Inoculation Platoon Training will be carried out. | Individual training not to be includ-ed in the four hours.<br><br>S.B.R's to be worn by details left in billets, from 10.00 to 11.00 hours daily. |
| Thursday 26th. | Bn. | | BRIGADE ROUTE MARCH. | |
| Friday 27th. | Bn. | | BATTALION TRAINING. | |
| Saturday 28th. | Bn. | | BRIGADE TRAINING. | |

Capt,
Adjt, 6th Lancs. Fusiliers.

SECRET

# 6th Lancashire Fusiliers Order No. 18.

## APPENDIX VIII

Copy No. 2

27th Sept 1918.

1. The Battalion will move to CORBIE on the 28th Sept 1918. as follows:—

| | |
|---|---|
| Breakfast: | 06.30 hours. |
| Hour of Start: | 10.30 " |
| Starting Point | Bn. H. Q. |
| Order of March: | Bn. Hd. "B" Drums, "C" "D" "A" |
| Route via | GIVENCHY - LE - NOBLE - VILLERS-SIR - SIMON - PENIN - TINQUES. where the Battalion will entrain for CORBIE. Probable length of train journey 4 to 5 hours. |

2. Water-bottles will be filled before starting and all ranks will be cautioned that no further supply of water can be obtained before arrival at CORBIE.

3. Blankets rolled and tied in bundles of ten and clearly labelled by platoons, Officers Kits, Mess boxes, camp kettles and stores will be stacked in the courtyard at Bn. H. Q. at 07.45 hours. Battalion Headquarters will furnish a party of 1 Officer and 30 ORs to load the baggage on to the Lorries at 08.00 hours. These Lorries will proceed under Brigade arrangements direct to the CORBIE Area.

4. The Supply arrangements for the move are as follows:—
   (a). Unexpended portion of days rations will be carried on the men
   (b). Rations for consumption on the 29th Sept will be issued in CORBIE Area.

5. Medical Arrangements.
   (a) Men who are certified by the Medical Officer as unfit for marching will be conveyed to TINQUES by Motor Ambulance.
   (b). A Motor Ambulance will be at the Station of Entrainment.

6. Billets in CORBIE Area will be notified at the station of detrainment.

7. Watches will be synchronised at Battalion Headquarters at 07.00 hours.

J. Franks
Captain.
Adjutant 6 Bn Lancashire Fusiliers

Issued at 1900 hrs

Copies to:
1 File
2 War Diary
3 OC A Company
4 " B "
5 " C "
6 " D "
7 Maj. [illegible] Townshend MC
8 Quartermaster
9 Spare
10 Sig Office

6/Lancashire Fusiliers Order No. 19.
Copy No 2
29th Sept 1918.

# APPENDIX IX

1. The Battalion will proceed by march route to billets in HARBONNIERES today as follows:—

Hour of Start. 1300 hours
Starting Point. BRIDGE over the SOMME S of CORBIE.
Order of March. "B" "C" Drums "D" "A" Bn HQ & Transport.
Route FOUILLOY - WAFUSEE - ABANCOURT HARBONNIERES.

Distances 100x between Companies
100x " Bn HQ & Transport
50x " each Section of 12 vehicles.
500x " Battalions

2 Water bottles will be carried filled.

3. Men certified by the Medical Officer as unfit to march with the battalion will parade at Bn HQ at 1215 hours under Lt C CHENEY. This party will leave Bn Headquarters at 1400 hours and proceed by march route to HARBONNIERES

3 but will not pass through WARLUS - ABANCOURT before 16·30 hours.

4 Watches will be synchronised at Bn H Q at 1100 hours.

J Franks Capt
Adjutant 8 Lancashire Fusiliers

Issued at :- 1035 hours
Copies to :- 1 File
2 War Diary
3 OC "A" Coy
4 " "B" "
5 " "C" "
6 " "D" "
7 Transport Officer
8 Quartermaster
9 Spare.

38.J.
68 sheets

(6339) Wt. W160/M3016 1,500,000 10/17 McA & W Ltd (E 1898) Forms W3091.

Army Form W.3091.

198/66

# Cover for Documents.

Confidential

Nature of Enclosures.

War Diary

of

6th Bn Lancashire Fusiliers.

from 1st Oct: 1918 to 31st Oct: 1918.

(Volume 4)

Notes, or Letters written.

DUPLICATE.

Instructions regarding War Diaries and Intelligence Summaries are contained in F. S. Regs., Part II. and the Staff Manual respectively. Title pages will be prepared in manuscript.

# WAR DIARY
or
# INTELLIGENCE SUMMARY.
(*Erase heading not required.*)

Army Form C. 2118.

| Place | Date | Hour | Summary of Events and Information | Remarks and references to Appendices |
|---|---|---|---|---|
| CAPPY | 1/10/18 | | Weather fine, but rather cold. Bn Order No 20 was issued to all concerned at 0345 hours. The Battalion moved to CAPPY in accordance with Order 20 (see appendix I attached) & arrived at 1405 hours. The Battalion are accommodated in Huts which have recently been occupied by the GERMANS needless to say they are in a very filthy condition | J.F. |
| — " — | 2/10/18 | | Weather fine during the morning light rainfall at night. The Battalion moved in accordance with Bn Order 21 (see appendix II attached) | |
| MOUNTABAN | | | The Brigade carried out a Tactical Operation in conjunction with the move this delayed our arrival in billets which we reached at 1730 hours. | J.F. |
| — " — | 3/10/18 | | Weather fine. Battalion Training | J.F. |
| | 4/10/18 | | Weather fine. Battalion Training. The Officers & Platoon Comdrs. carried | |

D. D. & L., London, E.C. (A8001) Wt. W1771/M2031 750,000 5/17 Sch. 52 Forms/C2118/14

Instructions regarding War Diaries and Intelligence Summaries are contained in F. S. Regs., Part II. and the Staff Manual respectively. Title pages will be prepared in manuscript.

# WAR DIARY
*or*
# INTELLIGENCE SUMMARY.
*(Erase heading not required.)*

Army Form C. 2118.

| Place | Date | Hour | Summary of Events and Information | Remarks and references to Appendices |
|---|---|---|---|---|
| MONTAUBAN | 4/10/18 | | out a Bde Tactical exercise at 1530 hours, at 1910 hours orders received from Bde that Battalion would move to MOULIANS at once. The Battalion moved at 1945 hours [illegible] arrived in billets at 0030 hours 5/10/18 | |
| MOULIANS | 5/10/18 | | Weather fine. Orders received at 0745 hours that Battalion would move to ST EMILIE at 1005 hours. The Battalion arrived at 1410 hours & were accommodated in a field 700x E of the town, only 15 tents allotted to the Battalion | |
| ST EMILIE | | | | |
| ST EMILIE | 6/10/18 | | Weather fine. Battalion resting. The Comdg Officer attended a conference at Bde HQ at 1115 hours. Orders to move to LE CATELET were received at 1000 hours, but were cancelled at 1140 hours | |
| | 7/10/18 | | Weather fine. The Battalion moved to LE CATELET area at 1100 hours and arrived at 1500 hours where we stayed in a Railway siding until 2300 | |

Instructions regarding War Diaries and Intelligence Summaries are contained in F. S. Regs., Part II. and the Staff Manual respectively. Title pages will be prepared in manuscript.

# WAR DIARY
*or*
# INTELLIGENCE SUMMARY.
*(Erase heading not required.)*

Army Form C. 2118.

| Place | Date | Hour | Summary of Events and Information | Remarks and references to Appendices |
|---|---|---|---|---|
| LE CATELET | 7/10/18 | | when we moved for to the Taped line in accordance with 198th Bde Order 115. | |
| On the Move | 8/10/18 | | Weather cold & windy. The Battalion formed up on the Taped line at 0200 hours in the following order: Diamond formation in file A Coy leading B Company 50x on Right flank C Company 50x on left flank D Coy 50x in rear of A Coy. Zero hour was at 0510 hours, but as the Battalion were in reserve it was not until 0545 that we moved from the point of assembly. From this point the distances were increased between Companies to 400x. At 0600 hours a message was received that the leading Battalions (6th DUBLIN FUSILIERS 5th INNISKILLING FUSILIERS) were pushing on satisfactorily on receipt of this message Battalion HQ moved forward to T.27 d. 5.0 MONTBREHAN Sheet. At 0642 hours our troops were opted to hold PETIT VERGER | JF |

D. D. & L., London, E.C. (A8001) Wt. W1771/M2031 750,000 5/17 Sch. 52 Forms/C2118/14

Army Form C. 2118.

Instructions regarding War Diaries and Intelligence Summaries are contained in F. S. Regs., Part II. and the Staff Manual respectively. Title pages will be prepared in manuscript.

# WAR DIARY
*or*
# INTELLIGENCE SUMMARY.
*(Erase heading not required.)*

| Place | Date | Hour | Summary of Events and Information | Remarks and references to Appendices |
|---|---|---|---|---|
| On the Move | 8/10/18 | | RIDGE and Bn HQ moved forward to a point 500x E of PETIT VERGER FARM. As the Division on our left had not yet taken VILLERS OUTREAUX the advance was held up 1150 hours when it was reported that VILLERS OUTREAUX had been captured. The Battalion moved forward to the GREEN LINE approx T.17.d. at 13.15 hours. Casualties Killed 3 [illegible] 2 Wounded 21. | JF |
| " " | 9/10/18 | | Weather fine. Orders received at 0230 hours that the Division would continue the advance today with 198 Bde on left 199 Bde on right. 6th Lancashire Fusiliers will form up in U.14.b Ref Sheet 57B S.W. $\frac{1}{20,000}$ and will advance so as to clear the E outskirts of ELINCOURT and will capture PINON WOODS. The Battalion moved off at 0300 hours in the following order D B C A Bn HQ and formed up at the place of assembly in U.14.b at | |

Instructions regarding War Diaries and Intelligence Summaries are contained in F. S. Regs., Part II. and the Staff Manual respectively. Title pages will be prepared in manuscript.

# WAR DIARY
*or*
# INTELLIGENCE SUMMARY.
(*Erase heading not required.*)

Army Form C. 2118.

| Place | Date | Hour | Summary of Events and Information | Remarks and references to Appendices |
|---|---|---|---|---|
| On the Move | 9/10/18 | | 0450 hours. The Battalion moved forward at Zero hour 0520 hours and advanced E of ELINCOURT. Our barrage was late in coming down and when it did eventually commence did so on our forward troops thereby causing ~~[illegible]~~ casualties. Owing to the dense mist the advance was stopped at 0600 hours and recommenced when the mist had lifted at 0715 hours. Our first objective (BOIS de PINON) was occupied at 0845 hours and the advance to our final objective MARETZ-CLARY Road commenced. Final objective reached at 1050 hours. Orders received from Brigade at 1600 hours that the Battalion were now in Divisional reserve. Casualties Killed 2 Died of wounds 1 Wounded 9 Missing 2 | [initials] |
| " " | 10/10/18 | | Weather changeable: sleet ~~[illegible]~~ with spells of sunshine alternating. At 0200 hours the Adjutant was called to Bde to take down orders and returned | |

D. D. & L., London, E.C.
(A8004) Wt. W2771/M2031 750,000 5/17 Sch. 52 Forms/C2118/14

Army Form C. 2118.

Instructions regarding War Diaries and Intelligence Summaries are contained in F. S. Regs., Part II. and the Staff Manual respectively. Title pages will be prepared in manuscript.

# WAR DIARY
*or*
# INTELLIGENCE SUMMARY.
*(Erase heading not required.)*

| Place | Date | Hour | Summary of Events and Information | Remarks and references to Appendices |
|---|---|---|---|---|
| In the Morn | 10/10/18 | | at 0240 hours with orders as follows:- The Brigade will move at 0300 hours and will move through S.A. Bde outpost at 0500 hours. Starting point LE PINETTE. 6 R.M.F.ns will lead followed by 5th INNISK Fus 6th D.F. Advance will be on a one Battalion front; each Battalion will have 3 Coys in the line. Owing to the late hour at which orders were received it was 0330 hours when the Battalion reached the starting point and as Brigade had not then arrived it was 0345 hours when the march commenced. The Battalion reached REUMONT at 0615 hours and formed up for the attack in the following order 'B' on the Right 'C' in the centre 'D' on the left 'A' Company in Reserve with Bn H.Q. and 1 one V.M.G. section. The advance commenced at 0645 hours 'C' Company directing and marching on a 45° true bearing. 'D' company were ordered to keep in touch with the Div on the left. At 0725 hours the forward companies came in for a heavy shelling and at 0736 the reserve company & H.Q. came into the enemy | |

D. D. & L., London, E.C. (A8001) Wt. W1771/M2031 750,000 5/17 Sch. 52 Forms/C2118/14

Instructions regarding War Diaries and Intelligence Summaries are contained in F. S. Regs., Part II. and the Staff Manual respectively. Title pages will be prepared in manuscript.

# WAR DIARY
*or*
# INTELLIGENCE SUMMARY.
*(Erase heading not required.)*

Army Form C. 2118.

| Place | Date | Hour | Summary of Events and Information | Remarks and references to Appendices |
|---|---|---|---|---|
| On the move | 10/10/18 | | barrage. At 0816 hours the three leading companies had reached the N side of the LE CATEAU – INCHY Road and Bn HQ K 26. c. 4. 3 Ref: 57.B. At 0935 hours the situation was as follows: B Company on line of road K 27. b. C Company line of road K 21. c Reserve Coy & Bn HQ K 27. c The position of 'D' Coy was obscure but believed to be K 21. b. 5 5. Companies had suffered fairly heavy casualties and reorganisation was necessary. These positions were maintained during remainder of day. At 1710 hours orders were received that the Battalion would attack MONTAY at 1700 hours and join up with R. Liverpools on high ground K 17. At 1730 hours 'A' Company moved down GULLY K 27 a and thence up track to K 27 b 5. 5. where advance on MONTAY commenced in the following order 'A' Company 6th L.F. attachment 'A' and S Highlanders A Company 5 INNISK, B Company 5th INNISK. Advance came in for a considerable amount of M.G. fire. Owing to darkness & late hour at which orders were received | |

Army Form C. 2118.

Instructions regarding War Diaries and Intelligence Summaries are contained in F. S. Regs., Part II. and the Staff Manual respectively. Title pages will be prepared in manuscript.

# WAR DIARY
*or*
# INTELLIGENCE SUMMARY.
*(Erase heading not required.)*

| Place | Date | Hour | Summary of Events and Information | Remarks and references to Appendices |
|---|---|---|---|---|
| On the Move | 10/10/18 | | Coy Comdrs did not have time to carry out a reconnaissance before moving to the attack ~~[illegible]~~ but 'A' and 'C' Companies of 6 L.F reached their objectives. The A and S.H. and two companies of 5th INNISK returned to K 27 b 5.5 at 2120 hours. 'B' and 'D' Companies 6 LF did not take part in the attack. Casualties Killed 2Lt C. JACKSON and 3 O.R. Wounded 2Lt J R SMITH-SAVILLE. 2/Lt H H SMITH. T.C MARRIOTT. 2/Lt P.BAKER and 59. O.R. Missing 68. O.R | J.F. |
| " " | 11/10/18 | | Weather fine, but cold. At 0005 hours a message was received from Capt R.A.V. WHITE O.C 'A' Company who was holding MONTAY that his position would be untenable in daylight and a message was despatched ordering A+C Coys to withdraw and rejoin Bn HQ in K 27 c at 0400 hours. At 0430 hours after A+C Companys had withdrawn a message (BM 229) was received from Brigade ordering MONTAY | |

D. D. & L. London, E.C. (A8001) Wt. W1571/M1031 750,000 5/17 Sch. 52 Forms/C2118/14

Instructions regarding War Diaries and Intelligence Summaries are contained in F. S. Regs., Part II. and the Staff Manual respectively. Title pages will be prepared in manuscript.

# WAR DIARY
*or*
# INTELLIGENCE SUMMARY.
*(Erase heading not required.)*

Army Form C. 2118.

| Place | Date | Hour | Summary of Events and Information | Remarks and references to Appendices |
|---|---|---|---|---|
| On the move | 11/10/18 | | to be held at all cost and "B" Company Commanded by Captain W.V. Jones were immediately dispatched to reoccupy the position at 0600 hours a message was received from O.C. "B" Company that he was in position in MONTAY. ~~with one Platoon~~ of the 5th INNISKILN FUSILIERS in position in the Sunken Road K 27.5.5 as a support to B Company in MONTAY. During the day the enemy artillery kept up counter Battery and indiscriminate fire on our positions with little effect. At 1430 hours the Comdg Officer and the Adjutant visited the outpost line in MONTAY and reorganised the defence. At 1600 hours BM 231 ordering the relief of the Battalion by the 6th D.F. was received, but this was cancelled at 1700 hours by B.O. 117 which reads as follows:- The 19th | |

D. D. & L., London, E.C.
(A8004) Wt. W1771/M1031 750,000 5/17 Sch. 52 Forms/C2118/14

Instructions regarding War Diaries and Intelligence Summaries are contained in F. S. Regs., Part II. and the Staff Manual respectively. Title pages will be prepared in manuscript.

# WAR DIARY
*or*
# INTELLIGENCE SUMMARY.
*(Erase heading not required.)*

Army Form C. 2118.

| Place | Date | Hour | Summary of Events and Information | Remarks and references to Appendices |
|---|---|---|---|---|
| On The Line | 11/10/18 | | Brigade will be relieved in the left sector of the 66th Division front by the 4th South African Battalion and a Coy 1st South African Battalion. 6th LANCASHIRE FUSILIERS will be relieved by one (1) Company 1st South African Infantry. The relief was completed at 1130 hours and the Battalion proceeded to Billets in REUMONT arriving at 0040 hours. | |
| | | | Casualties – 15 O.R. Wounded. | |
| | | | During the period 7th October up to date the Battalion have had a strenuous and trying time but all ranks have risen to the occasion and have done exceedingly well | [illegible] |

D. D. & L., London, E.C. (A7883) Wt. W203/M1672 350,000 4/17 Sch. 52a Forms/C/2118/14

Instructions regarding War Diaries and Intelligence Summaries are contained in F. S. Regs., Part II. and the Staff Manual respectively. Title pages will be prepared in manuscript.

# WAR DIARY
*or*
# INTELLIGENCE SUMMARY.
*(Erase heading not required.)*

Army Form C. 2118.

| Place | Date | Hour | Summary of Events and Information | Remarks and references to Appendices |
|---|---|---|---|---|
| On the Move | 12/10/18 | | Weather fine. Battalion resting cleaning up and reorganising. The men are accommodated in fairly good billets, but the place is under shell fire & there has been numerous casualties from Gas in the other Battalion occupying the village. | J.F. |
| " " | 13/10/18 | | Weather fine. Orders received at 0600 hours that the Bn would move to MARETZ at 0915 hours today. The Battalion moved in accordance with Bn Order (See APPENDIX III attached) at 0855 hours and arrived in billets at MARETZ at 1100 hours. Congratulatory wire (see APPENDIX IV attached) was received from Bde at 1500 hours. The "B" Teams of the Battalion who had been left out of action rejoined the Battalion viz: 7 Officers 108. O.R. Conference | |

D. D. & L., London, E.C. (A8001) Wt. W1771/M031 750,000 5/17 Sch. 52 Forms/C2118/14

Instructions regarding War Diaries and Intelligence Summaries are contained in F. S. Regs., Part II. and the Staff Manual respectively. Title pages will be prepared in manuscript.

# WAR DIARY
*or*
# INTELLIGENCE SUMMARY.
*(Erase heading not required.)*

Army Form C. 2118.

| Place | Date | Hour | Summary of Events and Information | Remarks and references to Appendices |
|---|---|---|---|---|
| 13/10/18 MARETZ. | | | for Coy Comdrs was held in Bn. H.Q. Mess at 1730 hours. Subject:- Interior Economy. | [illegible] |
| — " — | 14/10/18 | | Weather fine. Battalion resting & cleaning up. The Comdg Officer attended a conference at Brigade H.Q. at 1300 hours and afterwards rode over the area which the Battalion advanced over during the recent fighting. 2 O.R. proceeded on Leave to U.K. | [illegible] |
| — " — | 15/10/18 | | Weather changeable, light rainfall during morning, dull during afternoon. The Corps Commander visited the Battalion during the morning and inspected the men's billets. He expressed his appreciation of the good work carried out by the Battalion during the recent operations. Conference for Coy Comdrs was held in Bn. H.Q. Mess at 1400 hours. Subject Interior Economy | [illegible] |

D. D. & L., London, E.C. (A8004) Wt. W2771/M6031 750,000 5/17 Sch. 52 Forms/C2118/14

Instructions regarding War Diaries and Intelligence Summaries are contained in F. S. Regs., Part II. and the Staff Manual respectively. Title pages will be prepared in manuscript.

# WAR DIARY
*or*
# INTELLIGENCE SUMMARY.
*(Erase heading not required.)*

Army Form C. 2118.

| Place | Date | Hour | Summary of Events and Information | Remarks and references to Appendices |
|---|---|---|---|---|
| MARETZ<br>REUMONT | 16/10/18 | | Weather changeable light rainfall during morning. Warning Order received from Bde at 0030 hours that the Battalion would be prepared to move forward at 1015 hours. Coys were warned & all preparations made. Bde move order received at 0850 hours & Bn move order issued to all concerned at 0855 hours (see APPENDIX V attached). The Bn moved to REUMONT at 1000 hours & arrived at 1230 hours. The Comdg Officer attended a conference at Bde at 1200 hours. Conference for Coy Comdrs was held in Bn H.Q. Qrs at 1400 hours Subject forthcoming operations. At 1500 hours The Comdg Officer accompanied by the Bn I.O. & Coy Comdrs carried out a reconnaissance of the area into which the Battalion is moving into as Divisional Reserve. Bde Order 120 received at 1630 hours. Battalion moved to Q 7 a and c area at 1755 hours & arrived at 1900 hours. Ref Sheet 57B 1/40,000. Special instructions with B.O. 120 received at 1945 hours. The men slept in small holes in an open field & the officers managed to get a bivouac which we borrowed from the S Africans & made ourselves comfortable. | FF |

D. D. & L., London, E.C. (A8001) Wt. W1771/M2031 750,000 5/17 Sch. 52 Forms/C2118/14

Instructions regarding War Diaries and Intelligence Summaries are contained in F. S. Regs., Part II. and the Staff Manual respectively. Title pages will be prepared in manuscript.

# WAR DIARY
*or*
# INTELLIGENCE SUMMARY.
*(Erase heading not required.)*

Army Form C. 2118.

| Place | Date | Hour | Summary of Events and Information | Remarks and references to Appendices |
|---|---|---|---|---|
| On the Move | 17/10/18 | | Weather damp rather cold at night. At 1100 hours the Battalion was ordered to move forward & capture the Road Q4 a. 5.9. both inclusive. The advance was commenced at 1115 hours in the following order A.B.C.D Bn H.Q Companies at 300x distance and in artillery formation. At 1140 hours A Coy came under very heavy M.G. fire from direction of Q16. d. Ref Sheet 57B 1/40,000 and the remaining companies came under the same M.G fire on entering the La SELLE valley. At 1325 hours orders were received for the Battalion to withdraw and reassemble in Q7 but as the three leading companies had crossed the River La SELLE it was not until 1600 hours that the withdrawal was completed. The Battalion reassembled in Q7 where we spent the night there was no accommodation & as it was frightfully cold it was not at all comfortable. Casualties 10. O.R Wounded 1. O R Missing | [illegible] |

D. D. & L., London, E.C. (A8004) Wt. W1771/M2031 750,000 5/17 Sch. 52 Forms/C2118/14

Instructions regarding War Diaries and Intelligence Summaries are contained in F. S. Regs., Part II. and the Staff Manual respectively. Title pages will be prepared in manuscript.

# WAR DIARY
*or*
# INTELLIGENCE SUMMARY.
*(Erase heading not required.)*

Army Form C. 2118.

| Place | Date | Hour | Summary of Events and Information | Remarks and references to Appendices |
|---|---|---|---|---|
| On the Line | 16/10/18 | | Weather changeable with heavy fog most of the day. At 0145 hours orders were received for the Bn to relieve the 6th R.D.F. in LE CATEAU. The Battalion moved forward at 0245 hours arrived at 0340 hours but owing to the obscurity of the position it was not until 0710 hours that the relief commenced and relief was not completed until 1000 hours. "B" "C" and "D" Companies took over the line with "A" Coy in support. At 1410 hours the Battalion moved forward to Railway E of LE CATEAU K 35 d. and then took up position on high ground K 36 a. and c. At 1630 hours orders received for the Battalion to move forward to capture & consolidate Red Line approx K 36 central & 80. Advance was commenced at 1710 hours with B. C and D in the line "A" Company in support. The three Coys | |

Instructions regarding War Diaries and Intelligence Summaries are contained in F. S. Regs., Part II, and the Staff Manual respectively. Title pages will be prepared in manuscript.

# WAR DIARY
*or*
# INTELLIGENCE SUMMARY.
*(Erase heading not required.)*

Army Form C. 2118.

| Place | Date | Hour | Summary of Events and Information | Remarks and references to Appendices |
|---|---|---|---|---|
| On the spot | 18/9/18 | | in the line came in for heavy M.G. fire but in spite of this they pushed on & took the RED LINE at 1830 hours after capturing 35 prisoners and 6 M Guns and inflicting heavy casualties on the enemy, our own casualties being light:- Killed 4 O.R. Wounded 12 O.R. Missing 2 O.R. | |
| | | | 2/Lt R.F. HINSON was wounded earlier in the day & was evacuated. 2/Lt H.E. ATKINS was sent down suffering from shock. At 1930 hours BM 64 ordering a readjustment of the line was received. At 2315 hours the 9th MANCHESTERS arrived to relieve the Battalion & the relief was completed at 0145 hours. The Battalion should have side slipped to the Right on relief and taken over from the 2nd R.D.F. This relief however did not take place and the Battalion remained in support to the MANCHESTERS in R 35 d. & c. Casualties:- Killed 3 O.R. Wounded 18 O.R. | |

Instructions regarding War Diaries and Intelligence Summaries are contained in F. S. Regs., Part II. and the Staff Manual respectively. Title pages will be prepared in manuscript.

# WAR DIARY
*or*
# INTELLIGENCE SUMMARY.
*(Erase heading not required.)*

Army Form C. 2118.

| Place | Date | Hour | Summary of Events and Information | Remarks and references to Appendices |
|---|---|---|---|---|
| On the Tor | 19/10/18 | | Weather changeable light rainfall at intervals during the day. The Bde Major Staff Captain visited Bn H.Q at 0840 hours. 'A' Company moved forward and took up position in Q.6.a Sheet 57B. The Comdg Officer reconnoitred the line at 1100 hours and returned at 1230 hours. 'C' Company were ordered to move forward and take up position near 'A' Coy which they carried out at 1300 hours. The remainder of the day was uneventful. Casualties:— Missing 1. O.R. | J.F. |
| | | | See APPENDIX VI | |
| -"- | 20/10/18 | | Weather unsettled raining at intervals. At 0030 hours the Brigade Major rang up on the phone and told the Adjutant that the Battalion were | |

(A9475) Wt W2358/P360 600,000 12/17 D. D. & L. Sch. 52a. Forms/C2118/15

Instructions regarding War Diaries and Intelligence Summaries are contained in F. S. Regs., Part II, and the Staff Manual respectively. Title pages will be prepared in manuscript.

# WAR DIARY
*or*
# INTELLIGENCE SUMMARY.
*(Erase heading not required.)*

Army Form C. 2118.

| Place | Date | Hour | Summary of Events and Information | Remarks and references to Appendices |
|---|---|---|---|---|
| On the March | 20/10/18 | | taking over from the 9th Manchesters as far as K36.d o. Sheet 57B 1/40000 and that 2 Companies of the 5th INNISK would afterwards relieve the Battalion in present area & the Battalion would move to area Q.7. Sheet 57B. This relief was carried out and completed at 0400 hours. A and C companies withdrew to LE CATEAU where the Battalion had breakfast. The Battalion commenced to move to Q7 and at 0600 hours and arrived at 0705 hours. The roads were shelled during the march but the Battalion had no casualties. | |
| | | | The Battalion moved into billets in MAUROIS at 1515 hours in accordance with APPENDIX VII attached and arrived at 1630 hours | [initials] |

Instructions regarding War Diaries and Intelligence Summaries are contained in F. S. Regs., Part II. and the Staff Manual respectively. Title pages will be prepared in manuscript.

# WAR DIARY
*or*
# INTELLIGENCE SUMMARY.
(*Erase heading not required.*)

Army Form C. 2118.

| Place | Date | Hour | Summary of Events and Information | Remarks and references to Appendices |
|---|---|---|---|---|
| On the March | 21/10/18 | | Weather changeable with light rainfall at intervals. B.R.O. 123 received at 0010 hours ordering the Battalion to move to PREMONT. The Battalion moved to PREMONT in accordance with Bn. Order (see appendix VIII attached) and arrived at 1230 hours. The Companies took advantage of the afternoon to get the men billeted & generally cleaned up. | [illegible] |
| PREMONT | 22/10/18 | | Weather intermittent rainfall throughout the day, fine towards evening. The Battalion are resting & generally cleaning up. The Brigade Commander accompanied by the Bde Major visited the Bn. at 1130 hours. The Comdg Officer 2nd in Command & two Coy Comdrs attended a Tank Demonstration at 1430 hours. The Divisional Concert Party "The Lancashire Lads" gave a performance at 1730 hours | |

D. D. & L., London, E.C. (A5001) Wt. W1771/M2031 750,000 5/17 Sch. 52 Forms/C2118/14

Army Form C. 2118.

# WAR DIARY
*or*
# INTELLIGENCE SUMMARY.
*(Erase heading not required.)*

Instructions regarding War Diaries and Intelligence Summaries are contained in F. S. Regs., Part II. and the Staff Manual respectively. Title pages will be prepared in manuscript.

| Place | Date | Hour | Summary of Events and Information | Remarks and references to Appendices |
|---|---|---|---|---|
| PREMONT | 22/10/18 | | but owing to the limited accommodation of the concert room only 100 men from the Battalion were ~~allowed~~ able to attend | J.J. |
| — " — | 23/10/18 | | Weather, fine with sunshine most of the day. Battalion resting & generally cleaning up. The Comdg Officer inspected the Battalion in Drill Order at 1000 hours. A Congratulatory message was received from the Brigadier and read out to all ranks on Parade see APPENDIX IX attached. The Divisional Commander visited the Battalion at 1600 hours & had a long chat with the Comdg Officer. The Band played to the men from 1630 to 1730 hours. 100 O.R. attended a performance given by the 'Lancashire Lads' at the SERAIN Theatre. 2/Lt A. INGLIS B. Coy proceeded on leave to U.K. enroute for INDIA and is struck off the strength of the Battalion | J.J. |

D. D. & L., London, E.C. (A5001) Wt. W1771/M2031 750,000 5/17 Sch. 52 Forms/C2118/14

Instructions regarding War Diaries and Intelligence Summaries are contained in F. S. Regs., Part II. and the Staff Manual respectively. Title pages will be prepared in manuscript.

# WAR DIARY
*or*
# INTELLIGENCE SUMMARY.
*(Erase heading not required.)*

Army Form C. 2118.

| Place | Date | Hour | Summary of Events and Information | Remarks and references to Appendices |
|---|---|---|---|---|
| PREMONT | 24/10/18 | | Weather, fair. Battalion trained for two hours during the morning. The Cmdg Officer inspected the draft. L.G class commenced under the L.G.O. | [initials] |
| PREMONT | 25/10/18 | | Weather fine sunshine most of the day. The Batt. carried out a route march in clean fatigue with belts. Route. PREMONT – AVELU. Rd junction S of CLARY – ELINCOURT – SERAIN. The new L.G. class was continued under the L.G.O. A special order by the Divisional commander was received see APPENDIX X. The 198th Inf Brigade also issued a special report on the operations from 7/10/18 – 11/10/18 See APPENDIX XI. An American journalist visited the Batt. & stayed the night. He was one of a party of twelve, who were visiting the Division, during their tour of the whole battle front. 2/Lt. A.C GALLAWAY joined the Batt. & was posted to 'B' Coy. | [initials] |
| PREMONT | 26/10/18 | | Weather fine sunshine all day. The Batt carried out a route march in drill order, & steel helmets. ROUTE:– SERAIN – LES MARLICHES FARM – PETIT.VERGER FARM – T30.A.5.5 – PREMONT. (Sheet 57B 1/40000) The L.G classes attended the route march & carried on their special | [initials] |

D. D. & L., London, E.C. (A8001) Wt. W1771/M6031 750,000 5/17 Sch. 52 Forms/C2118/14

Army Form C. 2118.

Instructions regarding War Diaries and Intelligence Summaries are contained in F. S. Regs., Par. II. and the Staff Manual respectively. Title pages will be prepared in manuscript.

# WAR DIARY
*or*
# INTELLIGENCE SUMMARY.
*(Erase heading not required.)*

| Place | Date | Hour | Summary of Events and Information | Remarks and references to Appendices |
|---|---|---|---|---|
| PRÉMONT | 26/10/18 | | instruction during the afternoon. 2/Lt. H. WILSON and 2/Lt G.L WHITEHEAD joined for duty. and were posted to "B" & "C" Coys respectively. | J.F. |
| " | 27/10/18 | | Weather fine. Battalion resting. 2/Lts J.R. DAVIES and P.L. KEIGHLEY joined for duty and were posted to "C" & "D" Coys respectively. 53 O.R joined for duty & were posted to Coys as follows:- "A" 9. "B" 15. "C" 13. "D" 16. The Brigadier visited the Headquarters Mess at 1600 hours. | J.F. |
| " | 28/10/18 | | Weather fine. The Battalion attended a Brigade Route March at 0830 hours. Approx. Distance 11 Miles. Route (Ref. 57D 1/40000) U 21.d.6.9. PONCHAUX - MARINCOURT SERAIN. The Battalion returned to billets at 1300 hours. See APPENDIX XII | J.F. |
| | 29/10/18 | | Weather fine with bright sunshine all day. Companies | |

D. D. & L., London, E.C. (A8001) Wt. W1771/M2031 750,000 5/17 Sch. 52 Forms/C2118/14

Instructions regarding War Diaries and Intelligence Summaries are contained in F. S. Regs., Part II. and the Staff Manual respectively. Title pages will be prepared in manuscript.

# WAR DIARY
*or*
# INTELLIGENCE SUMMARY.
*(Erase heading not required.)*

Army Form C. 2118.

| Place | Date | Hour | Summary of Events and Information | Remarks and references to Appendices |
|---|---|---|---|---|
| PREMONT | 29/10/18 | | carried out three hours General Training during the morning and in the evening the Battalion attended a Brigade Gas Demonstration which owing to the changeable wind proved a failure. 2/L S.D. STEPHEN and 4 O.R. proceeded to U.K. on leave. Account of the recent Operations Parts IV. V. VI. received from Brigade & circulated to Coys for perusal see appendix XIII attached | J.F. |
| PREMONT | 30/10/18 | | Weather fine with bright sunshine. The Battalion carried out Tactical Training during the morning a conference for Coy Cmdrs was held in Bn. H.Q. Mess at 1700 hours to discuss the days training. The | |

D. D. & L., London, E.C. (A8004) Wt. W1771/M2031 750,000 5/17 Sch. 52 Forms/C2118/14

Instructions regarding War Diaries and Intelligence Summaries are contained in F. S. Regs., Part II. and the Staff Manual respectively. Title pages will be prepared in manuscript.

# WAR DIARY
*or*
# INTELLIGENCE SUMMARY.
(*Erase heading not required.*)

Army Form C. 2118.

| Place | Date | Hour | Summary of Events and Information | Remarks and references to Appendices |
|---|---|---|---|---|
| PRÉMONT | 30/10/18 | | Comdg Officer attended a Conference at Bde at 1830 hours and at 2030 hours a Conference for Coy Comdrs was held in Bn H.Q. Subject: Divisional Field Operations to be carried out on the 31/10/18 | J.F. |
| " | 31/10/18 | | Weather changeable cold during morning & but rain during the afternoon. The Battalion attended a Divisional Field Day. We marched out of Billets at 0745 hours and returned at 1800 hours. The men had dinner on return to Billets. 2/Lt J. A. McKECHNIE joined for duty and was posted to "A" Company. 2 O.R. joined for duty. The admissions to hospital | |

D. D. & L., London, E.C. (A8004) Wt. W2771/M2031 750,000 5/17 Sch. 52 Forms/C2118/14

Army Form C. 2118.

Instructions regarding War Diaries and Intelligence Summaries are contained in F. S. Regs., Part II. and the Staff Manual respectively. Title pages will be prepared in manuscript.

# WAR DIARY
*or*
# INTELLIGENCE SUMMARY.
*(Erase heading not required.)*

| Place | Date | Hour | Summary of Events and Information | Remarks and references to Appendices |
|---|---|---|---|---|
| PREMONT | 31/10/18 | | owing to sickness during the past month total 81. Total casualties in action:- Killed Wd Missing | |
| | | | Officers 1 " 5 " — | |
| | | | O. Ranks 22 " 179 " 16 | [illegible] |
| | | | 1/11/18 [signature] Lt Colonel Comdg 6th Lancashire Fusiliers | |

D. D. & L., London, E.C. (A8001) Wt. W1771/M2031 750,000 5/17 Sch. 52 Forms/C2118/14

6th Lancashire Fusiliers Order No 21.

Copy No 2

# APPENDIX II

3rd Oct 1918.

1. The Battalion will proceed by march route to GUILLEMONT area today as follows:-

Hour of Start: 10:20 hours

Starting Point. Junction of road leading to "D" Coy billets.

Order of March "D" "A" Drums Bn H.Q. "B" "C".

Route SUZANNE - MARICOURT.

2. Transport will be Brigaded and will march under orders of Brigade Transport Officer, except that Pack animals and L.G. Limbers will march with their companies.

J. Franks Captain

Adjutant 6th Lancashire Fusiliers

Issued at:- 06.30 [illegible]

Copies to:- File

2 War Diary

OC A Co

" B "

" C "

OC "D" Co

Transport Officer

Quartermaster

Spare.

6th Lancashire Fusiliers

Amend Order No 21. 2nd Oct. 1918
Copy No 2
as follows:-

(a) Para 1.
Hour of Start to read 10.50 hours

(b) "B" teams will not march with their companies but will march under Capt. I. S. Rutherford behind the 198th L.T.M.B.
Starting Point CAPPY Church 11-15 hours

(c) Steel helmets will be worn and S.B.R carried in the alert position.

Para 2
(a) Remaining transport will march under Bde T.O.
Hour of Start 11-20 hours
Starting Point CAPPY Church

Copies as Order No 21.

(Signed), F. Franks
Capt & Adjt
6 Lancs Fus

6th Lancashire Fusiliers. Order No 20
Copy No 2
1st Oct. 1918

# APPENDIX I

1. The Battalion will proceed by march route to CAPPY to day as follows:-

<u>Hour of Start</u>: 10.40 hours

<u>Starting Point</u>. Bn H.Q

<u>Order of march</u>: 'C', 'D', Drums. 'A', Bn HQ, 'B' Tpt.

<u>Route</u>. PROYART - FROISSY - Southern bank of Canal - CAPPY.

<u>Distances</u> 100x between Companies
100x " 'B' Coy & Transport
50x " each 12 vehicles

Continued

Order No 40 contd

2: (a) Blankets neatly rolled in bundles of ten, tied and clearly labelled by platoons, will be stacked outside Bn H.Q. by 07.00 hours.

(b) Officers kits, mess boxes & stores, will be stacked outside Battn H.Q. by 09-00 hours

3 Two Field ambulances will follow ½ mile in rear of the Brigade column.

4 Watches will be synchronised at Bn H.Q. at 06-30 hours

Issued at: 03-45 hours

J. Franks Capt.
Adjt. 6th Lancs Fusiliers

Copies to: 1 File
2 War Diary
3 OC 'A' Coy
4 'B' Coy
5 'C' Coy
6 'D' Coy
7 Transport Officer
8 Quartermaster
9 Spare (RSM)

6 Lancs Fus.

APPENDIX IX 20 Copies



6th Lancs. Fus.
5th R. Innis. Fus.
6th R. Dublin Fus.
198th L.T.M.B.
No. 3 Signal Section.
198th Inf. Bde. H.Q.

---

The B.G.C. wishes to congratulate the Brigade on their performances of the last 12 days.

During that period they have advanced 13¾ miles on 10½ of which they were actually in touch with the enemy, have captured 484 prisoners, 23 field guns, 3 heavy howitzers and a large number of machine guns, in addition to inflicting heavy casualties on the enemy. Their final effort was to clear the town of LE CATEAU, East of the River SELLE, so liberating over 1000 French civilians who have been under German domination for over four years.

This result has been attained by the hard work and unselfishness of all ranks, coupled with a determination to do their duty and get to grips with the enemy in spite of all deterrents.

The B.G.C. regrets the casualties sustained in fighting a stubborn enemy, but he knows that now the Brigade has got the measure of the enemy and that he can rely on them in future operations to do equally good work in bringing the war to a speedy and victorious conclusion.

21.10.18.
RHW

APPENDIX X

SPECIAL ORDER.

1. I wish heartily to congratulate all ranks of all arms and departments of the Division on the result of their first appearance on the Battle Field after their reorganisation as the 66th Division.

The operations between October 8th and October 19th which were in many respects as unique as they were successful may be summarised as follows :-

8th Oct. After a successful frontal attack at 05.00 by the S.A. Bde and 198th Bde on a first objective 3,800 yards in depth and 3,800 yards in width, 199th Bde went through and exploited the situation on the same frontage to a depth of a further 2,300 yards, finally capturing the village of SERAIN by 19.00.

9th Oct. During the night 8th/9th the Divisional front was reorganised and at 05.00 October 9th the pursuit was continued by 199th Bde on Right, 198th Bde on Left, and S.A. Bde in Reserve, each Bde advancing on a front of 1,500 yards narrowing to 1000 yards on the first objective, which was 5,000 yards distant. This objective was secured at 10.45. At 11.00 South African Bde passed through to continue the pursuit for a further 4,500 yards to a second objective which was secured about 14.00. Cavalry then passed through and held a line covering REUMONT and TROISVILLES. During the night the South African Bde threw out an outpost line astride the ROMAN ROAD in relief of the Cavalry immediately N.E. of REUMONT.

10th Oct. At 05.00 199th Bde on the Right and 198th Bde on the Left, each on a 1,000 yards front, passed through the South African Bde outpost line and took up the pursuit.

MONTAY and that portion of LE CATEAU West of the River SELLE, was secured by 10.00.

The Division had advanced 14 miles on a two mile front in 53 hours, taking many villages and ending up with LE CATEAU.

Prisoners were taken from eight Divisions, viz :- 2nd Guards, 8th Division, 21st Division, 21st Reserve Division, 38th Division, 119th Division, 121st Division, and 204th Division, also from 75th M.G. Marksman Detachment and from 4th Saxon Cyclist Brigade.

26 Officers (including 3 Battalion Commanders) and 1031 O.R. had been captured and also following materiel :- 62 ·77 guns and 4.2" Hows., 3 8" How., 3 5.9" How., 1 Anti-Aircraft gun, 15 T.Ms., 6 Anti-tank Rifles, 126 M.Gs. and 2 Motor cars.

Patrols were pushed into and had occupied the greater part of LE CATEAU East of the River by 10.00.

At 17.30 5th Bn Connaught Rangers rushed the town and secured a footing on the railway embankment East of the town, killing many enemy.

From conversation with the Mayor of LE CATEAU, it appears that the confusion and panic in the town was very great. A few dead of the Connaught Rangers were afterwards found on the high ground N.E. of the railway embankment about the RED Line of the attack on the 17th. Owing to the high ground on either flank remaining in the enemy's hands, we were however forced to withdraw.

/11th Oct....

11th Oct. On the night 11th/12th the S.A. Bde took over the Divisional front, less that portion north of the ROMAN ROAD which was relieved by the 9th Bn Glouc. R.

12th Oct. to 17th Oct. On 12th October to October 17th the S.A. Bde prepared for the attack on the high ground N.E. of LE CATEAU. The 17th Reserve Division had come into the line opposite the Division after seven weeks rest on the night 10th/11th Oct, and at once proceeded to organise the position E. of the River and the Eastern part of the town, even pushing patrols across to the Western bank.

17th Oct. At 05.20 the 50th Division, in conjunction with the rest of the Fourth Army, attacked on our Right. At this hour the South African Bde was assembled in its jumping off position N. of LE CATEAU, on the eastern bank of River SELLE having crossed by means of eight 30 foot bridges made and placed in position by the Divisional Engineers. The Brigade attacked at 08.05 having been covered meanwhile by a dense fog further thickened by smoke shell and bombs from Artillery, Aeroplanes and Mortars. The attack was so timed that the Left Bde of the 50th Division coming from a south-westerly direction should arrive at the railway embankment on the LE CATEAU - BASUEL Road simultaneously with the Right of the South African Bde.
The attack of the South African Bde came as a complete surprise to the enemy, who was unaware that it had crossed the river.
The enemy fought hard. The position was a very strong one and there were three belts of double apron fencing to be negotiated. Undeterred, the South African Brigade carried out its task and secured its objective. The 6th R.D.F. of 198th Bde were detailed to mop up LE CATEAU by a concentrated attack. This difficult work was most thoroughly accomplished with great dash.
198th Bde interposed one Battalion on the final objective between S.A. Bde and 50th Division on the Right.

18th-19th Oct. On the night of 18th/19th Oct. the 199th Bde took over the Divisional front and pushed out certain posts in front of the RED Line on the 20th.
Between 17th and 19th Oct. 4 Officers (including one Battalion Commander) and 265 O.Rs of 17th Reserve Division had been taken, also 2 .77 guns, 81 M.Gs., 5 lorries and 3 bicycles.

20th Oct. On the night of the 20th/21st the 18th Division relieved 66th Division.

2. The following are some of the points to which attention must be paid next time :-

(i) Communications. The axial line of communication is undoubtedly the only satisfactory system, and when properly run is invaluable. The same method must be applied in advance of Brigades where the communication arrangements were poor. Battalion runners had to go excessive distances which could have been obviated by the provision of Advance Report Centres.

(ii) Reports. The standard varied considerably. Ignorance of the situation in many instances caused

/unnecessary....

2. (ii)(cont.)
unnecessary delay and in several cases casualties to our own troops. Commanders of units must ensure by using every means at their disposal that they are in touch with the situation on their own fronts. Officers patrols were not enough used in this respect.

(iii) In future, no barrage will be put down in answer to S.O.S. Signal by day or night, and a protective barrage after gaining final objective will seldom be employed, as both these cramp the style of the Infantry.

F.O.Os will be attached to attacking battalions and will keep more in touch with the situation in the front line. They will regularly report direction of any hostile shelling for information of counter-battery work. Generally one Battery R.F.A. will be attached to each Brigade of Infantry, the Battery Commander usually remaining with the Brigade, and one Section being attached to each of the attacking Battalions. In this respect Training Leaflet No. 5 should be studied by all - it is being distributed down to Company Commanders.

(iv) Evacuation of wounded. Regimental Aid Posts will be pushed up closer to Battalions. This will allow of motor ambulances making full use of all passable roads and evacuating from as far forward as possible.

3. All ranks may justly be proud of the share they took in these operations, the great success of which was mainly due to :-

(i) The drive, marching and staying powers of the men.

(ii) The foresight and initiative displayed by junior officers and N.C.Os.

(iii) The quickness with which all commanders adapted themselves to the constantly changing situation and the rapidity with which orders were issued and carried out

(iv) The excellent co-operation of Artillery, Machine Guns, Tanks, Aeroplanes and Cavalry with the Infantry which largely contributed to the great pace with which the pursuit was pushed by the latter.

(v) The first rate performance of the R.E. in bridging the River SELLE, which alone rendered the trying operation of October 17th feasible
The good work done by the 9th Glouc. R. (Pioneers) throughout the operations both in making a dry weather track and holding MONTAY.

(vi) The untiring efforts of all the administrative services, resulting in the rapid evacuation of wounded, troops being fed, and ammunition supply secured.

(vii) The excellent spirit which pervaded all ranks in all conditions. In itself always a deterrent to sickness, it resulted in the number of sick in the Division being extremely small, some units being almost free from any wastage from this cause.

D.H.Q.,
24th October 1918.

H. Bethell.
Major-General,
Commanding 66th Division.

All Companies
6 Lancashire Fusiliers. Operation Order.
APPENDIX 3 13-10-18.

The Battalion will proceed by march route to MARETZ to-day as follows:–

para
1 Hour of Start: 08.55 hours

Starting Point: Cross roads P.22. c.7.7.

Order of march: B. C. D. HQ. A. Tpt.

Distances: 50 yds between platoons, and 50 yds between each 6 vehicles.

para
2. Blankets will be rolled in bundles of ten tied and clearly labelled by platoons, and will be stacked at Bn H.Q at 07.30 hours.
Officers Kits & mess boxes will be stacked at Bn H.Q mess at 08.10 hours.
Lewis Gun limbers will be packed at 08.00 hours under the supervision of 2/Lt C.W. Jones.
3. COOKERS. Water will be boiled on the march and tea served on arrival at MARETZ.

Acknowledge [signature] Capt & Adjt
6 Lancs Fusiliers

6th Lan. Fus. etc.,

APPENDIX IV

198th Inf. Bde.
No. B.M. 239.

Following from Army Commander begins aaa Will you please convey to the 66th and 25th Divisions my warm thanks for their gallantry and determination in driving back the enemy yesterday aaa I wish to congratulate the Corps and Divisional Staffs also on their success aaa All Staff arrangements particularly the Intelligence have worked most satisfactorily and the Artillery have done some most excellent work in getting forward their guns aaa Ends aaa The Corps Commander adds his congratulations to the above.

(Signed) A. Hunter
Brig. Gen.
198th Infantry Brigade.

11.10.18.

All Companies.
6th Lancs. Fus.

The above congratulatory telegram will be read out at the head of each [illegible] on Parade.

J. Banks
Captain & Adj[illegible]
6th Bn. Lancashire Fu[illegible]

13.10.18.

All Companies — Secret

6th Lancs Hrs — APPENDIX V

1. The Battalion will move to REUMONT to-day as follows:-

Hour of Start: 0955 hours.

Starting Point: Bn H.Q. Mess

Order of March: B.H.Q. A-B-C-D

Distances: 50x between platoons

2. Each man will carry one blanket.

3. Transport will move under the Bde Transport Officer.

4. Acknowledge

0855 hours

16.10.18

J. Franks Capt & Adjt
6th Lancs Hrs.

# APPENDIX VI L743

All Companies
6th Lancs. Fus.

1. The Battalion responsible for the main line of defence which runs from Q.6.B.6.0 — K.36.D.2.6.

2. A and C companies will continue to consolidate their present position

3. The Battalion will construct strong points as follows.
   (a) B Coy. at the eastern apex of Railway triangle
   (b) "D" Coy. at approximate K.35C.9.3.

   Each company will be assisted by one section 431 Field Coy. R.E. Details to be notified later

4. The 5th Inniskilling Fus. in conjunction with 13th Black Watch on the our right and 9th Manchesters on our left will be responsible for patrolling the line of the RICHEMONT RIVER.

5. In the event of the RICHEMONT RIVER line being reached it will constitute the outpost line.

(5) Contd.
and will run:– The Mill Rd. exclusive – GARDE MILL inclusive and will be held by the 5th Innis. Fus.

Issued at 1950 hrs.

Copies to A Coy 1
B "
C "
D "

J Franks
Capt. & Adjt.
6/Lancashire Fusiliers

19.10.18

APPENDIX VII LF 46

All Companies
6 LAN F.us

1. The Battalion will proceed by march route to MAUROIS today as follows

Hour of Start 1515 hours
Starting Point Bldg Patrum C Coy
Order of March Bn. H.Q. C. D. B. A

Distances 100x between companies

2. L Guns and L.G equipment will be stacked near the main road at once exact site to be pointed out by the R.S.M. Each company will leave one L Gunner to take charge of the guns until the limbers arrive

3. Waterproof capes will be worn

1440 hours

20/10/18

J Franks
Capt. Adjt.
6 LAN Fus

L.O. 719

6 Lancashire Fusiliers

All Companies.
T.O. QM.

APPENDIX VIII

1. Battalion will move by route march to PREMONT to-day, 21st inst.

2 Hour of Start 10.00 hours

3. Starting Point X Roads 100* North of Bn. H.Q.

4 Order of March H.Q, Drums A-B-C-D.

5 Route MARETZ - V18.C.0.2. PREMONT

6. 100* will be maintained between Companies during the march

[signature] Capt.
6 Lanc. Fusiliers

21-10-18

All Coys. No. 720.

Amendment to Movement Order. Ref. L.O. 719

Men will wear their ~~groundsheets~~ Waterproof-capes

J. Franks Capt.

21/10/18. Adjt. 6 Lan. Fusrs.

All Companies
Bn H.Q

L.O. 792

APPENDIX XII

1. The Battalion will parade for Brigade Route march on the 28th October 1918 as follows:-

Hour of Start: 08.30 hours

Starting Point: Bn H.Q

Order of March: Drums - "D" - H.Q - "A" - "B" - "C".

Route: U21.d.6.9 PONCHAUX-MALINCOURT SERAIN.

2. Dress: Full Battle Order

3. Exemptions:- Bn H. 1 Officers cook
1 mens cook
1 Mess Corporal
1 Sanitary man
1 M.O's Orderly

Each Coy:
1 Officers + 1 mens Cook = 2
Sanitary = 2

4. Distances: 100x between Companies.

[signature]
Capt + Adjt
6 Lancs Fusiliers

27-10-18.

APPENDIX XIII

# ACCOUNT OF OPERATIONS.

## PART IV.

12th October, 1918 - 12.00 18th October, 1918.

THE CLEARING OF LE CATEAU.

-:-:-:-:-

## PART V.

12.00 18th October - 18.00 18th October, 1918

THE ADVANCE TO THE RED LINE.

-:-:-:-:-

## PART VI.

18.00 18th October, 1918 - 20th October, 1918.

PATROLS AND RELIEF.

-:-:-:-:-

# P A R T   I V.

## 13th October, 1918 - 12.00 18th October, 1918.

-:-:-:-:-:-

After the relief by South African Brigade, described in Part III, the 198th Infantry Brigade went into Divisional Reserve - first at REUMONT at 2 hours notice, then at MAUROIS and finally at MARETZ where the Brigade was settled in Billets at 14,00 on 13th October.

The Brigade remained at MARETZ till the morning of the 16th when it moved to REUMONT, Later in the day it moved again and took up positions as follows :-

| Unit. | Position. | In relief of. | Remarks. |
|---|---|---|---|
| Brigade H.Q. | Q.7.a. | S.A. Brigade H.Q. | |
| 1 Coy., R. Innis. Fus. | Q.3 & Q.8. | S.A. Brigade. | Front Line posts. |
| R.Dub. Fus. less 2 Cos. | W. of LE CATEAU. | S.A. Brigade. | Front Line posts. |

/2 Cos., R. Dub. Fus.

| | | | |
|---|---|---|---|
| 2 Cos., 6 R.Dub.Fus. | Q.3.central. | - | For clearing LE CATEAU from the N. & N.E. & E. |
| 5 R.Innis.Fus. less 2 Cos. | Roman Road to N.W.end of MONTAY. | 9 Glouc. Regt. | Front Line posts. |
| 1 Co., 5 R.Innis.Fus. | Q.7. | - | Brigade Reserve. |
| Lancs. Fus. | Q.7. | - | Divl. Reserve. |
| 198 L.T.M.B. | With R.Dub.Fus. | | For clearing LE CATEAU. |

On conclusion of relief, the S.A. Brigade concentrated in the ravines in K.26 and 27 preparatory to forcing the crossing of the SELLE and taking the Red Line K.36.d.0.5 to BAILLON FARM, with a defensive flank to the North.

The two Companies 6th R. Dublin Fus. were to follow close behind them and start mopping up LE CATEAU from the N.E. and E. - when they had made some progress the remainder of 6 R. Dublin Fus. were to press in from the West and finally the Eastern outskirts of the town were to be put in a state of defence.

The 50th Divn. on our right were to take the red dotted line which included the Railway Station and the triangle in Q.5 before the S.A. attack and the mopping up of LE CATEAU were to begin. On their reaching this line the Coy. of 5th R. Innis. Fus. in Q.3 and Q.9 would be unnecessary and the plan was for them and the Coy. in Brigade Reserve to move up and take the place of the Dublins W. of LE CATEAU.

In spite of the 50th Division not getting either the station or triangle, the S.A. attack was launched and the mopping-up Companies of the Dublins were put in. They had considerable difficulty in their task and first one and then the other Company of 5th R. Innis. Fus. were sent up to 6th R. Dublin Fus. so as to release more men of the Dublins for the mopping up of the town - which was urgent as S.A. Brigade were being much troubled by M.G. fire and small counter attacks along the railway

/from the road crossing

from the road crossing K.35.c.9.3 northwards. Messages were received from Division authorising the employment of all the Dublins in this mopping up (the force had been limited to two Companies at the outset) and eventually all the Dublins and a platoon or two of Inniskillings were employed.

At [illegible] a telephone message from the Divisional Commander placed 6th Lancs. Fus. at Brigade disposal with instruc ions that as 50th Division had taken the station and triangle, 6th Lancs. Fus. were to cross the R. SELLE at ST. BENIN or north of it and attack the objective - road crossing K.35.c.9.3. to K.35.c.0.5 - with the idea of completing the clearing of LE CATEAU promptly.

The Battalion was therefore sent off, and succeeded in passing two companies across the river at Mins. de Pont Chapelle in Q.9.b. The station and ra lway triangle which dominate the valley entirely were <u>not</u> in our hands. This was reported by 6th Lancs. Fus. and eventually instructions were received from Division to withdraw them again into Divisional Reserve. This was done and completed at [illegible] at the cost of some dozen casualties and a certain amount of fatigue to the battalion.

The mopping up of LE CATEAU was going on slowly in the mean-time and section after section of the town was reported in our hands.- till the whole of the main town was ours at 17.50 the Faubourg de Landrecies being however still distinctly German, and commanded from the Railway Triangle and the embankment and crossing at K.35.c.9.3.

Throughout the night the situation on our right at the Railway Triangle and the Station was obscure. Notification was received of an attack being in preparation to capture these two points by the division on our right but this attack was postponed . Under instructions from Division orders were therefore issued at 23.45 to the 6th Lancs. Fus. (who were placed at the disposal of G.O.C. at this timeand ceased to be in Divisional Reserve) to get into touch with the 6th R. Dublin Fus. and reconnoitre with a

/view to

view to

(a) Taking over the line from the 6th R.Dublin Fus. and establishing their line from K.33.central - Road and railway crossing K.35.c.9.3 - Q.4.b.3.1 - River with advanced posts pushed forward to road junction K.35.d.6.0.

(b) To assemble on approximate front K.35.central - K.35.c.7.0 for an attack on the objective K.36.d.3.7 - Cross Roads K.36.a.00 95.

The task (b) was only to be undertaken in the event of the capture of the railway triangle by the Division on our right.

At 00.50 on the 18th orders were issued for Task (a) to be carried out. During the night and previous to relief the 6th R. Dublin Fus. completed the mopping up of the FAUBOURG de LANDRECIES except that the railway crossing at K.35.c.9.3 could not be captured as long as the enemy held Railway Triangle.

Touch was obtained with the South African Brigade on the railway in K.35.central.

The relief of 6th R. Dublin Fus. by the 6th Lancs. Fus. in LE CATEAU proved very difficult to carry out. The enemy shelled the West end of the town throughout the night with a large proportion of gas shell of all kinds, and the difficulties of relieving posts and patrols scattered all over the town were very great. A mist added to the difficulties of relief. In spite of this the relief was complete shortly after 09.00.

Meanwhile the Division on our right attacked at dawn and captured the Railway Triangle about 06.30.

The 6th Lancs. Fus. immediately got into touch with the 13th Black Watch on their right who carried out this attack and pushed forward and seized the road and railway crossing at K.35.c.9.3.

This position was an extremely strong one and owing to the Railway Triangle not having been captured had resisted all our efforts to capture it throughout the 17th.

At 10.00 on the 18th the Brigade was therefore disposed as follows :-

<u>6th Lancs. Fus.</u>

Two Companies in depth along line of Railway from K.35.central where in touch with S.A. Brigade - K.35.c.9.0.

One Company in close Support in Eastern outskirts of LE CATEAU.

One Company in Reserve near Battalion H.Q. at K.33.b.5.4.

<u>5th R. Inniskilling Fus.</u>

In support in Q.2.

<u>6th R. Dublin Fus.</u>

In Brigade Reserve in Q.7.

---

198th L.T.M.B. was attached to the 6th R. Dublin Fus. to assist in the mopping up of LE CATEAU.

2 Guns were attached to the 2 Companies of 6th R.D.F. who worked round from the N. and N.E., and 2 Guns to the 2 Companies that worked into LE CATEAU from the West.

They were of considerable assistance in dealing with hostile M.G. posts in houses in LE CATEAU.

About 100 rounds were fired in all during the 17th, and 18th instant.

---

The total casualties sustained by the 6th R.Dub.Fus. during the mopping up of LE CATEAU, were :-

Killed - 13.
Wounded - 64 (including 3 at duty)
Missing - 9.

Captured during this action were :-

| | Prisoners. | Lorries. | M.G's. | |
|---|---|---|---|---|
| 6 R. Dub.Fus. | 95 | 3 | ? | x |
| 6 Lancs.Fus. | 12 | - | - | |
| 5 Innis. Fus. | - | - | 2 | |

x All material found in LE CATEAU is claimed and this includes many more M.G's, the number of which it is impossible to estimate.

# P A R T V.

## The Advance to the RED LINE.

### 12.00, 18th October to 18.00, 18th October, 1918.

-:-:-:-:-:-:-:-:-

After the capture of the line of the Railway, the 6th Lancs.Fus. pushed on towards the RED Line and at 16.30 held the following line with three Companies in depth:-
K.36.c.3.3. - K.35.b.5.5.
One Company and Battalion H.Q., at K.35.d.4.4.

On reaching this line the 6th Lancs.Fus. came under hostile machine gun fire. The Battalion accordingly halted for 45 minutes while arrangements were made for the co-operation of troops of the 25th Division on the Right for the final advance to the RED Line. This halt of 45 minutes also enabled the advance to be continued at dusk.

At 17.15 the advance was resumed and was very successful. The bad light hampered the enemy Machine Gunners, prisoners from whom afterwards stated that they were unable to see our men until they were right up to them.
The RED Line was reached from K.36.d.0.6. - K.36.a.0.9., 5 Machine Guns and 35 prisoners were captured, and severe casualties were inflicted on the enemy.

This engagement furnished an interesting instance of the vulnerability of hostile machine guns against infantry employing their own weapons skillfully and making the best use of ground.
More enemy could undoubtedly have been killed and captured had any Cavalry or fresh Infantry been available to exploit the success. Large numbers of enemy and some transport were seen retreating hurriedly eastwards.

The 6th Lancs.Fus. then consolidated the RED Line and pushed forward patrols towards RICHEMONT River. These patrols soon got into touch with more hostile Machine Guns

/ The 5th R.Innis.Fus

The 5th R.Innis.Fus. ~~pushed on~~ moved up to RAILWAY TRIANGLE (Q.5.) at 18.00 to be in Support to the 6th Lancs.Fus.

From the time of their relief of 6th R.Dublin Fus. until the capture of the RED Line, on the evening of the 18th, the 6th Lancs.Fus. captured 5 Machine Guns, and 47 prisoners (25 of whom were captured in the final advance to the RED Line).

In the same period they suffered the following casualties :-

Killed - 4 O.R.
Wounded - 16 O.R.

## PART VI.

**18.00 18th October, 1918 - 20th October, 1918.**

-:-:-:-:-:-

Under instructions received from Division, orders were issued to the 6th Lancs. Fus. at 18.15 on 18th October to re-adjust their front as follows :-

(a) To hand over the Red Line from K.36.central to K.36.a.0.9 to the 9th Manchester Regt. Relief to be complete as soon as possible after dusk.

(b) To take over the Red Line from K.36.central to Q.6.b.6.0 from 13th Black Watch (Scottish Horse) of 50th Division, as soon as the latter were definitely in possession of that portion of the Red Line.

The relief of 6th Lancs. Fus. by 9th Manchester Regt. was not complete until 02.00 on the 19th instant. In the meantime reports had been received from the 149th Infantry Brigade that the 13th Black Watch were not on the Red Line.

Orders were accordingly sent to the 6th Lancs. Fus. to side slip to their right on relief by 9th Manchester Regt. and establish themselves as far as possible on the Red Line from K.36.central to Q.6.b.6.0.

On reconnoitring to carry out this order 6th Lancs. Fus. found troops of the Gloucesters of the 25th Division on this portion of the Red Line.

As the Red Line was held throughout its length and relief by 9th Manchester Regt. could not be completed till very late at night O.C., 6th Lancs. Fus. decided to concentrate his Battalion about K.35.d.1.4. and carry out the relief of whoever was holding his portion of the Red Line as soon as possible after daylight. While 6th Lancs. Fus. were concentrating the Gloucesters of the 25th Division were withdrawn and the 13th Black Watch took over a portion only of their front establishing a post on the North side of the LE CATEAU - BAZUEL road about Q.3.b.2.2.

The 9th Manchester Regt. filled this gap by placing a post about Q.6.b.3.9.

Shortly after daylight 6th Lancs. Fus. took over their sector of the Red Line from the road at Q.6.b.5.0 where they were in touch with the 13th Black Watch to K.36.d.0.6. where they were in touch with 9th Manchester Regt.

The morning of the 19th instant was very quiet. There was practically no hostile artillery fire. Some hostile machine guns were active from about the line of road K.36.d.9.2 - K.36.d.8.9.

Arrangements were then made for 5th R. Inniskilling Fus. to push out strong patrols to the RICHEMONT River at dusk and to secure the line of the river as an outpost line from the Mill at R.2.a.1.5 to GARDE MILL (L.31.a.90.85).

One Battery of 83rd Brigade, R.F.A. was detailed to assist 5th R. Innis. Fus. in their to the outpost line, and a liaison officer for this purpose reported to this Battalion.

Verbal orders were received from Division at 23.00 on 19th instant that the advance to the line of the RICHEMONT River would be carried out under an artillery barrage at 07.00 on 20th instant in conjunction with an advance by 1st Infantry Brigade. Orders were accordingly issued to 5th R. Innis. Fus. to report by 03.00 on the 20th the position of their patrols. If no report was received by that hour patrols would have to withdraw to the Red Line and advance under cover of the barrage at 07.00 in conjunction with 1st Infantry Brigade. There is

/little doubt

little doubt that patrols of 5th R. Inniskilling Fus. wouldhave reached the line of the RICHEMONT river solely by the use of infantry weapons and without the assistance of an artillery barrage as the enemy had only a few machine gun posts along the line of the road K.36.d.[illegible].2 - K.36.d.8.[illegible]. These were not dug in and could be enfiladed from the road at Q.6.b.6.0. Arrangements had already been made for enfilade fire to be brought to bear on them from a post at this point.

At 23.30 on the 19th instant verbal instructions were received from the Divisional Commander that the 1[illegible]th Infantry Brigade would take over the front held by this Brigade at once from the Northern Brigade Boundary to K.36.d.6.0., and that the Southern portion of the Brigade front would be taken over at once by 25th Division.

The advance to the RICHEMONT River would be carried out by 1[illegible]th Infantry Brigade on the whole Divisional front.

Patrols of 5th R. Inniskilling Fus. were accordingly withdrawn at once.

In order to enable the 6th Lancs. Fus. to be withdrawn without delay, the 5th R. Inniskilling Fus. (less two Companies) were instructed to take over the Southern portion of the Brigade front pending relief by the 25th Division.

6th Lancs. Fus. were relieved in the northern portion of the Brigade front by the [illegible]th Manchester Regt, and the whole battalion was concentrated by 07.00 on 20th October in Q.7.

6th R. Dublin Fus. meanwhile moved from Q.2. to REUMONT and 2 Coys. 5th R. Innis. Fus. moved to Q.2.

The whole of the Brigade was thus relieved by 03.[illegible] on 20th October except the 5th R. Innis. Fus. (less two Companies) who were awaiting relief by troops of the 25th Division.

This relief was considerably delayed and when finally arrangements were made for 20th Manchesters to carry out this relief the battalion reported that the relief could not be carried out until dusk owing to hostile machine gun fire.

/Relief accordingly took plac

Relief accordingly took place at dusk on 20th October and the 5th R. Inniskilling Fus. (less two Companies) reached MAUROIS at 23.30 on 20th instant.

The remainder of the Brigade marched to MAUROIS on the afternoon of the 20th instant.

---

The following are the casualties sustained by this Brigade from the 18th October to 20th October, both dates inclusive :-

| | Officers. | | | O.R. | | |
|---|---|---|---|---|---|---|
| | K. | W. | M. | K. | W. | M. |
| 6th Lancs. Fus. | .. | 1 | .. | 4 | 38 x | 2. |
| 5th Innis.Fus. | .. | 1 | .. | .. | 29 ∅ | 8 |
| 6th R.D.F. | 1 | 3 | .. | 12 | 61 ∅ | 9 |
| | 1 | 5 | .. | 16 | 128 | 19. |

∅ Includes 3 at duty.
x " 5 " "

TOTAL CAPTURES (from 18th to 20th inst.)

| Prisoners. | Lorries. | M.G's. |
|---|---|---|
| 107. | 3 | 8 x |

x All material found in LE CATEAU is claimed and this includes many more M.G's, the numbers of which it is impossible to estimate.

Secret

APPENDIX XI

198TH INFANTRY BRIGADE.

REPORT ON OPERATIONS.

7.10.18 - 12.10.18.

----:----

PART I.

7.10.18 - 18.00 8.10.18.

----:----

1. ASSEMBLY.

On 7th October the 198th Infantry Brigade Group moved by march route to the vicinity of LE CATELET and occupied their assembly position in the LE CATELET - NAUROY line.

Battalions were distributed as follows :-

| | |
|---|---|
| 5th R.Inniskilling Fus. | RIGHT. |
| 6th R. Dublin Fus. | LEFT. |
| 6th Lancs. Fus. | RESERVE, in the GOUY - BELLICOURT railway cutting. |

198th Infantry Brigade H.Q. RAILWAY RIDGE.

2. DEPLOYMENT. See Map A Position 1.

On the evening of 7th October units began their march to position of deployment at 22.00. Rain began about 19.00 and fell heavily till 22.00. The 'going' was as a result very slippery. In spite of this all units moved forward very well and were approaching their tapes in good time.

At 01.00 an attack on VILLERS OUTREAUX resulted in a heavy hostile barrage being put down on our positions of deployment.

The 6th R. Dublin Fus. were lining up on their tapes and the 5th R. Inniskilling Fus. were just nearing them when the barrage came down.

Both battalions suffered considerable casualties and were correspondingly disorganised.

/Heavy shelling continued

Heavy shelling continued throughout the period of deployment.

At 04.45 however, both battalions were in position on their tapes ready to advance.

The 6th Bn. Lancashire Fus. had meanwhile assembled in Reserve without ~~any~~ much difficulty.

One Section of 198th L.T.M.B. was allotted to each Battalion, and the guns with 28 rounds of ammunition were brought up on pack mules and off loaded at the positions of deployment.

3. ATTACK.

At 05.10 our barrage opened and the infantry advanced to the attack.

On the whole the enemy showed little tendency to fight, and often ran away before our troops could get to grips with him, with the exception of M.G. nests which fought stoutly.

From the earliest stages of the attack the 6th R. Dublin Fus. were troubled by machine gun fire on their left flank.

As the attack progressed this became more serious as VILLERS OUTREAUX was not taken and the enemy had therefore a perfect target for enfilade M.G. fire. In spite of these difficulties the 6th R. Dublin Fus. pushed on and captured PETIT VERGER Farm and MARLICHES Farm. The latter they were unable to hold owing to enfilade M.G. fire.

The 6th R. Dublin Fus. then established a defensive flank along the ridge in T.23.b. This flank was further extended by four posts which were established by the 6th Bn. Lancashire Fus. in T.23.c.

On the right the 5th R. Inniskilling Fus. continued their advance and established themselves on the RED LINE.

There was some fighting in HAMAGE FARM and HAMAGE WOOD but, with the assistance of tanks, the wood was soon cleared and a battery of 77 mm. was captured.

/The position at 09.15

The position at 09.15 was approximately as shown on attached map. (Map A Position 2).

At 09.45 the enemy counter attacked N. of HAMAGE FARM. This counter attack was repulsed with the assistance of two tanks.

During the next hour there were several minor actions along the WALLINCOURT - AUDIGNY Line, the enemy attempting to debouch from there to counter attack our troops establishing themselves on the RED LINE. All these local counter attacks were repulsed with loss to the enemy.

At 10.30 the 6th R. Dublin Fus. established touch with the battalion on their left the 4th K.R.R.C. of the 50th Division.

As our troops advanced along the S.E. side of VILLERS OUTREAUX the 6th R. Dublin Fus. advanced again and captured MARLICHES FARM (11.30) and established themselves along the line of their final objective (Green Line on attached Map "A"). At the same time the 5th R. Innis. Fus. continued their advance, captured LAMPE FARM, and established themselvs on the GReen Line. (Map A Position 3)

PART II.

18.00 8.10.18 - 18.00 9.10.18.

----:----

1. RELIEF OF PORTION OF 199th Infantry Brigade FRONT.

About 17.00 on 8th October orders were received from the Divisional Commander that the Brigade would take over a portion of the front of 199th Infantry Brigade who were carrying out a minor operation with a view to re-adjusting their front before an attack the next morning.

Unfortunately G.O.C., 199th Infantry Brigade and his Brigade Major were both in the line arranging for this minor operation, and details for relief could not be arranged till 19.00. It was then decided that the 5th R. Innis. Fus. should relieve the 9th Manchester Regt., less 1 Coy. in U.7.central and LAMPE POST to be relieved by 6th R. Dublin Fus.

The latter portion of the relief was carried out, but owing to a misunderstanding the three Coys., 9th Manchester Regt., were not relieved by 5th R. Inniskilling Fus.

2. ORDERS FOR ATTACK ON 9TH OCTOBER.

About 00.15 on 9th October orders were received for an attack the next morning.

It was decided that the 6th Lancs. Fus. would lead the attack with 5th R. Inniskilling Fus. in Support and 6th R. Dublin Fus. in Reserve.

3. ATTACK.

6th Lancs. Fus. were formed up at 04.50 and advanced at 05.20 clearing the eastern outskirts of ELINCOURT.

Two Coys. of 5th R. Inniskilling Fus. followed up and entered ELINCOURT from the South and East. The remaining Companies were late reaching their assembly position.

It soon became evident that the enemy had withdrawn and would offer no serious resistance in ELINCOURT.

/The 6th R. Dublin Fus. entered

The 6th R. Dublin Fus. entered the village from the West and with the assistance of the 5th R. Inniskilling Fus. rapidly cleared the village capturing some dozen prisoners. (See Map B. Position 5)

A section of R.E. were detailed to search for booby traps and mines in ELINCOURT.

They discovered an unexploded charge under the Railway Crossing at the Southern exit of the village.

Considerable delay was caused by a very dense fog which lasted from 06.00 to 07.15 when the 6th Lancs. Fus. continued their advance without meeting organized any opposition, captured the BOIS DE PINON and IRIS COPSE and reached their final objective - the MAUREZ-CLARY Road at 10.50, sending patrols to S. exit of CLARY to gain touch with Brigade on our left.

The 5th R. Inniskilling Fus. then moved up into Support sending one Company to IRIS FARM to secure their left flank, and the 6th R. Dublin Fus. into Reserve.

The South African Brigade who had been following up close in rear of the Brigade then passed through the 6th Lancs. Fus. and continued the advance.

At 12.00 the Brigade was therefore distributed in accordance with attached map "B". (Position 6

4. BRIGADE IN DIVISIONAL RESERVE.

Orders were received at 13.00 that the Brigade was in Divisional Reserve and would hold the RED LINE (final objective of 198 and 199 Infantry Brigades) in the event of a hostile counter attack.

All units were ordered to be prepared to move at ½ hours notice, and O.C., "A" Coy., 25th M.G. Battalion was ordered to place eight guns in position covering the southern portion of the Red Line in addition to the eight already in position in the Northern Sub-sector. (Map B Position 7)

PART III.

18.00 9.10.18 - 05.00 11.10.18.

----:----

1. ORDERS FOR ATTACK.

At 00.30 the Divisional Commander dictated to the G.O.C. on the telephone orders for attack at 06.00 10th October.

2. APPROACH MARCH.

At 03.30 10th October the Brigade marched through MARETZ and MAUROIS to REUMONT.

3. ADVANCE.

East of REUMONT the Brigade deployed at 06.15 N. of REUMONT - LE CATEAU Road. The advance was carried out on a one battalion front with three Companies in the line.

The 6th Lancs. Fus. again led the attack with the 5th R. Inniskilling Fus. in Support and the 6th R. Dublin Fus. in Reserve.

Touch was obtained with 199th Infantry Brigade on the right, and with the 2nd Argyle and Sutherland Highlanders of the 33rd Division on the left. 199th Infantry Brigade were deployed before this Brigade as they led the march to the position of deployment. 199th Infantry Brigade accordingly advanced slowly in order to allow this Brigade to get into line with them.

Owing to the very short time available in which to make arrangements for this attack it was impossible to arrange for artillery co-operation.

The Brigade advanced accordingly without artillery Support.

At the outset of the attack little opposition was encountered either from hostile shell or machine gun fire, but as our troops neared LE CATEAU the shelling became heavy.

The enemy had evidently several batteries, chiefly 5.9, ready in position, and the 6th Lancs. Fus. in particular suffered casualties from shell fire.

/77 mm. firing over open sights

77 mm. firing over open sights on the forward slopes in K.21 and K.27 were particularly troublesome.

In spite of these difficulties the 6th Lancs. Fus. pushed on and captured the high ground in K.27,b. and d.

The high ground and the line of the INCHY - LE CATEAU Railway were very heavily shelled and it became evident that a further advance without more artillery support and without counter-battery work would be difficult.

The enemy was holding the line of the River SELLE in strength.

The situation at 12.00 was as shown on attached map "C".

4. ATTACK ON MONTAY.

At 16.25 verbal orders were received by the G.O.C. from the Divisional Commander that the Brigade would attack and capture MONTAY at 17.00.

This order was communicated verbally to O.C., 6th Lancashire Fus. by the Brigade Major at 16.45 and at 17.30 the 6th Lancs. Fus. advanced on MONTAY.

The advance came under heavy machine gun fire from the Eastern bank of the river.

In spite of this the 6th Lancs. Fus. pressed on and entered MONTAY supported by two Coys. 5th R. Inniskilling Fus.

Touch was established with 18th K.L. on the right but it was found impossible to cross the river as the bridges were broken and the river was unfordable. (22.55).

Our line then ran as shown on attached map "D".

5. Throughout the 11th the situation remained approximately unchanged. Some casualties were suffered from the enemy's shell fire which was still very heavy.

Arrangements were made for the relief of the 6th Lancs. Fus. and the 6th R. Dublin Fus. during the night 11th/12th and instructions were given to

/O.C., 6th R. Dublin Fus.

O.C., 6th R. Dublin Fus. to endeavour to cross the river SELLE, and get into touch with troops of the 33rd Division on the high ground East of the river.

At 17.00 orders were received that the Brigade would be relieved that night by a portion of the South African Brigade.

The relief was effected without incident, though the shell fire was heavy, and the Brigade concentrated in billets in REUMONT.

To sum up the Brigade were in action practically continuously from dawn 8th Oct. to dawn 12th Oct. During this period the Brigade advanced 13 miles, 9 miles of which were realised fighting.

26 guns and a number of prisoners were captured and two villages were liberated.

Total captures made during this period were :-

| 77mm. Guns. | 5.9" How. | Anti-Tank Rifles. | T.Ms. | A.A. Guns. | M.Gs. counted. |
|---|---|---|---|---|---|
| 23 | 3 | 3 | 2 | 1 | 48. |

Prisoners - 342 O.R.

Total casualties during this period were :-

| Officers. | | O.R. | | | |
|---|---|---|---|---|---|
| K. | W. | K. | W. | NYD. | M. |
| 4 | 26 | 71 | 579 | 1 | 125 ⊗ |

Practically all these have been accounted for, either K, W, or M, i.e.,

| K. | W. | M. |
|---|---|---|
| 13 | 59 | 53x. |

x. All these 53 must be either killed or wounded in our hands. No men fell into enemy hands as far as is known.

# 198TH INFANTRY BRIGADE.

| | |
|---|---|
| Brigade Commander. | Brigadier General A.J. HUNTER, D.S.O., M.C. |
| Brigade Major. | Captain R.A. EDEN, M.C. |
| Staff Captain. | Captain F. INGLESON, M.C. |
| Brigade Intell. Offr. | Captain T.H.G. GREY, M.C. |
| Signalling Officer. | Lieut. A.T. TERRY. |

## 6th LANCASHIRE FUSILIERS.

| | |
|---|---|
| Commanding Officer. | Lieut. Colonel R.F. GROSS, D.S.O. |
| Second-in-Command. | Major J.S. TOWNSHEND, M.C. |
| Adjutant. | Captain F. FRANKS, M.C. |
| O.C., "A" Coy. | Captain R.A.V. WHITE. |
| O.C., "B" Coy. | Captain J.S. RUTHERFORD. |
| O.C., "C" Coy. | Captain L.B.L. SECKHAM, M.C. |
| O.C., "D" Coy. | Captain C.H. POTTER, M.C. |

## 5TH R. INNISKILLING FUS.

| | |
|---|---|
| Commanding Officer. | Lieut. Colonel A.W.S. PATERSON, D.S.O. |
| Second-in-Command. | Major G.M. KIDD, M.C. |
| Adjutant. | Captain H.J. EASTWOOD, M.C. |
| O.C., "A" Coy. | Captain G.R. ROCHE-KELLY. |
| O.C., "B" Coy. | Captain W.C.G. BOLITHO. |
| O.C., "C" Coy. | Captain W.R. GALLWAY. |
| O.C., "D" Coy. | Captain T.T.H. VERSCHOYLE. |

## 6TH R. DUBLIN FUSILIERS.

| | |
|---|---|
| Commanding Officer. | Lieut. Colonel W.B. LITTLE, D.S.O., M.C. |
| Second-in-Command. | Major W. VANCE, M.C. |
| Adjutant. | Captain J. ESMONDE, M.C. |
| O.C., "A" Coy. | Captain H.J. HOYE. |
| O.C., "B" Coy. | Captain H.A. SHADFORTH. |
| O.C., "C" Coy. | Captain H.J. GAFFNEY, M.C. |
| O.C., "D" Coy. | Captain W.B. ENGLISH. |

## 198TH L.T.M.B.

| | |
|---|---|
| Officer Commanding. | A/Captain F.J. ROE. |

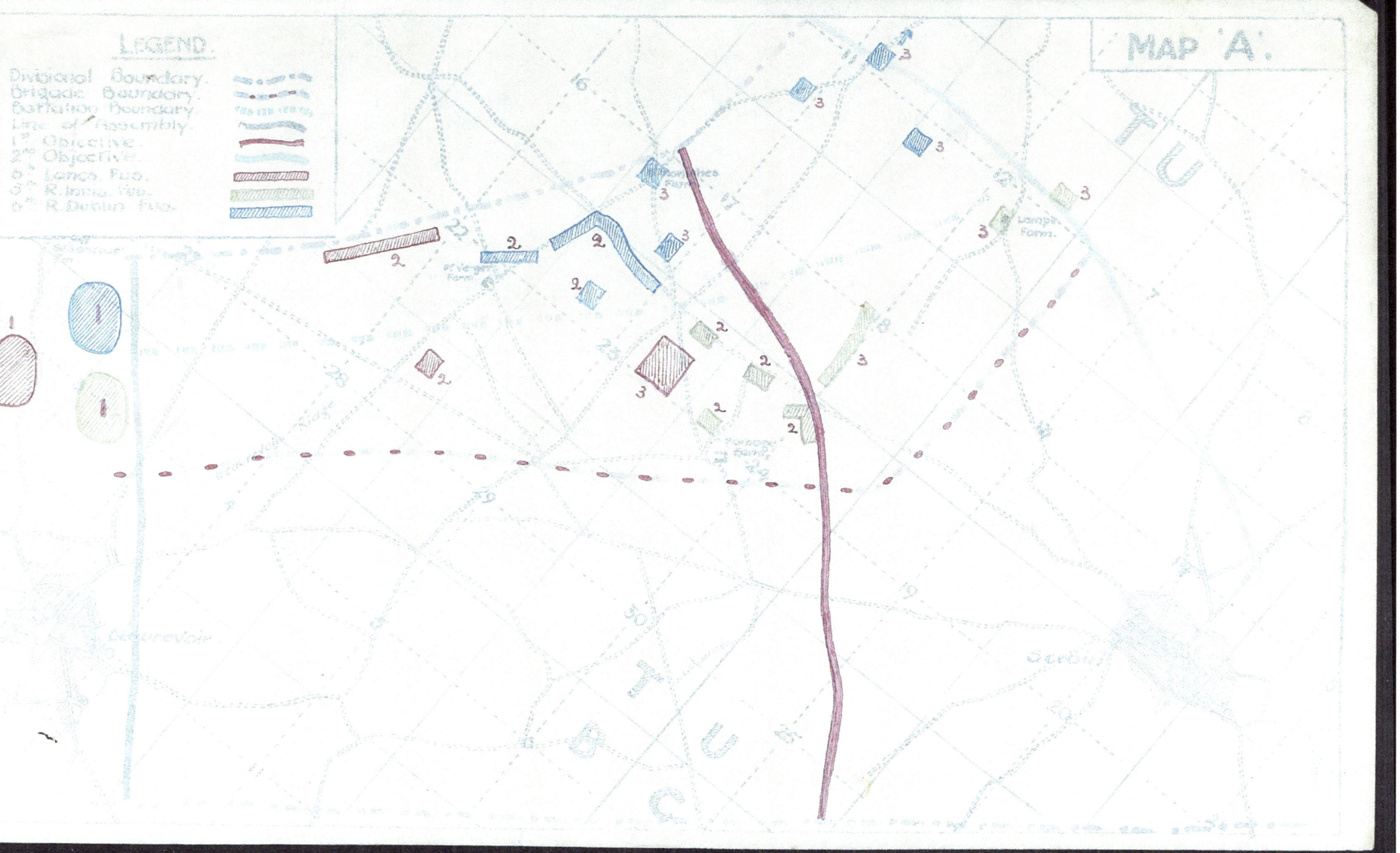

MAP 'A'.
LEGEND.
Divisional Boundary.
Brigade Boundary.
Battalion Boundary.
Line of Assembly.
1st Objective.
2nd Objective.
6th Lancs. Fus.
5th R. Innis. Fus.
6th R. Dublin Fus.
Lampe Farm.

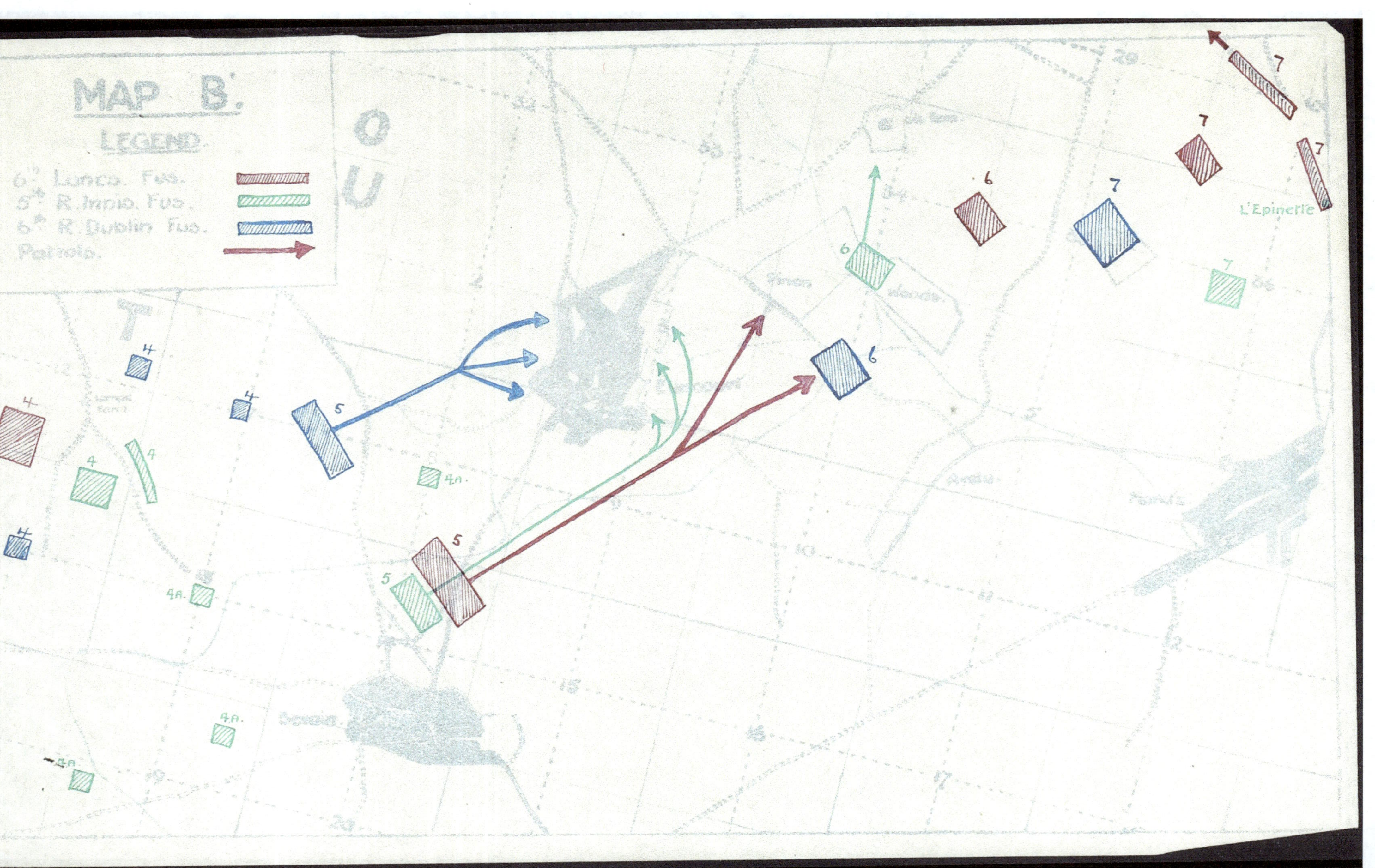
MAP B.
LEGEND
6th Lancs. Fus.
5th R. Innis. Fus.
6th R. Dublin Fus.
Patrols.
O
U
T
L'Epinette

# MAP 'C'

LEGEND.

6th Lancs. Fus.
5th R. Innis. Fus.
6th R. Dublin Fus.

1:20,000

Parts of 57B NE / 57B SE

Montay

Rouvillers Farm

Five Valleys Bridge

LE CATEAU

Troisvilles

J K P Q

1:20,000

# MAP 'D'.

LEGEND.

| | |
|---|---|
| 6th Lancs. Fus. | (red) |
| 5th R. Innis. Fus. | (green) |
| 6th R. Dublin Fus. | (blue) |

Monfoy

Bolton Farm

Four Valleys Bridge.

Rte Cambrai

LE CATEAU

Troisvilles

J K

P Q

39.J.
55 sheets

(6339) Wt. W160/M3016 1,500,000 10/17 McA & W Ltd (E 1898) Forms W3091.

Army Form W.3091.

22

# Cover for Documents.

198/66

Confidential

WO

**Nature of Enclosures.**

War Diary
of
6th Bn. Lancashire Fusiliers

from 1st Nov. 1918 to 30th Nov. 1918.

(Volume 5)

**Notes, or Letters written.**

Instructions regarding War Diaries and Intelligence Summaries are contained in F. S. Regs., Part II. and the Staff Manual respectively. Title pages will be prepared in manuscript.

# WAR DIARY
*or*
# INTELLIGENCE SUMMARY.
*(Erase heading not required.)*

Army Form C. 2118.

| Place | Date | Hour | Summary of Events and Information | Remarks and references to Appendices |
|---|---|---|---|---|
| PRÉMONT | 1/11/18 | | Weather fine with sunshine all day. Battalion resting & cleaning up. All Lewis Gunners were given instruction in the method of firing an Enemy M.G. The Brigade Commander visited Bn H.Q. at 1140 hours. Conference for Coy Comdrs was held in Bn H.Q. mess at 1400 hours. Brigade Order No 135 received at 1815 hours. Bn Order No 23 was issued to all concerned at 1915 hours. For details see APPENDIX I attached. 2/Lt P.L. KEIGHLEY was admitted to hospital | |
| [illegible] | 2/11/18 | | Weather changeable with rain at intervals. The Battalion proceeded to HONNECHY in accordance with Bn Order No 23 (see appendix I attached) and arrived at 1200 hours. The Battalion was accommodated in Billets. At 1530 hours 2/Lt C.W. JONES proceeded to LE CATEAU to arrange billets for the Battalion. Conference for Coy Comdrs was held [illegible] Bn H.Q. [illegible] at 1400 hours subject | [illegible] |

D. D. & L., London, E.C. (A7883) Wt. W803/M1672 350,000 4/17 Sch. 52a Forms/C/2118/14

Instructions regarding War Diaries and Intelligence Summaries are contained in F. S. Regs., Part II, and the Staff Manual respectively. Title pages will be prepared in manuscript.

# WAR DIARY
or
# INTELLIGENCE SUMMARY.
(*Erase heading not required.*)

Army Form C. 2118.

| Place | Date | Hour | Summary of Events and Information | Remarks and references to Appendices |
|---|---|---|---|---|
| On the Move | 2/11/18 | | Forthcoming Operations. 198th Bde Instructions No 1 issued with B.O. 127 received. The following instructions under No 1758/284 were received from Brigade:- "Instruct Major J. S. TOWNSEND M.C. [illegible] 5th Bn Royal INNISK Fus forthwith to assume duties as Second-in-Command of that battalion. Capt L. B. L. SECKHAM M.C. will assume duties as Second-in-Command of the unit under your Command from to-day." These instructions were complied with at 1900 hours. Bn Order No 23 was issued to all concerned at 2145 hours see APPENDIX II attached | [illegible] |
| On the Move | 3/11/18 | | Weather fine. 198th Bde Instructions No 2 issued with B.O. 127 received at 1000 hours. Conference for Coy Comdrs was held in Bn H.Q. Mess at 1000 hours. Subject:- Forthcoming Operations. The Battalion proceeded to LE CATEAU in accordance with Bn Order 23 (see APPENDIX II attached) and arrived in Billets at 1720 hours. | [illegible] |

(A9175) Wt W2358/P560 600,000 12/17 D. D. & L. Sch. 52a. Forms C2118/15

Instructions regarding War Diaries and Intelligence Summaries are contained in F. S. Regs., Part II. and the Staff Manual respectively. Title pages will be prepared in manuscript.

# WAR DIARY
*or*
# INTELLIGENCE SUMMARY.
*(Erase heading not required.)*

Army Form C. 2118.

| Place | Date | Hour | Summary of Events and Information | Remarks and references to Appendices |
|---|---|---|---|---|
| On The Move | 4/6/18 | | Weather fine. At 0030 hours Bde Warning Order for move to POMMEREUIL was received and at 0630 hours Brigade Order No 129 was received. Bn Order No 24 was issued to all concerned at 0700 hours. For details of which see APPENDIX III attached. At 1040 hours verbal orders received from the Staff Captain that the move was postponed until the afternoon and at 1540 hours orders were received that the Battalion would pass the starting point at 1615 hours. The Battalion left billets at 1600 hours and arrived in billets at POMMEREUIL at 1715 hours. Conference for Coy Comdrs was held in Bn H.Q. Mess at 1130 and 1400 hours. Subject:- forthcoming operations. | |
| On The Move | 5/6/18 | | Weather changeable, rain at intervals throughout the day. At 0010 hours Warning Order for move to G.g area was received and at 0300 hours Bde Order No 130. Bn Order No 25 was issued to all concerned at 0345 hours (see appendix IV attached) The Battalion moved | |

(A9175) Wt W2358/P360 600,000 12/17 D. D. & L. Sch. 52a. Forms/C2118/15.

Instructions regarding War Diaries and Intelligence Summaries are contained in F. S. Regs., Part II and the Staff Manual respectively. Title pages will be prepared in manuscript.

# WAR DIARY
*or*
# INTELLIGENCE SUMMARY.
(*Erase heading not required.*)

Army Form C. 2118.

| Place | Date | Hour | Summary of Events and Information | Remarks and references to Appendices |
|---|---|---|---|---|
| On the Move | 5/11/18 | | at 0830 hours and arrived in Q.9 area, Ref: Sheet 57A 1/40000, at 0950 hours where the battalion stayed until 1505 hours and then moved into billets near the Station at P.9 G.16.a in the N. Western outskirts of LANDRECIES. The Divisional Comdr visited Bn HQ at 1715 hours. | J.T. |
| " | 6/11/18 | | Weather changeable. The Battalion moved to BASSE NOYELLES at 1630 hours and arrived at [illegible] hours. | |
| " | 7/11/18 | | Weather changeable. The Battalion moved at 1800 hours to DOMPIERRE and arrived at 1810 hours. At 1900 hours orders were received for the battalion to relieve the 9th DEVONS who were in support to the main line in I.3.d.9 area Ref 57A 1/40000. The battalion moved forward at 2045 hours and the relief was completed at 2330 hours. | |
| " | 8/11/18 | | Weather changeable. Conference for Coy Commanders was held in Bn HQ at I.3.a.1.3 at [illegible] hours. Subject: To-day's operations. Bn Order No 26 were issued to all concerned at 0530 hours (For details see APPENDIX V attached). At 0700 hours the Battalion assembled | |

22

Instructions regarding War Diaries and Intelligence Summaries are contained in F. S. Regs., Part II. and the Staff Manual respectively. Title pages will be prepared in manuscript.

# WAR DIARY
*or*
# INTELLIGENCE SUMMARY.
*(Erase heading not required.)*

Army Form C. 2118.

| Place | Date | Hour | Summary of Events and Information | Remarks and references to Appendices |
|---|---|---|---|---|
| On the Line | 8/11/18 | | In accordance with Bn Order 56 and at 0845 hours Bn HQ B and D Companies moved forward to LA CROISELLES FME. A and C Companies having moved up in close support to 5th INNISK FUS. At 0910 hours Bn HQ was established at LA CROISELLES FME with B and D Companies. At 1030 hours Advanced Bn HQ and B Company moved forward to J.6.c.4.0 and at 1115 hours Bn HQ and D Company moved to same point. At 1125 hours Bn HQ was established at J.6.c.4.0 and Advanced Bn HQ moved forward to FME LA JONQUIERE at 1300 hours. At 1120 hours O.C. A Company (Right Company) reported that he was in close support to 5th INNISKS (who were held up by MG fire in J.12.a.5.5) and in touch with the LIVERPOOL (199th Bde) on Right. O.C. C Company reported at the same hour that he was in close support to left Company 5th INNISKS (who were held up in front of W[illegible] J.6.b) but was not in touch with troops on left. At 1215 hours 5th INNISKS were reported to have crossed the AVESNES – MAUBEUGE Road in K.1.d. and at | |

(A9475) Wt W2358/P360 600,000 12/17 D. D. & L. Sch. 52a. Forms/C.2118/15.

Instructions regarding War Diaries and Intelligence Summaries are contained in F. S. Regs., Part II. and the Staff Manual respectively. Title pages will be prepared in manuscript.

# WAR DIARY
*or*
# INTELLIGENCE SUMMARY.
*(Erase heading not required.)*

Army Form C. 2118.

| Place | Date | Hour | Summary of Events and Information | Remarks and references to Appendices |
|---|---|---|---|---|
| [illegible] | 8/11/18 | | 1255 hours information was received that our line was established on the AVESNES – MAUBEUGE Road along the whole Divisional front. At 1300 hours 'B' Company moved forward and took up position in the centre of "A" and "C" Companies on the AVESNES – MAUBEUGE Road and at 1310 hours "A" "B" and "C" Companies were instructed to commence the advance on the final objective at 1400 hours. The Brigade Comdr visited Bn HQ at 1300 hours and as the 5th CONNAUGHTS were held up on our right the Brigade Comdr ordered one section 100th MG Coy to report to the Battalion to be used as necessary to form a defensive flank to the Right. At 1430 hours "A" "B" and "C" Companies commenced the advance from the AVESNES – MAUBEUGE Road on to their final objective and Bn HQ moved forward and established [illegible] in FME LA JONQUIERE at 1455 hours. At 1530 hours information was received from OC "C" Company that the enemy were holding the HOUSES in E 26 d with M.guns and that one Platoon had suffered heavy casualties | |

Instructions regarding War Diaries and Intelligence Summaries are contained in F. S. Regs., Part II. and the Staff Manual respectively. Title pages will be prepared in manuscript.

# WAR DIARY
*or*
# INTELLIGENCE SUMMARY.
*(Erase heading not required.)*

Army Form C. 2118.

| Place | Date | Hour | Summary of Events and Information | Remarks and references to Appendices |
|---|---|---|---|---|
| On the Line | 8/11/18 | | and required support. At 1525 hours one Platoon 6th R.S.F. moved forward to assist the left flank of C Company and O.C. C Company was informed that a further Platoon would be sent if necessary. At 1545 hours O.C. C Company replied that the Platoon of the 6th R.S.F. were in line with his company and were pushing forward, but that he was not in touch with B Company on his Right. No information had been received from either A or B Companies since 1400 hours and orderlies who had been sent forward with messages returned at 1535 hours having failed to locate either company. At 1855 hours information was received from A and B Companies that they were held up by M.G. fire during the afternoon (Locality and Estaires) and as the troops on the Right and left flank were not in line they were unable to push forward to final objective. The situation at 1930 hours was as follows:- A, B and C Companies holding line approx. K.8.b.5.6 – K.2 central – E.26.c.4.3 no touch | |

(A9475) Wt W2358/P360 600,000 12/17 D. D. & L. Sch. 52a. Forms/C2118/15

Instructions regarding War Diaries and Intelligence Summaries are contained in F. S. Regs., Part II. and the Staff Manual respectively. Title pages will be prepared in manuscript.

# WAR DIARY
*or*
# INTELLIGENCE SUMMARY.
*(Erase heading not required.)*

Army Form C. 2118.

| Place | Date | Hour | Summary of Events and Information | Remarks and references to Appendices |
|---|---|---|---|---|
| On the [illegible] | 8/11/18 | | with troops on Right and Left. 2nd Line of Defence held by V.M.G. and Lewis Guns AVESNES – MAUBEUGE Road K.7.c.1.9 – E.25.c.8.2. R.D.F. had been withdrawn into Reserve Dispositions as follows: 3 Companies in line approx K.1.c.8 to K.1.a.2.9. One Company at K.1.b.3.8. One Section T.M. and one Section V.M.G. in Reserve in FME de JONQUIERE with Bn. H.Q. At 2130 hours touch was gained with [illegible] on our left. | |
| | | | Casualties – Killed 2/Lt E H WILSON and 5. O.R. | |
| | | | Wounded ——— 31. O.R. | [illegible] |
| " " | 9/11/18 | | Weather fine with bright sunshine all day. At 0315 hours information was received from Brigade (G.71) that Division on the left had advanced to E.11 and E.17 without opposition and were anxious about their Right flank and the platoon of "C" Company under 2/Lt L.G. GIBSON were ordered to move forward along the SARS POTERIES Road, [illegible] of the enemy | |

(A9475) Wt W2358/P36c 600,000 12/17 D. D. & L. Sch. 52a. Forms/C.2118/15.

Instructions regarding War Diaries and Intelligence Summaries are contained in F. S. Regs., Part II. and the Staff Manual respectively. Title pages will be prepared in manuscript.

# WAR DIARY
*or*
# INTELLIGENCE SUMMARY.
*(Erase heading not required.)*

Army Form C. 2118.

| Place | Date | Hour | Summary of Events and Information | Remarks and references to Appendices |
|---|---|---|---|---|
| | 9/11/18 | | had withdrawn from our front and to establish a strong Point at E edge of BOIS des BEUGNIES at the same time A and B Companies were ordered to send out strong patrols to the line of the Road K.9.a.2.6 – E 26.d.6.7 and if it was found that the enemy were not holding this Road, our patrols were to remain on the line of the Road for the remainder of the night. At 0700 hours "C" Company had established a strong point at E 28.a.6.4 and were in touch with the Scottish Horse at E 22.c.2.4. "D" Company moved forward from Bn Reserve in FME de JONQUIERE at 0700 hours with the object of establishing position on Road K 4.c – E 27.b. "A" Company were ordered to assemble at HOUSE K.3.c.2.2 and "B" Company were ordered to assemble at HOUSE K.2.b.9.2. Both moves to take place immediately. "D" Company had crossed Road K.9.d – E 26.d. Advanced Bn H.Q. moved forward to K 3.a.1.3 at 0700 hours and at 0800 hours | |

(A9475) Wt W2358/P360 600,000 12/17 D. D. & L. Sch. 52a. Forms/C2118/15.

Instructions regarding War Diaries and Intelligence Summaries are contained in F. S. Regs., Part II, and the Staff Manual respectively. Title pages will be prepared in manuscript.

# WAR DIARY
or
# INTELLIGENCE SUMMARY.
(*Erase heading not required.*)

Army Form C. 2118.

| Place | Date | Hour | Summary of Events and Information | Remarks and references to Appendices |
|---|---|---|---|---|
| | | | a message was received from Advanced H.Q. reporting that 'D' Company crossed the Road K.9.a – E.26.d at 0745 hours without opposition. At 0900 hours Advanced H.Q. reported that 'D' Company had reached final objective at 0825 hours without opposition. Bn H.Q. moved forward to FARM in K 2.b.9.4 at 0945 hours and on arrival a Conference of Coy Comdrs of 'A' 'B' and 'C' Companies was held. After discussing the situation 'A' Coy was ordered to remain in Reserve in FARM in K.3.c.0.2. and 'C' Coy in Reserve in FARM E.26.d.5.3. Bn H.Q. moved forward and established in FARM E.27.d.7.2. at 1135 hours and 'B' Company moved up in support to 'D' Company and occupied buildings at E.28.c.3.3 at 1215 hours a report was received from D.C. XII Lancers patrol that FELLERIES was clear of the enemy and that enemy were holding with M.Guns the buildings in F.26.d central. Enemy were retiring across Country towards WOOD | |

(A9475) Wt W2358/P360 600,000 12/17 D. D. & L. Sch. 52a. Forms/C2118/15.

Instructions regarding War Diaries and Intelligence Summaries are contained in F. S. Regs., Part II, and the Staff Manual respectively. Title pages will be prepared in manuscript.

# WAR DIARY
*or*
# INTELLIGENCE SUMMARY.
*(Erase heading not required.)*

Army Form C. 2118.

| Place | Date | Hour | Summary of Events and Information | Remarks and references to Appendices |
|---|---|---|---|---|
| | 9/11/18 | | E 27 and F 28. Railway bridge at L 1 d 9 7 blown up and blocking road. At 1300 hours the situation was as follows:– 'D' Company holding line approx K 10 C 8 0 – K 5 C 5 8 – E 29 C 0 5 in touch with Scottish Horse at E 29 a 3 7. 'B' Company in Support in building E 28 C 2 2. Bn HQ in FARM E 27 d 7 2. 'A' Company in Reserve in FARM K 3 C 0 2. 'C' Company in FARM E 26 d 5 3. At 1430 hours the Comdg Officer accompanied by the Bn L G Officer and an Officer of the 100 M.G. Coy went round the whole line and organised the defence. At 1730 hours D Company and 100 M.G. Coy were ordered to withdraw all posts and assembly in BARRIER K 4 b 3 6 and E 28 C 2 2 respectively where they would stay the night it being unnecessary to hold the line as there was a Flying Column billeted in BEUGNIES. Casualties Nil. | [initials] |

(A9175) Wt W2358/P360 600,000 12/17 D. D. & L. Sch. 52a. Forms/C 2118/15.

# WAR DIARY
*or*
# INTELLIGENCE SUMMARY.
*(Erase heading not required.)*

Army Form C. 2118.

Instructions regarding War Diaries and Intelligence Summaries are contained in F. S. Regs., Part II. and the Staff Manual respectively. Title pages will be prepared in manuscript.

| Place | Date | Hour | Summary of Events and Information | Remarks and references to Appendices |
|---|---|---|---|---|
| On the March | 10/11/18 | | Weather fine with bright sunshine all day. At 0100 hours Bde Order No 137 was received and at 0130 hours Bn Order No 27 was issued to all concerned (for details see APPENDIX VI attached). The Battalion moved to ST HILAIRE SUR-HELPE and arrived in billets at 1100 hours. Conference for [illegible] Cards was held in Bn HQ Mess at 1730 hours. Subject: Interior Economy and Work for tomorrow. | |
| ST HILAIRE SUR-HELPE | 11/11/18 | | Weather fine and bright sunshine. The Battalion carried out work on the Roads, each Company working for two hours. The remainder of the day was devoted to Bathing and generally cleaning up. The Brigadier [illegible] at 1200 hours. 13th Corps wire received at 1900 hrs see APPENDIX VII. | |
| On the March | 12/11/18 | | Weather fine, cold N wind. Bn Order No 28* was issued to all concerned at 0600 hours and the Battalion moved to BEUGNIES at 0915 hours and arrived at 1145 hours. 2nd Lt A GRAVES joined the Battalion for duty and was | * see appendix VIII |

Instructions regarding War Diaries and Intelligence Summaries are contained in F. S. Regs., Part II, and the Staff Manual respectively. Title pages will be prepared in manuscript.

# WAR DIARY
*or*
# INTELLIGENCE SUMMARY.
*(Erase heading not required.)*

Army Form C. 2118.

| Place | Date | Hour | Summary of Events and Information | Remarks and references to Appendices |
|---|---|---|---|---|
| BEUGNIES | 12/11/18 | | posted to "B" Company. Draft of 58 O.R. arrived from ENGLAND and were posted to companies as follows:- A Coy 19. B Coy 13. C Coy 13. D Coy 13. | [illegible] |
| — " — | 13/11/18 | | Weather cold during the morning, sunshine most of the day. Companies carried out work on the Roads and devoted [illegible] time to Billeting generally cleaning up. The Comdg Officer inspected the Draft of 58 OR (who arrived [illegible] day) at 1000 hours and afterwards inspected the Company billets. Copy of XIII Corps wire G X 105 12 was received at 0800 hours. For details see APPENDIX IX attached. | [illegible] |
| — " — | 14/11/18 | | Weather fine but cold. The Battalion were employed in unloading trains at FELLERIES and cleaning Roads in BEUGNIES. A Guard of Honour composed as follows paraded at Bn HQ at 1030 hours and proceeded by march route to SOLRE LE CHATEAU where they were inspected by the ~~Army~~ XIII Corps Commander. | |

(A9475) Wt W2358/P360 600,000 12/17 D. D. & L. Sch. 52a. Forms/C2118/15.

Army Form C. 2118.

# WAR DIARY
*or*
# INTELLIGENCE SUMMARY.
*(Erase heading not required.)*

Instructions regarding War Diaries and Intelligence Summaries are contained in F. S. Regs., Part II. and the Staff Manual respectively. Title pages will be prepared in manuscript.

| Place | Date | Hour | Summary of Events and Information | Remarks and references to Appendices |
|---|---|---|---|---|
| BEUGNIES | 14/11/18 | | Composition of the Guard of Honour:- | |
| | | | Major L.B.L. SECKHAM M.C. | |
| | | | Capt C.H. POTTER M.C. | |
| | | | " D. PENNINGTON M.C. | |
| | | | R.S.M. J. ECCLES | |
| | | | C.S.M. R. BATEMAN | |
| | | | C.S.M. A. STOUT | |
| | | | Sergt E. CLUELOW and 42 O.R. | |
| | | | After the inspection the Corps Commander presented Ribbons to the following men:- | |
| | | | 25869 Pte E. GWILLIM M.M. | |
| | | | 6051 " C. CREIGHTON M.M. | |
| | | | Lt Col R.F. GROSS D.S.O. was in command of the Guards of Honour of the 198 Infy Bde. The Battalion moved into billets at SARS-POTERIES at 14.30 hours. Conference of Coy | |
| | | | Commanders was held in Bn HQ Mess at [illegible] hours. | |

(A9475) Wt W2358/P560 600,000 12/17 D. D. & L. Sch. 52a. Forms C/2118/15.

Instructions regarding War Diaries and Intelligence Summaries are contained in F. S. Regs., Part II, and the Staff Manual respectively. Title pages will be prepared in manuscript.

# WAR DIARY
or
# INTELLIGENCE SUMMARY.
(*Erase heading not required.*)

Army Form C. 2118.

| Place | Date | Hour | Summary of Events and Information | Remarks and references to Appendices |
|---|---|---|---|---|
| En SARS-POTERIES | 15/11/18 | | Weather fine, but cold. 'A' and 'B' Companies carried out work on the Roads. 'C' and 'D' Companies devoted the morning to Bathing and cleaning up. The Battalion paraded for inspection by the Brigade Commander at 1115 hours but the inspection was cancelled. Major Turner gave a lecture on Demobilization at 1530 hours and all Officers and N.C.O's attended. Conference for Coy Cmdrs was held in Bn H.Q. Mess at 1730 hours. Subject: Interior economy and the March to the Rhine. Bn. Order No. 29 was issued to all concerned at 2300 hours. For details see APPENDIX X attached. Special Order by Lt Gen Sir T.L.N. MORLAND K.C.B. K.C.M.G. D.S.O. Comdg XIII Corps was issued and read out to all troops on parade. See APPENDIX XI. | |
| [illegible] | 16/11/18 | | Weather fine, but cold. The Battalion moved to L'EPINE DE HARNAUT and arrived at 1300 hours. Continues | |

(A9175) Wt W2358/P360 600,000 12/17 D. D. & L. Sch. 52a. Forms C2118/5

Army Form C. 2118.

Instructions regarding War Diaries and Intelligence Summaries are contained in F. S. Regs., Part I. and the Staff Manual respectively. Title pages will be prepared in manuscript.

# WAR DIARY
or
# INTELLIGENCE SUMMARY.
(*Erase heading not required.*)

| Place | Date | Hour | Summary of Events and Information | Remarks and references to Appendices |
|---|---|---|---|---|
| | | | for Coy Comdrs was held in Bn HQ Mess at 1600 hours. Subject: Interior Economy. | [initials] |
| On the move | 17/11/18 | | Weather fine, but cold. Bn Order No 30 was issued to all concerned at 0530 hours and the Battalion marched to RANCE and arrived in billets at 1415 hours. The Brigadier visited the Battalion at 1630 hours and after complimenting the Battalion on its good work during the fighting 8th October to 11th Nov 1918 lectured the men on their behaviour during the forthcoming march to the Rhine. A Reprint from the Morning Post dated Oct 11th is attached as APPENDIX XIII | See APPENDIX XII<br>[initials] |
| RANCE | 18/11/18 | | Weather cold, light snowfall during the morning. Companies bathing & generally cleaning up. The Battalion attended Divine Service C of E in the RANCE Church at 1530 hours. The Brigade Comdr was in attendance. Bn Order No 31 was issued to all concerned at 2310 hours. | [initials] |

Army Form C. 2118.

Instructions regarding War Diaries and Intelligence Summaries are contained in F. S. Regs., Part II. and the Staff Manual respectively. Title pages will be prepared in manuscript.

# WAR DIARY
*or*
# INTELLIGENCE SUMMARY.
*(Erase heading not required.)*

| Place | Date | Hour | Summary of Events and Information | Remarks and references to Appendices |
|---|---|---|---|---|
| On the move | 19/11/18 | | Weather fine, but cold. The Battalion moved in accordance with Bn Order 31 see APPENDIX XIV attached and arrived in billets at JAMAGNE at 1500 hours | J.F. |
| JAMAGNE | 20/11/18 | | Weather fine, but cold. The Battalion carried out bathing under company arrangements & devoted the day to general cleaning up. | J.F. |
| -"- | 21/11/18 | | Weather fine, cold N wind. One Officer and 20 men per company carried out work on the Roads during the afternoon. Each Company and Bn HQ carried out one hours training. | J.F. |
| -"- | 22/11/18 | | Weather fine, but cold. One officer and 20 men per Company carried out work on the Roads. Each Company carried out one hours training during the morning. Bn Order No 32 was issued to all concerned at 1545 hours. | J.F. |
| MORVILLE | 23/11/18 | | Weather fine, bright sunshine all day. The Battalion moved to ROSÉE in accordance with Bn Order No 32 see APPENDIX XV attached but on arrival were ordered to proceed to MERVILLE where we arrived in billets at 1140 hours | |

(A9475) Wt W2358/P560 600,000 12/17 D. D. & L. Sch. 52a. Forms/C.2118/15.

Army Form C. 2118.

Instructions regarding War Diaries and Intelligence Summaries are contained in F. S. Regs., Part II. and the Staff Manual respectively. Title Pages will be prepared in manuscript.

# WAR DIARY
*or*
# INTELLIGENCE SUMMARY
*(Erase heading not required.)*

| Place | Date | Hour | Summary of Events and Information | Remarks and references to Appendices |
|---|---|---|---|---|
| MORVILLE | 23/11/18 | | at 1500 hours, all the Officers and N.C.O.s of the Battalion and those of the 5th INNISK Fus paraded in the Square near the Church to receive an official welcome from the inhabitants of the village. The speech was translated by Capt A.O. BISSON R.A.M.C. and Lt Col PATTERSON. D.S.O. (5/Innis Fusiliers) replied his reply being translated by Capt A.O. BISSON R.A.M.C. The inhabitants then gave three cheers which were reciprocated by the troops. Bn Order No 33 was issued to all concerned at 0600 hours 24/11/18. | JF |
| On the move | 24/11/18 | | Weather fine, but cold. The Battalion moved in accordance with Bn Order 33 (see APPENDIX XVI) and arrived in billets at NEFFE at 1500 hours. 66th Div Special Order was issued to Companies for circulation among the men. For details see APPENDIX XVII | JF |
| NEFFE | 25/11/18 | | Weather damp & cold. The Companies carried out one hours training during the morning & devoted the remainder of the day to bathing | |

2449 Wt. W14957/M90 750,000 1/16 J.B.C. & A. Forms/C.2118/12.

Instructions regarding War Diaries and Intelligence Summaries are contained in F. S. Regs., Part II. and the Staff Manual respectively. Title pages will be prepared in manuscript.

# WAR DIARY
*or*
# INTELLIGENCE SUMMARY.
(*Erase heading not required.*)

Army Form C. 2118.

| Place | Date | Hour | Summary of Events and Information | Remarks and references to Appendices |
|---|---|---|---|---|
| NEFFE | 25/11/18 | | and generally cleaning up. The Brigade Commander visited Bn. H.Q at 1145 hours. The Comdg Officer inspected the Battalions Billets during the morning. Capt R.A.V. WHITE returned from leave to U.K. | [initials] |
| " | 26/11/18 | | Weather fine, but dull. Companies carried out one hours training during the morning and devoted the remainder of the day to bathing & cleaning up. | [initials] |
| " | 27/11/18 | | Weather changeable with slight rainfall during the morning. Parades were cancelled owing to the weather and companies carried out bathing & generally cleaning up. 2/Lt S.D. STEPHEN rejoined from leave to U.K. | [initials] |
| " | 28/11/18 | | Weather changeable. Companies carried out one hours training during the morning. Following order received from B.de:- | |

D. D. & L., London, E.C. (A5001) Wt. W1771/M2031 750,000 5/17 Sch. 52 Forms/C2118/14

Army Form C. 2118.

Instructions regarding War Diaries and Intelligence Summaries are contained in F. S. Regs., Par. II. and the Staff Manual respectively. Title pages will be prepared in manuscript.

# WAR DIARY
*or*
# INTELLIGENCE SUMMARY.

*(Erase heading not required.)*

| Place | Date | Hour | Summary of Events and Information | Remarks and references to Appendices |
|---|---|---|---|---|
| NEFFE | 28/11/18 | | 66th Division will be transferred from IX Corps to X Corps at 23.59 hours on November 28th 1918. The Brigade Comdr visited Bn H.Q at 1515 hours. | |
| " | 29/11/18 | | Weather fine but dull. Companies carried out the usual hours training and 100 men were employed at DINANT station offloading supplies. The Brigade Comdr visited Bn H.Q at 1205 hours. | |
| " | 30/11/18 | | Weather fine. The Battalion paraded for Route March at 0900 hours and returned to billets at 1200 hours. During the afternoon Companies carried out bathing.<br>The admissions to hospital through sickness during the past month is as follows:- Officers Nil, O. Ranks 87 | |

Lt Colonel
Comdg 6 LAN FUS

D. D. & L., London, E.C. (A8001) Wt. W2771/M2031 750,000 5/17 Sch. 52 Forms/C2.18/14

SECRET. APPENDIX I Copy. No 1

6th Lancashire Fusiliers.

Order No 22. 1st Nov. 1918

1. The Battalion will proceed by march route to HONNECHY on the 2nd November 1918 as follows :-

Hour of Start: 09.00 hours.

Starting Point: "A" Coy H.Q. Mess.

Order of march: D. A. Drums. Bn H.Q. B. C. Transport.

Route. x Roads 29.b.4.8. - x Roads V27.b.70.9. - BUSIGNY.

Distances: 500x between Battalions, 100x between Coys.

2. Dress: Battle order. Jerkins will be carried in the Pack.

3. Lieut. P. Tyson, Sergt. Woodward and each C.Q.M.S. will leave Bn H.Q at 0800 hours, and proceed by cycle to HONNECHY to arrange billets.

4. (a) Blankets + Greatcoats rolled in bundles of ten each and clearly labelled by Platoons will be stacked at the Q.M Stores by 0700 hours.

(b) Officers kits + mess stores will be stacked at the Q.M. Stores by 08.15 hours.

Issued at: 19.15 hours.

Copies to: 1 War Diary.
2 File.
3 H.Q.
4 A. Coy
5 B.
6 C.
7 D.
8 T.O.
9 QM.

J Franks
Capt & Adjt
6 L.F.

SECRET. Copy No 1

8 Lancashire Fusiliers

Order No 23. 2nd Nov. 1918.

APPENDIX II

1. The Battalion will proceed by march route to LE CATEAU on the 3rd November 1918 as follows:-

Hour of Start: 15~~30~~ 15 hours.

Starting Point: ~~Cross roads~~ ~~P.29.a.4.8~~ "B" Coy: Billets

Order of March: A. Bn HQ. Drums. B.C.D.

Route: Station (P.29.d.) Q.4.

Distances: 500x between Battalions 100x between Coys

2. Dress: Battle order. Jerkins will be carried in the pack.

3. (a) 2/Lt C.W. Jones, Sgt Woodward Cpl Hoyle, and each C.Q.M.S. will leave Bn H.Qs at 0800 hrs and proceed by cycle to LE CATEAU to arrange billets. 2/Lt C.W. Jones will arrange for guides to meet Battn and Transport at the cross roads

~~4.~~ Q4.b.5.0.

(b) One guide from each platoon will report to Battn H.Q. at 0900 hours and proceed under Sgt Mead by march route to LE CATEAU and will report to 2/Lt C.W. Jones. On the arrival of the Battn these men will guide their platoons into their respective billets.

Order No. 23. Sheet 2.

4 (a) Blankets and greatcoats rolled in bundles of 10 each, clearly labelled by platoons will be stacked at the QM Stores by 0800 hours.

(b) Officers Kits & Mess Stores will be stacked at the QM Stores by 1400 hours.

5. Transport will be Brigaded and will march under the orders of Brigade Transport Officer
Hour of Start: 1635 hours.
Starting Point: P29. a. 4. 8.

J. Franks
Capt & Adjt
6 Lancs Fusiliers.

Issued at 21.45 hours
Copies to. 1 War Diary
2 File
3 HQ.
4 A. Coy
5 B
6 C
7 D
8 T.O
9 QM.

SECRET

APPENDIX III Copy No 1

6th Lancs Fusiliers III 7-11-18.
Order No 24.

1. The Battalion will proceed by march route to POMMEREUIL to-day as follows:-
Hour of Start: 1100 hours
Starting Point: Bn H.Q.
Order of march. Bn H.Q - B - C - D - A.
Route. Q5. b. 60. 95 - L. 31.
Distances. 500^x between Battalions, 100^x between Coys.

2 Dress: Battle Orders. Jerkins will be carried in the pack. Blankets will be carried rolled horseshoe fashion round the pack.

3. 2/Lt C.W. Jones, Sgt Woodward, L/Cpl Hoyle and each C.Q.M.S will leave Bn H.Q at 08-30 hours and proceed by cycle to POMMEREUIL to arrange billets.

4 (a) Greatcoats rolled in bundles of 10 clearly labelled by platoons will be stacked at the Q.M. Stores by 0830 hours.
(b) Officers Kits & Mess Stores will be stacked at the Q.M. Stores by 09.30 hours

5 All surplus kit will be dumped near Brigade H.Q. Dumping may commence at 0800 hours.

6 "B" Teams will remain in LE CATEAU. They will retain their greatcoats.

7 Transport will be brigaded and will march under the orders of Brigade Transport Officer.
Hour of start: 11.50 hours
Starting Point: X roads K35. c. 0.6.

Issued at: 0700 hours
Copies to
1 War Diary
2 File
3 H.Q.
4 A
5 B
6 C
7 D
8 T.O
9 QM

[signature]
Capt & Adjt
6th Lancs Fusiliers

Secret | 6 Lancs Fusiliers | Copy No 1

Ref. 1/40.000 | Order No 25 | 5/11/18

APPENDIX IV

1. The Battalion will proceed by march route to the Valley in G. 9. a and b to-day as follows:-
Hour of Start. 0800 hours
Starting Point. Road junction L. 27. c. 2. 5
Route x roads L. 20. b. 2. 0 - fork road L. 16. b - x roads L. 11. c. - road junction G. 7. b. - G. 8. d. 7. 5.
Distances 500x between Battns 100x between Coys

2. Dress Battle Order, jerkins to be carried in the pack.

3. Lewis Gun limbers will march in rear of their Coys. Remaining transport except G. S wagons will march in rear of the Battalion.
G. S. wagons & Q. M. Stores will remain in POMMEREUIL

4 Blankets rolled in bundles of 10, clearly labelled by platoons, & securely tied, officers kits & stores, will be stacked at the Q. M. Stores by 0700 hours.

5. The Q. M. will arrange for the blankets & officers kits to be dumped at the present Brigade H.Q. Dumping will commence at 08.30 hours.

6. Breakfast will be served to the men at 0600 hours mid day meals will be prepared on the line of march.

Issued at 03.45 hours
Copies to War Diary
File
A
B
C
D
HQ
TO
QM

J Franks
Capt & Adjt
6 Lancs Fus

LANCASHIRE FUSILIERS
ORDER NO 26

APPENDIX V

REF: Sheet 57A 1/40000

1 Enemy are believed to be still holding with M Guns the East bank of Stream (D. 30. c. to J. 10. d.) The position of our own troops is as shewn on the Map.

2 The 66th Division in cooperation with the troops on the Right and Left will continue to drive the enemy in an Easterly direction today. 199 Bde on the Right 198 Bde on the Left.

3 Brigade boundaries are as shewn on the Map

4 The Brigade advance will be carried out in two phases
1st Phase The 5th INNISK FUS supported by the 6th LANFUS

will make good that par.
of the AVESNES-MAUBERG
Road as shewn on the map
2nd Phase The 6th LAN FUS
supported by the 6th DUBLIN
FUSILIERS will make good
the line as shewn on the map
5 The Battalion will be disposed
as follows during the first
and second phases:-
(a)
1st Phase: 'A' Company will
advance in close support of
the Right Company of the 5th
INNISK
'C' Company will advance in
close support of the Left Coy
5th INNISK
The role of these two companies
is
1 To protect the flanks and
to support the attack in the
event of it being held up

These two companies will be assembled and ready to advance by 0730 hours.
"A" Company Northern end of WOOD J.3.d.9.0.
"C" Company Road Junction J.4.b.2.6.
"B" Company and "D" Company will form Battalion Reserve and will be assembled at Bn. H.Q. by 0730 hours.
(b) 2nd Phase. The Battalion will advance on a three company front to the final objective as follows:-
"A" Company on the Right moving with its Right on the Southern Brigade Boundary
"B" Company in the Centre advancing on the HOUSE K.4.b.2.5.

'C' Company on the left advancing on CHATEAUX COPREAUX.
On reaching the final objective Patrols will be sent out as follows:-
'A' Company to the Eastern edge of the BOIS de LA VILLETTE
'B' Company to SPUR at N.E. corner of the same WOOD E 29. d.
'C' Company to X Roads at E 29. b. 5. 9.

6 The final objective when captured will be organized in a series of strong points

7 As soon as the final objective has been gained Cavalry Patrols will reconnoitre FELLERIES and BEUGNIES

8 One section A/331 F A Bde will be attached to the Battalion

9 Success signals will be fired as follows:–

(a) 5 INNISK FUS will fire two RED Very lights in quick succession after the capture of the final objective

(b) D LANI FUS will fire three RED Very lights after capture of final objective

10 Troops in the front line will be on the look out for contact planes and ensure that their signals are responded to.

1 Battalion Report and A R C will be as follows:-

| Report Centre | A Report Centre |
|---|---|
| FARM (J 3. C. 8. 3.) | LA CROISETTE FME J 5. C. 2. 0. |
| LA CROISETTE FME | Road Junction J. 6. C. 4. 2 |
| Road Junction J. 6. C. 4. 2. | FME LA JONQUIERE |
| FME LA JONQUIERE | HOUSES K. 2. & 9. 2 |
| HOUSES K. 2 & 9. 2 | FME KOPREAUX |
| FME KOPREAUX | |

12 Zero hour will be 0730 hours

[illegible]
Capt & Adj
6 L.F.

8th November 1918

SECRET APPENDIX VI order 27

All Companies

6th Lancashire Fusiliers.

Nov. 10th 1918

1. The 18th King's Liverpool Regiment will take over the present area at 08.00 hours 10th November 1918.

2. The Battalion will proceed to ST. HILAIRE-SUR-HELPE as follows –

Hour of Start 0815 hours.
Starting Point X Roads E26.d.7.6.
Order of March Bn. H.Q. B. D. C. A.
Route X Roads E26.d.1.9 – K1.b.5.1. Track to J.6.a.3.6. – LA TUILLERIE
Distances 100x between companies

3 Lt P. Tyson and C.Q.M.S. of B.C.D will leave road junction E26.d.7.6 at 0800hs and proceed by cycle to ST. HILAIRE-SUR-HELPE to arrange billets for the Battalion

4 Transport will march in rear of the Battalion

5. Breakfast will be served to the men at 06.30hrs. Midday meal will be prepared on the march.

6 Acknowledge

Issued at 0130hrs.

Copies to File
War Diary
H.Q.
A
B
C
D
{T.O.
{Q.M.

(Sd.) F. Franks
Capt. & Adjt
6th Lancashire Fusiliers

APPENDIX VIII

Following wire received :-

66th Division "G"
Hostilities will cease at 11.0 hours to-day Nov.11. aaa
Troops will stand fast on line reached at that hour
which will be reported by wire to advanced Army H.Q. aaa
Defensive precautions will be maintained aaa There will
be no intercourse of any description with the enemy
until receipt of instructions from Army H.Q. aaa
Further instructions follows

13th Corps.
07.00

Captain,
Brigade Major,
199th Infantry Brigade.

11.11.18.
RV.

SECRET. APPENDIX VIII Copy. No

12.11.18

6th Lancs Fus. ORDER No. 28

1. The Battalion will move to BEUGNIES to-day as follows:-

Hour of Start. 0915 hours
Starting Point. Bn H.Q
Order of March. Bn HQ, C. D. A. B.
Route: via J. 17. b. 2. 2. – BAS LIEU
E26. d. 9. 7
Distances. 100x between Companies.

2. Transport will march in rear of the Battalion under the Transport officer.

2

3 Dress. Battle order. jerkins will be carried in the pack.

4. Blankets rolled in bundles of ten clearly labelled by platoons. Officers Kits, mess boxes & stores will be stacked outside QM Stores by 0800 hours.

5 Acknowledge

Immediate 0600 hours.
Copies to 1 War Diary
2 File
3 A
4 B
5 C
6 D
7 T.O
8 HQ
9 QM.

[signature] Franks
Major Cmdg.
6 Lanc Fusiliers

APPENDIX IX All Companies

A
B
C
D

To :- 198 Brigade. 13/11/18.
GX 105. 12. -
Following wire received from Corps aaa Begins aaa There is to be no unauthorised intercourse or fraternising of any description with the enemy aaa He will NOT be permitted to approach our lines and attempt to do so, will be immediately stopped if necessary by fire aaa Any parties of the enemy coming over to our line under white flag will be made prisoners and report sent Divisional H.Q. aaa Enemy aircraft will NOT be permitted to cross the line aaa Should any attempt to do so they will be attacked by fire from ground and air aaa No civilians will be permitted to cross our line in either direction aaa Ends.

4th Army Adv. Guard. 18.15.

---

6th Lancs. Fus. -
5th R. Innis. Fus.
6th R. Dublin Fus.
198th L.T.M.B.

198th Inf. Bde.
No. G. 95/8.

---

Forwarded for information and necessary action.

Captain,
Brigade Major,
198th Infantry Brigade.

12.11.18.
RHW*

ORDERLY ROOM
6th BATT. LANCS. FUSILIERS
Date 13/11/18

Ref. 1/100,000 NAMUR APPENDIX X copy

6 Lan. Fusiliers
Order No 29

1 The Battalion will move to L'EPINE HERNAUT on the 16.11.18 as follows:-

Hour of Start. 0915 hours
Starting Point. A. Coy H.Q. Mess.
Order of march. Bn H.Q., A, B, Drums, C. D. Transport
Route. X Roads L'EPINE HERNAUT, LES FONTAINES
Distances. 100x between Companies

2 Dress. Battle order. Jerkins in the pack. Blankets will be carried rolled horseshoe fashion round the pack.

3 Officers Kits + Mess Stores will be stacked at the Q.M. Stores by 0815 hours

4 Lt. ? Tyson Sgt Woodward, Cpl Hoyle and each C.Q.M.S. will be at Bn H.Q. at 0800 hours + proceed by cycle to L'EPINE HERNAUT to arrange billets for the Battalion.

5 Acknowledge

Issued at ~~1100~~ 2300 hours

Captain Adjt
6 Lan. Fusiliers

Copies to
1 War Diary
2 File
3 HQ Coy
4 A
5 B
6 C
7 D
8 T.O
9 QM

S P E C I A L   O R D E R S

APPENDIX XI

by

Lieut. - General Sir T.L.N. MORLAND, K.C.B., K.C.M.G., D.S.O.

COMMANDING XIII CORPS.



12 copies

---

On the conclusion of hostilities and in the hour of decisive victory, I wish to express to General Officers Commanding, their Staffs and to Regimental Officers and men of all arms and departments my hearty congratulations on the results of their splendid efforts.

During the period 3rd October to 11th November, troops of XIII Corps have fought a series of successful actions, have advanced a distance of 50 miles meeting and defeating 16 actual enemy divisions. During this period they have captured 8,300 prisoners (of 26 Divisions) 260 guns and enormous quantities of stores of all sorts. These results are due to the fine leading of subordinate commanders, the gallantry and devotion of all ranks, and the close co-operation between the various arms - Cavalry, Infantry, Field and Heavy Artillery, Royal Engineers, Royal Air Force and Tank Corps - in the actual fighting, and also to the indefatigible efforts of the auxiliary services under great difficulties.

I wish to express to each individual officer, N.C.O. and man my thanks for the part he has taken in the final victory.

H.Q., XIII Corps,
[illegible]th November, '18.

-2-

66th Division on their leaving XIII Corps.

---

I wish to express to the G.O.C. and all ranks of the 66th Division my appreciation of their gallant and distinguished service during the recent operations, which have resulted in complete victory.

To each individual of the British, Irish and South African Troops comprising the Division, I express my hearty thanks for his splendid efforts.

H.Q., XIII Corps,
[illegible]th November, '18.

SECRET.
Ref. 1/100,000 NAMUR

APPENDIX XII begs N

6th Lan. Fusiliers
Order No 30.

17.11.18

The Battalion will proceed by march route to RANCE to-day as follows:–

1 Hour of Start. 1000 hours.
Starting point. Bn HQ. C + D Coys will join the column at the X roads 100x S of the first N in L'EPINE HERNAUT.
Order of march. Bn HQ – A – B – Drums – C – D – Transport.
Route. Road junction 200x N of first E in SOLRE-LE-CHATEAU – BEAURIEUX – SIVRY
Distance. 100x between Coys

2 Dress. ~~Battle~~ Marching order, jerkins & blankets in the pack. Steel helmets worn

3 Greatcoats rolled in bundles of 10 clearly labelled by platoons, Officers kits & mess Stores, will be stacked at the Q.M. Stores by 0845 hours

4 [illegible] Jones, Sgt Woodward, Cpl Hoyle, & each C.Q.M.S. will leave Bn HQ at 0900 hours & proceed by cycle to RANCE to arrange billets for the Battalion

5 Loading party. OC 'A' Coy will detail 1 Sergt & 10 men to remain behind at QM Stores to load the greatcoats on to the G.S. wagons, and to march with them to RANCE

6 Acknowledge.

J Franks
Capt & Adj
6 Lan Fus.

Issued at 0530 hours

Copies to: War Diary
– 2 file
3 A
4 B
5 C
6 D
7 HQ
TO
QM
S
Spare

APPENDIX XIII

REPRINTED FROM "THE MORNING POST" OF FRIDAY, OCTOBER 11th, 1918.

# THE FIGHT FOR LE CATEAU.

## *FAMOUS BATTLEFIELD.*

## RESISTANCE SWIFTLY OVERCOME.

## *A RAPID ADVANCE.*

BRITISH FRONT, Oct. 10.

Le Cateau, a name which, with that of Mons, will be historic in British military annals, has now come into the battle front. Two British divisions, the Sixty-sixth and Twenty-fifth, were close to the western edge of the town this afternoon ready for the counter-attack which would indicate a fresh attempt on the part of the Hun to stay his retreating Second Army while fresh defences are being prepared. It is a gratifying fact—one which the tired but eager infantry can hardly yet grasp—that they are actually within rifle shot of Le Cateau and close to the graves of those British soldiers who fell in the fighting of four years ago.

They have made a wonderful journey from the now deserted trenches of the Hindenburg Line and the battlefield by the canal. Village after village has passed into their hands. They are now living in a land where civilians still occupy their homes, and the houses have unbroken windows, and little children play about the streets. It is hardly to be wondered at that a great wave of enthusiasm has passed over the fighting armies. The men, though footsore and dazed from want of sleep, are anxious to press on. I do not think that a single Fusilier or Connaught Ranger hugging the damp earth within view of Le Cateau would willingly yield his place if he thought he would miss its capture.

The approach to Le Cateau is the most interesting development of the advance. Cambrai, partially ruined and still devastated by fire, seems already to have slipped into the background. The front has swung forward so rapidly that only high velocity shells are being thrown into the littered streets, for the German light batteries are well beyond range. Caudry, a factory town half the size of Cambrai, lying midway on the road to Le Cateau, has taken its place in the battle picture.

### SWIFT ADVANCE ON LE CATEAU.

Our advance on Le Cateau has been swift, and until its environs were reached the only resistance encountered was that of a dispirited rearguard. I heard a partial account of the journey in the area of the Sixty-sixth Division to-day. The General was very proud of his men and of their rapid progress. They took Serain on Tuesday morning, when the American Thirtieth Division was attacking Prémont, and rescued the villagers from their cellars, where they had lived for more than a week. Our troops swept over the hills with such force that the Germans, representing five different divisions, simply fled through the town. They abandoned their field gunners and a battery of heavy howitzers which had not dreamed of suddenly finding itself in No Man's Land. I saw some of these derelict guns to-day with the bodies of their gunners lying about them and dead horses strewn over the field just as they fell when gun teams were galloped up in a vain effort to effect a rescue.

The loss of three 8-inch howitzers was too serious to be accepted without a protest, so the disheartened Germans were assembled on the far side of Serain and forced to counter-attack. Before their machine-gun fire the Connaught Rangers fell back to the outskirts of the village. The occupants of the cellars could hear the Germans shouting and running overhead, and dragging up their machine-guns as the officers cursed volubly and urged greater speed. They were in Serain for only a few minutes. The Rangers came on again, and drove the Germans back in disorder, taking a number of prisoners. Then the village was held, while other British troops and Americans were still fighting in the villages on either side.

Elincourt, a mile to the north, remained in the enemy's hands all day, and our line swung around Serain in an erratic way. Elincourt was abandoned by the Germans shortly after midnight. Early yesterday morning the 66th Division resumed its attack. The Connaught Rangers, Dublins, and Inniskillens, with Manchesters, Lancashires, and three battalions of Fusiliers on their flanks, carried the line beyond Maretz. Then other troops went through them and took Maurois and Bertry, an advance during the day of between five and six miles. They captured nearly one hundred and fifty prisoners of the Eighth Division, and a battalion commander of the 72nd Regiment. The latter was astounded by the fresh British attack. He said that Germany had offered advantageous peace terms, and that he had heard that "peace was to be signed at six o'clock that night." All the prisoners had been assured that the Allies would agree to an armistice, since German's offer comprised everything they demanded, and some of them considered the war as good as over.

### THE FINAL DEFENCE.

To-day the troops of the 66th Division had reached the environs of Le Cateau. The cavalry, which pushed forward yesterday nearly to the town met strong machine-gun fire, and did not attempt to enter it. On the right the 25th Division advanced south of the Roman Road without much opposition until near St. Benin, which the Germans held with the usual machine-gun force. They fired from the railway station and along the railway embankment, and showed considerable vigour. The 66th, advancing astride the Roman Road, reached the outlying buildings of Le Cateau on the Cambrai highway. The troops on their left met with similar resistance. The German Second Army appeared to be standing on the line Solesmes-Amerval and along the high ground immediately east of Le Cateau and the railway south of the town. The artillery fire was heavier, and it is evident that the rearguard intends doing what it can to hold us up in front of the town. But the fighting now in progress may result in its capture before the day is over. When I came back from the front we had not attempted to enter the town.

Between Le Cateau and Cambrai the Canadians continued their advance east of the Scheldt Canal and occupied Naves, while the 11th Division, on their left, cleared Paillencourt, on the Sensée. The Canadians think that their surprise attack at half-past one yesterday morning completely disarranged the enemy plans. The Germans had not intended falling back at least for some hours, but the result of the night advance was their prompt retirement, leaving nearly four hundred prisoners in Canadian hands.

### STOICAL PEASANTRY.

Much could be written about the scenes in the region where our troops are now fighting. I passed to-day through Beaurevoir, Serain, and many other villages which still retain their evidences of German occupation. The civilians contribute a strange note to the picture. It was something of a shock, after driving through miles of deserted, devastated country, suddenly to come upon trim red cottages and see women quietly washing clothes and children playing with a dog. Nearly fifty inhabitants of Serain—old men, women, and children—remained in their homes to greet the British, and to-day they were going about their usual occupations as though they had not been through a battle and seen men killed in their kitchen gardens. There are several hundred people still in Selvigny, and they have no desire to leave, although they hear the thunder of great guns which are still quite near, and the farms around them are dotted with dead and the wreckage of battle. The parish priest tells some moving stories of the sufferings of his flock under German rule.

### A HEROIC PADRE.

The priest is a true hero, for he braved death to save his church from destruction. Several days before the Germans began retiring he watched soldiers bringing up bombs and laying them around the church, while other men filled the belfry and interior with explosives. Wires were connected, and the soldiers told him that the church would be blown up. Not knowing the British were so near, but hoping that the Germans were really in retreat, the old priest got up in the middle of the night and cut the wires. Many brutal acts were committed by order of the German army commanders, but the foulest was the deliberate destruction of all the lace-making and embroidery machinery by which the people of the region make a living. Nearly every cottage had its machine, a delicate and costly affair valued often at fifty thousands francs. All the machines in Selvigny were smashed, and I am told that the neighbouring villages as well as the larger towns, including Bohain, Busigny, and Caudry, whose populations subsisted almost entirely on this industry, were similarly paralysed by the Hun.

APPENDIX XVII

# SPECIAL ORDER.

66th Division, I take this opportunity, on the eve of our march to the Rhine, to thank every one of you, Officer, N.C.O. and man, for your hard work during the past months, and for the cheerful, determined spirit in which you have tackled and dealt with any and all situations.

It is entirely owing to this spirit, combined with hard work, that the Division has been uniformly successful, whether in exterminating the malaria and fitting itself for battle, or in exterminating the enemy in battle itself.

It is this spirit to which the word "impossible" is unknown, that has enabled the Division to make a name for itself in the British Army in so short a time. Above all, it is this spirit which will stand you in most stead throughout your lives, however employed.

Fortunate in great opportunities and weather, the Division has exploited both to the full. To it fell the honour of retaking Le Cateau. Forming part of the Fourth Army Advanced Guard, it was the last Division of this Army to be in action with the enemy. At 11.00, 11th November, 1918, on the termination of hostilities, it was holding the Fourth Army front, and in close touch with the enemy. It is now about to advance to the Rhine on the right of the British Army.

South Africans, Irishmen and Englishmen, you have proved yourselves all to be magnificent infantry.

Engineers and Pioneers, you have shown yourselves to be of the same metal as your infantry.

Artillery, you have been away from us for a long time, but you returned with excellent reports from the Corps and Division with whom you had been serving and where you had well upheld the name of the Division.

Signal Service, you have steadily improved throughout the year, and your work in the late fighting was splendid. The task of keeping communication during the latter stages was one of extraordinary difficulty and could only have been coped with as successfully as it was by indefatigable efforts on the parts of all ranks of your Company.

Train and M.T., with you as with the infantry, there has been no "impossible." Your untiring efforts have contributed in no small way to success, and have been greatly appreciated by the troops.

Medical Services, in and out of battle, your work has been consistently excellent. The very low sick wastage in the Division is largely the result of your continuous efforts.

Machine Gun Battalion, though not long with the Division, your work up to date, in or out of action, confirms the very good report with which you came to us.

Commanders and Staffs, you have had a most difficult and anxious time. The cheerful wholehearted way in which you tackled every new combination, whether of training Cadres and American Divisions, or later of Battalions, making a success of all, foretold the results you have now obtained.

The Division has now been selected as one of those Divisions to carry out the march to the Rhine preparatory to the occupation of German territory in accordance with the terms of the Armistice.

Remember that we are on the right of the British line and about to pass through country where British troops have never been seen. French troops are on our right, the 1st Division is on our left. By our appearance and conduct the Imperial Army will be judged for years to come.

I expect every one of you in the same cheeful determined spirit, by the excellence of your discipline and turnout, and by your soldierly behaviour, to maintain the name of the 66th Division as high in peace as you have set it in war.

**H. K. BETHELL,** *Major-General,*
*Commanding 66th Division.*

*Divisional Headquarters,*
*17th November, 1918.*

Field Survey Bn., R.E. 4490—1000—20-11-18.

APPENDIX XIV

6th Lancashire Fusiliers

Order No 31 18-11-18

1 The Battalion will proceed in march route to PHILIPPE VILLE on the 19-11-18 as follows

Hour of Start: 0800

Starting Point: × roads 200× E of Battn H.Q.

Order of March: Bn HQ. B - C - Drums - D - A Transport.

Route: FROID CHAPELLE - CERFONTAINE - SENZEILLE - 9 on SILENRIEUX - PHILIPPEVILLE Road.

Distances: 10× between Coys 50× between Battalions. Transport 20× in rear of Battn. 20× between each 12 vehicles

2 Dress: Marching Order, jerkins will be carried rolled on top of the pack. S.B.R under left arm + on top of jerkin.

3 Lieut P. Tyson Sgt Worwood, Cpl Stoyle, + each C.Q.M.S will leave Battn HQ at 0700 hours + proceed by cycle to × roads 200× W of PHILIPVILLE + report to Staff Captain at 0930 hours when billets for Battn will be alloted

4 Companies will be responsible for loading their own Transport and that drivers report to the Transport Officer at the Bn starting point at 0755 hours.

5 a. Brigade Report Centre on arrival Square PHILIPVILLE

b. Meeting point for supply wagons × roads 200× W of PHILIPPE VILLE

6. Midday halt will be from 11-50 to 1300 hours

7 ACKNOWLEDGE.

Signed at 2310 hours

Copies to: 1 [illegible]

J. Franks

[illegible]

APPENDIX XV

SECRET                6th LANCASHIRE FUSILIERS.                Copy No. 1

Ref. Map NAMUR, 1/100000.                ORDER No.32.                22.11.18.

---

1. The Battalion will proceed by march route to ROSEE on the 23rd November 1918 as follows:-

   Breakfast: 0515 hours.

   Hour of Start: 0715 hours.

   Starting Point: RAILWAY BRIDGE near "D" Coy billets.

   Order of March: Bn.H.Q. D. C. Drums. A. B. Transport.

   Route. PHILIPVILLE - ROSEE Road.

   Distances. 100yds between Coys. Transport 100yds in rear of the Battalion. 50yds between each 12 vehicles.

2. DRESS: MARCHING ORDER. Jerkins rolled and carried on top of the pack.

3. Company Commanders will ensure that their transport is properly loaded, and that the drivers rport to the transport Officer ready to move off at 0710 hours.

4. Lieut.P.Tyson, Sgt.Woodward, Cpl.Hoyle, and each C.Q.M.S will leave Battn.H.Q. at 0630 hours, and proceed by cycle to x roads 200 yds N.of ROSEE Church, and report to the Staff Captain, when billets will be allotted for the Battalion.

5. (a) Brigade report centre on arrival :- x roads 200 yds N.of ROSEE Church.

   (b) Meeting point for supply wagons, x roads 200 yds N of ROSEE Church.

6. Acknowledge.

J. Franks
Capt. & Adjt,
6th Lancs.Fusiliers.

Issued at 1515 hours.

Copies to 1 War Diary.
2 file.
3 A.Coy.
4 B.
5 C.
6 D.
7 H.Q.
8 T.O.
9 Q.M.
10 Spare.

R.L.

SECRET.
Ref: Map NAMUR, 1/100000.

6th Bn. LANCASHIRE FUSILIERS.

ORDER NO. 33.

Copy No

23.11.18.

APPENDIX XVI

1. The Battalion, less "A" and "D" Companies will form the Advanced Guard to the 198th Inf. Bde on the 24th Nov. 1918 as follows:-

(a) Advanced Guard, Commander: Lt. Col. R. F. GROSS. DSO.

(1) Van Guard. Commander: Capt. F. A. RIDLER, MC.
"C" Coy (less 2 platoons)
2 S.A.A. Pack mules.
1 L.G. Limber. 3 cyclists 431 Fd Coy R.E.

(2) Main Guard. Commander: Capt. I. S. RUTHERFORD.
2 platoons "C" Coy.
"B" Coy.
Bn. H.Q.
4 S.A.A. Pack Mules. ) All under
1 L.G. Limber "C" Coy. )
2 L.G. Limbers "B" Coy. ) Sgt. I. Hesketh.
2 L.G. Limbers Bn. H.Q. )

Breakfast for the Battalion: 0600 hours

Hour of start: 0830 hours

Starting Point: MORVILLE Church.

Order of March. Van Guard, Main Guard.

Route: x roads ½ mile N of M in MORVILLE - ANTHEE - HASTIERE LAVAUX.

2. Remainder of the Battalion, Commander, Major L. B. L. SECKHAM, MC.

Hour of start: 0908 hours.
Starting Point: MORVILLE Church.
Order of March: Drums, A. Coy, D. Coy, remainder of Bn. transport under the Transport Officer.

3. Dress: Marching Order, jerkins neatly rolled and carried on top of the pack.

4. 2/Lt. C. W. Jones, Sgt. Woodward, Cpl. Hoyle, and each C.Q.M.S. will leave Bn. H.Q. at 0700 hours, and proceed by cycle to 5th kilo stone on the HASTIERE - ANTHEE Road, and report to the Staff Captain, when billets will be allotted for the Battalion.

5. (a) Brigade Report Centre on arrival: HASTIERE LAVAUX Church.

(b) Meeting point for Supply Wagons: to be notified later.

6. Acknowledge.

[signature]
Capt. & Adjt,
6th Lancs. Fusiliers.

Issued at 0600 hours.

Copies to
1 War Diary.
2 File.
3 Maj. L. B. L. Seckham. MC.
4 Bn. H.Q.
5 A. Coy.
6 B. Coy.
7 C. "
8 D "
9 T.O.
10 Q.M.

[initials]

APPENDIX XVIII

# ACCOUNT OF OPERATIONS.

## PART VII.

2nd November, 1918 - 11th November, 1918.

-:-:-:-:-:-:-:-:-:-:-

PART VII.

2nd November - 11th November, 1918.

Reference Map Sheet.
57A, 1/40,000.

---

On 2nd November the Brigade marched from PREMONT to HONNECHY.

On 3rd November the march was continued to LE GATEAU, which was reached at about 18.00.

On 4th November an attack was delivered on a front of about 50 miles. The attack involved troops of the First, Thirs and Fourth British Armies and the First French Army.

XIII Corps attacked with the 25th and 50th Divisions.

66th Division was in Corps Reserve ready to go through the 25th Division and continue the advance. The Brigade marched to POMMEREUIL on the evening of the 4th November.

The attack was completely successful and on the morning of 5th November the Brigade Group, constituted as follows, moved to the valley in G.9.a and c.

198th Bde. H.Q. & No. 3 Signal Section.
6th Lancs. Fus.
5th R. Innis. Fus.
6th R. Dublin Fus.
198th L.T.M.B.
431 Field Co., R.E.

A/331 Bty., R.F.A., and a troop of 12th Lancers and 1 section, 100 M.G. Battn., joined the Brigade Group on arrival in the valley.

/As the enemy offered little

As the enemy offered little resistance to the advance of the 25th Division the 66th Division were not committed to the attack and the Brigade moved to the portion of LANDRECIES, West of the Canal on the evening of the 5th November.

Troops of 12th Lancers rejoined their Regiment early on the morning of 6th November.

On 6th November XIII Corps continued their advance with the 25th and 50th Divisions.

At 14.30 a message was received from Division that the Brigade Group would not move on the 6th. At 14.45 further orders were received for a move that evening to BASSE NOYELLES.

The conditions for the march were very bad. Traffic on the roads was hopelessly congested and it was raining hard and became very dark soon after 17.30. In spite of this all troops of the Brigade reached their billets in BASSE NOYELLES by 22.30.

On the afternoon of the following day the Brigade Group moved to DOMPIERRE. Orders were received from Division while on the march that the Brigade was to take over the front held by 7th Brigade and continue the advance as far as the AVESNES - MAUBEGE Road, at 07.00 on the 8th if this line had not already been reached by the 7th Brigade.

Orders were accordingly issued for 5th R. Innis. Fus. to take over the line held by 21st Manchesters and for 6th Lancs. Fus. to take over the Support position on the road from J.2.ccn. - J.3.d.C.O.

6th R. Dublin Fus., 198th L.T.M.B., Section 100 Bn., M.G.C., and A/331 Bty., R.F.A. remained in DOMPIERRE.

The line to be taken over by 5th R. Innis. Fus. was roughly along the road through J.10.b. J.4.d. and b. O.C., 5th R. Innis. Fus. was given instructions to use his own discretion as to taking over any posts in front of this line.

The relief was successfully carried out, but was rather delayed owing to the deviation round the demolished road bridge at DOMPIERRE STATION being so deep in mud that Lewis Guns had to be off loaded from limbers and carried forward by hand.

During the night the locationsof enemy M.G's. were reported by 5th R. Innis. Fus. Most of these were on our right flankopposite 199th Infantry Brigade. These locations were given to 199 Infantry Brigade.

At 07.30 on 4th Nov. the attack began in a thickish mist, which however soon thinned, on which enemy M.G. fire bacame considerable, particularly from the right flank; taking our advance with oblique fire. The centre and left, however, got well forward and the threat of envelopment eased the situation on the right. (This was the general tendency during the whole advance up to the AVESNES - MAUBEGE Road.)

The AVESNES - ST. AUBIN Road was the enemy's next M.G. position, and whilst this was being dealt with he brought a few guns into action.

This position was carried quickly, enveloping tactics being used where necessary, and our troops were reported entering the wood in J.6.b. and d. at 09.40.

Brigade H.Q., which had moved at 0840 to a house at J.3.d.0.3, then moved forward to TUILERIE in J.10.d. On arrival there reports were receivved from both attacking and Support Battalions that the right flank was being fired into from flank and rear, from the spur in J.12.c. and J.18.a.

/One section, 100 Bn.,

One Section, 100 Bn., M.G.C., was therefore sent up by the TUILERIE - J.6.c.cen. road to occupy the high ground and houses in J.12.a. to protect the right flank.

The left flank, which had never got touch with 150 Brigade was also reported moving forward. The reason for this lack of touch was that 150 Brigade had made an encircling movement avoiding the marshy ground in D.29. and 30.

At ~~13.40~~ 10.30 the right flank of the 199 Brigade was much held up, as the Division on their right were still fighting in the neighbourhood of LE BALDAQUIN (J.30.)

There was a certain amount of desultory fighting on the wood in J.6.b. and d., but the enemy's next line of defence was obviously the AVESNES - MAUBEGE Road . His M.G. resistance stiffened there and it was only after considerable fighting that the line of the road was gained. The enemy had mean time ceased troubling the right flank from the spur in J. 12 and 18 but was enfilading the main road badly from BASLIEU and the high ground to the E. of it. In consequence the right Company of 5th R. Innis. Fus. spread out to the right, and sent one platoon down to the houses in K.13.a. On the way they captured a lorry and an abandoned tractor and also disturbed some pioneers who were busy about the culvert in K.18.a., but unfortunately were not able to prevent them blowing the mine there. This platoon was preparing to attack the high ground E. of BAS LIEU but as the Company was already very much extended the Coy. Commander gave orders that it was not to go further S. but to engage the enemy M.G's. there with L.G. fire and so to enable the troops on our right (who were unable to advance down the Eastern slopes of the spur in J.18, and who were digging in there) to get forward. This was successful and on their arrival the Company front was shortened by withdrawing troops to the North.

/Meantime arrangements had

Meantime arrangements had been made with 199 Infantry Brigade for their Support Battalion (Connaught Rangers) to be put through as soon as 6th Lancs. Fus. were ready to advance from the AVESNES - MAUBEGE Road. It was further arranged that Connaughts should start as soon as 6th Lancs. Fus. reported ready and that 6th Lancs. Fus. should be launched ½ hour later, as 6th Connaughts had further to go, being assembled near the TUILERIE.

At 12.55 the success signal went up from the left Co. of 5th R. Innis. Fus. who had been having some trouble with M.G. nests round the road junction TROIS PAVES (E.25.d.)

6th Lancs. Fus. then moved forward and were prepared to advance at 14.00.

Meantime, as the situation had eased somewhat on the right it was arranged that Connaughts should start at once (13.20). Moving round through K.7.c. and d. with the intention of seizing high ground in K.9 and 10 and so threatening the retreat of the enemy in AVESNES, who were still holding out, 6th Lancs. Fus. meanwhile going for their final objective which included the high ground in K.3. and 4.

Enemy resistance had, however, stiffened considerably. The 200th Jaeger Division fighting well and placing their M.G's., of which they had a great number, with considerable skill.

The short day was also a disadvantage as by 16.30 what with lack of light and mist it was impossible to locate friend or foe with any certainty .

The chief resistance was from the road in K.3.c. and 2.b., which is sunken for most of its length, and a particularly strong concentration of M.G's. in and round LA CORNELLE.

Orders were issued for the continuation of the attack by 6th R. Dublin Fus. on the morning of 9th October at 00.00.

The advance of 199 Brigade on the right was timed to begin 45 minutes earlier in order to

/ensure the capture

ensure the capture of the high ground in K.18. and K.8. before the advance of the 6th R. Dublin Fus. was begun.

Patrols were sent out by 6th Lancs. Fus. at dawn, and it was quickly discovered that the enemy had withdrawn during the night.

6th Lancs. Fus. were accordingly instructed to continue the advance to the final objective and to push out patrols, as far as the FELLERIES - LES CROUPIAUX - BEUGNIER road.

A troop of 12th Lancers was attached to 6th Lancs. Fus. This troop patrolled well forward of the infantry, and encountered no enemy opposition.

6th Lancs. Fus. reached the final objective at 10.00.

6th R. Dublin Fus. remained in support on the AVESNES - MAUBEGE Road and 5th R. Innis. Fus. in Reserve on the AVESNES - ST. AUBAN Road in J.6.

At 17.00 the South African Brigade forming part of the Fourth Army Advanced Guard passed through the line held by 6th Lancs. Fus. and billetted in BEUGNIES.

Early on the morning of 9th November the 199 Infantry Brigade took over the Brigade front, the 18th K. L'pools. taking over the line of resistance held by 6th Lancs. Fus.

By 14.00 on 9th November the Brigade was disposed as follows :-

| | |
|---|---|
| 198th Brigade H.Q. | DOMPIERRE. |
| 6th Lancs. Fus. | ST. HILAIRE-SUR-HELPE |
| 5th R. Innis. Fus. & 198th L.T.M.B. | MAUBEGE - AVESNES Road in J.6. |
| 6th R. Dublin Fus. | DOMPIERRE (E. of the Railway). |

The Brigade disposed as above until 11.00 on the 11th November, when the armistice brought hostilities to an end.

---

## TOTAL CAPTURES, 1st Nov. - 11th Nov., 1918.

### PRISONERS.

| Off. | O.R. |
|---|---|
| 1 | 6 |

### OTHER MATERIAL.

| M.G's. | A.T. Rifle. | Motor Lorry. | Steam Engine. | G.S. Wagon. |
|---|---|---|---|---|
| 7 | 1 | 1 | 1 | 1 |

---

## TOTAL CASUALTIES, 1st Nov. - 11th Nov. 1918.

| | KILLED. | | WOUNDED. | |
|---|---|---|---|---|
| | Off. | O.R. | Off. | O.R. |
| 6th Lancs. Fus. | 1 | 5 | - | 31 |
| 5th R. Innis.Fus. | - | 6 | - | 27 |
| 6th R. Dublin F. | - | - | - | 3 |

---

VR 23 Lo 1317

CONFIDENTIAL

WAR DIARY

OF

6TH LANCASHIRE FUSILIERS

VOLUME VI

FROM 1-12-15 TO 31-12-18

W H Clay.
Major for O.C.
6th Lancashire Fusiliers

20 J.
13 ...

Instructions regarding War Diaries and Intelligence Summaries are contained in F. S. Regs., Part II. and the Staff Manual respectively. Title pages will be prepared in manuscript.

# WAR DIARY
*or*
# INTELLIGENCE SUMMARY.
*(Erase heading not required.)*

Army Form C. 2118.

| Place | Date | Hour | Summary of Events and Information | Remarks and references to Appendices |
|---|---|---|---|---|
| NEFFE | 1/12/18 | | Weather fine. The Battalion carried out training during the morning | FH |
| " | 2/12/18 | | Weather fine. Companies carried out one hours training in the morning & devoted the afternoon to bathing. | FH |
| " | 3/12/18 | | Weather fine. Companies carried out the usual training. | |
| " | 4/12/18 | | Weather fine. The Battalion carried out a Route March leaving Bn H.Q. at 0830 hours & returning to Billets at 1150 hours. | FH |
| " | 5/12/18 | | Weather fine and mild. Companies carried out the usual training. | FH |
| " | 6/12/18 | | Weather fine and mild. Companies carried out the usual training. Major L.B.L. SECKHAM M.C. visited the ROCHFORT area | FH |

D. D. & L., London, E.C. A'o3.) Wt. [illegible] 71/M2031 750,000 5/17 Sch. 52 Forms C2.10/14

Instructions regarding War Diaries and Intelligence Summaries are contained in F. S. Regs., Part II. and the Staff Manual respectively. Title pages will be prepared in manuscript.

# WAR DIARY
*or*
# INTELLIGENCE SUMMARY.
*(Erase heading not required.)*

Army Form C. 2118.

| Place | Date | Hour | Summary of Events and Information | Remarks and references to Appendices |
|---|---|---|---|---|
| NEFFE | 7/12/18 | | Weather changeable. The Battalion carried out a Route March from 0830 hours to 1400 hours. No 61374 Pte R. Pickersgill was tried by F.G.C.M. for consuming a portion of his Emergency Rations and sentenced to undergo 28 Days F.P. No 1. | J.H. |
| " " | 8/12/18 | | Weather fine and mild. Battalion resting. Divine Services were held during the day. | J.H. |
| " " | 9/12/18 | | Weather, intermittent rainfall throughout the day. Owing to the state of the weather all training was cancelled. | J.H. |
| " " | 10/12/18 | | Weather unsettled light rainfall during the afternoon. Companies carried out the usual hours training. Major L.B.L. Seckham M.C. visited the ROCHEFORT area. | J.H. |
| " " | 11/12/18 | | Weather changeable. Each company carried out a three hours Route March | J.H. |

D. D. & L. London, E.C. (A'oo) Wt. 1771/2031 750,000 5/17 Sch. 52 Forms C2118/14

Army Form C. 2118.

Instructions regarding War Diaries and Intelligence Summaries are contained in F. S. Regs., Part II. and the Staff Manual respectively. Title pages will be prepared in manuscript.

# WAR DIARY
*or*
# INTELLIGENCE SUMMARY.
*(Erase heading not required.)*

| Place | Date | Hour | Summary of Events and Information | Remarks and references to Appendices |
|---|---|---|---|---|
| NEFFE | 12/12/18 | | Weather intermittent rainfall throughout the day. | |
| | | | Training was cancelled on account of the weather. | |
| | | | An advanced party consisting of Maj L.B.L. SECKHAM. M.C. and | |
| | | | 8. O.R. proceeded to ON to take over billets for the battalion. | [initials] |
| NEFFE | 13/12/18 | | Weather changeable with rainfall at intervals. | |
| | | | Training was cancelled owing to the state of the weather. | |
| | | | Major W.H. CLAY. M.C. joined for duty and assumed duty | |
| | | | as 2nd in Command to the Battalion. | |
| | | | Bn Order No 34 and Administrative Instructions No | |
| | | | I were issued to all concerned at 1800 hours. For details | [initials] |
| | | | see APPENDIX I attached. | |
| – " – | 14/12/18 | | Weather showery. Companies devoted the day to cleaning of | |

D. D. & L., London, E.C. (A7093) Wt. W1271/M2031 750,000 5/17 Sch. 52 Forms C2118/14

Army Form C. 2118.

Instructions regarding War Diaries and Intelligence Summaries are contained in F. S. Regs., Part II. and the Staff Manual respectively. Title pages will be prepared in manuscript.

# WAR DIARY
*or*
# INTELLIGENCE SUMMARY.
*(Erase heading not required.)*

| Place | Date | Hour | Summary of Events and Information | Remarks and references to Appendices |
|---|---|---|---|---|
| NEFFE | 14/12/18 | | billets' equipment. | J.H. |
| On the move | 15/12/18 | | Weather fine. The Battalion moved to CIERGNON in accordance with Bn Order No 34 (see appendix I attached) arrived in billets at 1315 hours. Order No 35 issued to all concerned at 1700 hrs. | J.H. |
| " | 16/12/18 | | Weather showery. The Battalion moved in accordance with Bn Order No 35 (see appendix II attached) arrived in billets at ON at 1315 hours. The billets on the whole are good, but companies are scattered. | J.H. |
| " | 17/12/18 | | Weather showery. The Comdg Officer proceeded to 66th Div H.Q. at 0930 hours to take up the temporary duties of AA+QMG. Maj W.H. CLAY. M.C. assumed acting command of the Bn. | J.H. |

D. L. & L., London, E.C. (A 9051) Wt. W1771/M2031 750,000 5/17 Sch. 52 Forms C2118/14

Instructions regarding War Diaries and Intelligence Summaries are contained in F. S. Regs., Part II. and the Staff Manual respectively. Title pages will be prepared in manuscript.

# WAR DIARY
*or*
# INTELLIGENCE SUMMARY.
*(Erase heading not required.)*

Army Form C. 2118.

| Place | Date | Hour | Summary of Events and Information | Remarks and references to Appendices |
|---|---|---|---|---|
| ON | 18/12/18 | | Weather changeable. The Companies carried out Salvage Work & one hours training. | [illegible] |
| – " – | 19/12/18 | | Weather intermittent rain & snowfall throughout the day. Companies carried out Salvage Work & the usual training. The Brigade Comdr inspected the Billets of the Bn during the morning & expressed his appreciation of the arrangements in general. In the Brigade Soccer League "C" Company were defeated by the 6th Dublin Fusiliers by 3 – 0. In a friendly game "B" Coy beat "A" Coy 2 – 0. | [illegible] |
| – " – | 20/12/18 | | Weather changeable. Companies continued work on Salvage & carried out the usual hours training. | [illegible] |

Instructions regarding War Diaries and Intelligence Summaries are contained in F. S. Regs., Part II. and the Staff Manual respectively. Title pages will be prepared in manuscript.

# WAR DIARY
*or*
# INTELLIGENCE SUMMARY.
*(Erase heading not required.)*

Army Form C. 2118.

| Place | Date | Hour | Summary of Events and Information | Remarks and references to Appendices |
|---|---|---|---|---|
| ON | 21/12/18 | | Weather changeable. Companies carried out the usual training. | JH |
| " | 22/12/18 | | Weather fine during the morning, light rainfall towards evening. 19. O.R. proceeded to U.K. for demobilization | JH |
| " | 23/12/18 | | Weather very unsettled. Route march was ordered, but had to be cancelled on account of the weather. Companies carried out the usual training. | |
| | | | Capt I.S. Rutherford & 14. O.R. proceeded to U.K. | JH |
| " | 24/12/18 | | Weather fine with spells of sunshine. The battalion carried out an eight mile route march. 24. O.R. proceeded to U.K. for demobilization. | |
| " | 25/12/18 | | Weather fine, but cold. The Battalion attended Divine Service (C of E) in the Square. ON. at 1000 hours | |

D. D. & L., London, E.C. (A7005) Wt. W1771/M2031 750,000 5/17 Sch. 52 Forms C2118/14

Army Form C. 2118.

Instructions regarding War Diaries and Intelligence Summaries are contained in F. S. Regs., Part II. and the Staff Manual respectively. Title pages will be prepared in manuscript.

# WAR DIARY
*or*
# INTELLIGENCE SUMMARY.
*(Erase heading not required.)*

| Place | Date | Hour | Summary of Events and Information | Remarks and references to Appendices |
|---|---|---|---|---|
| ON | 25/12/18 | | The Comdg Officer visited the mens dinners at 1200 hours & addressed a few cheery words to all. | [illegible] |
| " | 26/12/18 | | Weather fine with spells of sunshine. 25 O.R. proceeded to U.K. for demobilization | |
| " | 27/12/18 | | Weather Intermittent rainfall throughout day. Companies carried out the usual hours training. An Officers Dance was held in the local schoolroom at 2000 hours. A large number of civilians attended & it was a great success. The Brigade Comdr inspected the transport of the battalion at 1000 hours. | [illegible] |
| " | 28/12/18 | | Weather Intermittent rainfall throughout the day. Training was cancelled on account of the inclement weather | |

D. D. & L., London, E.C. (A7001) Wt. W1771/M2031 750,000 5/17 Sch. 52 Forms C2118/4

Army Form C. 2118.

# WAR DIARY
*or*
# INTELLIGENCE SUMMARY.
*(Erase heading not required.)*

Instructions regarding War Diaries and Intelligence Summaries are contained in F. S. Regs., Part II. and the Staff Manual respectively. Title pages will be prepared in manuscript.

| Place | Date | Hour | Summary of Events and Information | Remarks and references to Appendices |
|---|---|---|---|---|
| ON | 29/12/18 | | Weather very bad - showers all day. Church parade cancelled owing to rain | |
| | 30/12/18 | | Fine day. Bn platoon competition took place. | |
| | 31/12/18 | | Weather dull but fine. Officers of the brigade gave a ball in the town hall ROCHEFORT. | |
| | | | Number sent to hospital during the month 1 officer & 39 ORs. | |
| | | | W.H. Clay Major for O.C. 6th Lancashire Fusiliers | |
| | | | 2/1/1919 | |

D. D. & L., London, E.C. (A6031) Wt. W1771 M2031 750,000 5/17 Sch. 52 Forms C2118/14

APPENDIX I

SECRET. 6th LANCASHIRE FUSILIERS. Copy No. 1.

Ref. maps. ORDER No.34. 13.12.18.
NAMUR 1/100.000
MARCHE 1/100.00.

---

1. The Battalion will march to CIERGNON on the 15.12.18, in accordance with the following time table :-

| Unit. | Date. | Break-fast. | Hour of Start. | Starting Point. | Order of March. | Route. | Remarks |
|---|---|---|---|---|---|---|---|
| Transport (less D.Coy Transport) | 15/Dec. | 0630. | 0830. | Battn. Recreat^n. Room. | | [illegible] | via DINANT. |
| Battalion, (less D.Coy & Transport) | 15/Dec. | 0630. | 0845. | Battn. H.Q. Mess. | ( Bn.H.Q. ( A-B-C. | CELLES CIERGNON. | via ANSEREMME. |
| D.Coy & Transport. | 15/Dec. | 0630. | 0900. | ANSEREMME CHURCH. | | | D.Coy will march in rear of Tpt. and act as Baggage guard. |

2. DRESS. Marching order, jerkins will be carried inside the pack. Steel helmets will be worn.

3. DISTANCES. 10 yds between Companies. 10 yds between vehicles.

4. ACKNOWLEDGE.

J. Franks
Capt & Adjt.
6th Lancs.Fusiliers.

Issued at 1800 hours.

Copies to
1 War Diary.
2 File.
3 A.Coy.
4 B.
5 C.
6 D.
Bn.H.Q.
T.O.
Q.M.
10 Spare.

Secret. 6th Lancs. Fusiliers Copy No. 1

Order No 35

1. The Battalion will proceed by march Route to ON on the 16-12-18 as follows:-

Breakfast: 07.15 hours.

Hour of Start: Transport, + 1 platoon ~~[illegible]~~ of A Coy who will act as Baggage Guard — 09.00 hrs

Battn (less Tpt + 1 platoon of A Coy) 09.20 hrs

Starting Point: Bridge 100x E of CIERGNON

Order of march: D-B-Drums-C-A-HQ.

APPENDIX II

2. Blankets, Kits & Stores will be packed on the same wagons as to-day.

3. All blankets less "D" Coy will be handed in to the Q.M at the Transport lines at 06.45 hours.

4 Dress marching order, jerkins in the pack.

J Franks
Capt Adjt
6 Lancs Fus.

15.12.18

Issued at 1700 hours
Copies to 1 War Diary
file
HQ
A
B
C
D
T.O
QM
Spare

SECRET

SECRET.

6th LANCASHIRE FUSILIERS.

ADMINISTRATIVE INSTRUCTIONS . No.1.

Issued in connection with 6th Lancashire Fusiliers ORDER No.34 dated 13.12.18.

1. Baggage to be sent forward per lorry convoy.

(a) Greatcoats neatly rolled in bundles of 10, securely tied and clearly labelled, will be handed in to the Q.M.Stores at 1400 hours 14.12.18.

(b) Bivouac sheets, Company stationery boxes, fire buckets & boxes, and any Company miscellaneous stores, will be handed in to the Q.M.Stores at 1500 hours 14.12.18.

(c) The R.S.M. will arrange to collect and hand in to the Q.M.Stores by 1530 hours 14.12.18 the following :-

All signalling stores.
Half the Bn.reserve S.A.A (77 boxes)
Sports gear.
School requisites.
Forms from the Men's Recreation Room & Officers Mess.
Orderly room boxes.

"D" Coy will send in their greatcoats & stores per returning ration limbers on 14.12.18.

2. BLANKETS.

All blankets, less "D" Coy, neatly rolled in bundles of 10 securely tied and clearly labelled, will be stacked outside the Q.M.Stores by 0645 hours 15.12.18.
The Q.M. will arrange for these blankets to be loaded.

3. TRANSPORT for the move is allotted as follows:-

(a) 2 G.S.wagons to carry 2 blankets per man, less D.Coy.
1 G.S.limber to carry 2 blankets per man for D.Coy.
Company L.G.limbers for L.Gs and officers' kits.

(b) 1 G.S.limber to carry Bn.H.Q. officer's kits.

4. TRANSPORT will report to Companies as follows:-

(a) 2 L.G. and 1 blanket limbers to "D" Coy at 1600 h. 14.12.18
These limbers with drivers and teams complete will remain with D.Coy on the night 14/15th Dec.1918, and will join the column on the morning of 15.12.18 at the road junction at 30th kilo stone on ANSERAMME - DINANT Rd.

(b) Transport allotted to remainder of the battalion, at 0715 hours 15.12.18.

5. ADVANCED PARTIES. 2/Lt.C.W.JONES.M.C., L/Cpl.J.Brown, and Company Q.M.Sergts. will leave Bn.H.Q. at 1130 hours 14.12.18 and proceed by cycle to CINERGNON and arrange billets for the battalion for the night 15/16th Dec.1918.

P.T.O.

6. GUARDS.

(a) The following guards will remain behind until relieved, when they will rejoin the battalion.

Guard of 1 N.C.O and 10 men at ANSEREMME Station.
-"- 2 N.C.O.s " 12 " " NEFFE "
-"- 1 N.C.O " 3 " " DINANT "

These guards will be rationed up to the 21st inst inclusive.

(b) The guard furnished by "D" Coy over the ANSEREMME Bridge will dismount in time to march with the Company on the 15.12.18.

Capt & Adjt,
6th Lancs. Fusiliers.

Issued at hours.

Copies to 1 War Diary.
2 File.
3 Bn.HQ.
4 A.Coy.
5 B.
6 C.
7 D.
8 Tpt.
9 Q.M.
Spare.

Army Form C. 2118.

# WAR DIARY
*or*
# ~~INTELLIGENCE SUMMARY.~~
*(Erase heading not required.)*

6th Lancashire Fus.

Instructions regarding War Diaries and Intelligence Summaries are contained in F. S. Regs., Part II. and the Staff Manual respectively. Title pages will be prepared in manuscript.

| Place | Date | Hour | Summary of Events and Information | Remarks and references to Appendices |
|---|---|---|---|---|
| ON | 1/1/19 | | The Battalion carried out a Route March from 0900 hrs to 1045 hrs. Weather fine. | |
| " | 2/1/19 | | Weather changeable. Companies carried out the usual hours training during the morning & devoted the afternoon to sports. | J.F. |
| " | 3/1/19 | | Weather changeable. Companies training as usual. 'C' Company defeated 'A' Coy 6th R.D.F. by 6 goals to love. | J.F. |
| " | 4/1/19 | | Weather intermittent rainfall throughout the day. The battalion carried out a nine mile Route march. | J.F. |
| " | 5/1/19 | | Weather changeable. The Battalion attended Divine Service in the CINEMA HALL JEUELLE at 1045 hours. | J.F. |
| " | 6/1/19 | | Weather fine but cold. Companies carried out the usual training. 2/Lt F. HORN proceeded to HAVRE + assumed the | |

P. D. & L., London, E.C. (A7033) Wt. W1 7/1 M2031 750,000 5/17 Sch. 53 Forms C2./18/14

WAR DIARY
*or*
# ~~INTELLIGENCE SUMMARY.~~

Instructions regarding War Diaries and Intelligence Summaries are contained in F. S. Regs., Part II. and the Staff Manual respectively. Title pages will be prepared in manuscript.

(*Erase heading not required.*) 6th Lancashire Fus

Army Form C. 2118.

| Place | Date | Hour | Summary of Events and Information | Remarks and references to Appendices |
|---|---|---|---|---|
| ON | 6/1/19 | | duties of Area Commandant. Lieut C. G. E. HELDER proceeded on leave to U.K. | [illegible] |
| — " — | 7/1/19 | | Weather fine with sunshine most of the day. Companies carried out a 10 mile Route March | [illegible] |
| — " — | 8/1/19 | | Weather fine with sunshine all day. Most of the battalion visited the Rugger Match played at MARCHE between the SA Bde & the Australians. | [illegible] |
| — " — | 9/1/19 | | Weather intermittent rainfall throughout day. Companies carried out the usual hours training. In the Bde League 'C' Company defeated 'C' Coy 6 R.D.F. by 4 goals to 2. | [illegible] |
| — " — | 10/1/19 | | Weather fine with sunshine most of the day. The battalion carried out a Rehearsal for Presentation of Colours at 11.00 hours. 2. O.R. proceeded to U.K. for demobilization. | [illegible] |

D. D. & L., London, E.C. (A7003) Wt. W1771/M2031 750,000 5/17 Sch. 52 Forms C2118/14

Instructions regarding War Diaries and Intelligence Summaries are contained in F. S. Regs., Part II. and the Staff Manual respectively. Title pages will be prepared in manuscript.

# WAR DIARY
*or*
# ~~INTELLIGENCE SUMMARY.~~

(Erase heading not required) 6th Lancashire Fus

Army Form C. 2118.

| Place | Date | Hour | Summary of Events and Information | Remarks and references to Appendices |
|---|---|---|---|---|
| ON | 11/1/19 | | Weather intermittent rainfall throughout the day. The Battalion carried out a 10 mile Route March. Lieut A.G.B. MANSON. 2/Lts S.D. STEPHEN. A. GRAVES. J.R. DAVIES. J. McKEECHNIE proceeded to U.K. for demobilization | |
| ON | 12/1/19 | | Weather fine. The Battalion attended Divine Service in the Square ON at 1100 hours. | |
| — · — | 13/1/19 | | Weather fine. The Battalion carried out an 8 mile route march. CAPT F FRANKS proceeded on leave to UK. | JaR |
| — · — | 14/1/19 | | Weather fine. Usual Company training | JaR |
| — · — | 15/1/19 | | Weather intermittent rainfall. Most of the Batt: visited the Association football match played at LIEGNON between the Batt: & 330th Bde RFA. Result The Batt defeated 330th Bde RFA 1-0. | JaR |

Army Form C. 2118.

# WAR DIARY
*or*
# ~~INTELLIGENCE SUMMARY.~~
(*Erase heading not required.*) 6/Lancashire Fus

Instructions regarding War Diaries and Intelligence Summaries are contained in F. S. Regs., Part II. and the Staff Manual respectively. Title pages will be prepared in manuscript.

| Place | Date | Hour | Summary of Events and Information | Remarks and references to Appendices |
|---|---|---|---|---|
| ON | 16/1/19 | | Weather fine. Usual company training | [initials] |
| ON | 17/1/19 | | Weather intermittent rainfall. Usual company training | [initials] |
| ON | 18/1/19 | | Weather fine. Coy kit inspections. | [initials] |
| ON | 19/1/19 | | Weather fine. The Battalion attended Divine Service in the Square ON at 11.00 hours. In the afternoon the following Bde league football matches were played 'A' Coy 6th LF v 'B' Coy 6th LF :- result draw 2 goals each 'C' Coy 6 Lancs Fus v 'O' Coy 5th R Innis Fus :- result 'O' Coy R.I.F won 5-1. 'D' Coy 6 Lancs Fus v 'A' Coy 6th R Dublin Fus :- result 'A' Coy R.D.F won 3-0 | [initials] |
| ON | 20/1/19 | | Weather fine. Usual Coy training. The Commanding Officer inspected 'D' Coy billetts. CAPT. C.H. POTTER. M.C. + 2/LT. W.J. MOORE + 16 O.R proceeded to U.K for demobilisation | [initials] |
| ON | 21/1/19 | | Weather fine. Usual Coy training. The Battalion boxing competition took place at the CINEMA HALL JEMELLE at 18.00 hours. Major L.B.L. SECKHAM M.C proceeded to take up Command of the 9th Glosters. | [initials] |
| ON | 22/1/19 | | Weather fine. Usual Coy training. The following Div league football match to place at ROCHEFORT. 6th Btn Lancs Fus V 5th Royal Innis Fusiliers Result 5th R.I.F won 2-0. | [initials] |

D. D. & L., London, E.C. (A7091) Wt. W1771/M2031 750,000 5/17 Sch. 52 Forms C2118/14

Instructions regarding War Diaries and Intelligence Summaries are contained in F. S. Regs., Part II. and the Staff Manual respectively. Title pages will be prepared in manuscript.

# WAR DIARY
*or*
# INTELLIGENCE ~~SUMMARY~~.
*(Erase heading not required.)*

6 Lancashire Fus

Army Form C. 2118.

| Place | Date | Hour | Summary of Events and Information | Remarks and references to Appendices |
|---|---|---|---|---|
| ON | 23/1/19 | | Weather fine & frosty. Usual Company training | JaR |
| ON | 24/1/19 | | Weather fine & frosty. Usual Company training | JaR |
| ON | 25/1/19 | | Weather fine & frosty. The Batt took part in a Bde rehearsal for the presentation of colours | JaR |
| ON | 26/1/19 | | The Batt. attended divine service in the square ON at 1100 hours. Snow fell fairly heavily during the afternoon and evening. 69 O.R. proceeded to [illegible] for demobilisation. | JaR |
| ON | 27/1/19 | | Weather fine & frosty. Usual Coy training. | JaR |
| ON | 28/1/19 | | Weather fine & frosty. Usual Coy training. Batt employed in clearing snow from the roads. 2/Lt. N.J. GIBSON proceeded on leave to UK | JaR |
| ON | 29/1/19 | | Weather fine & frosty. Usual Coy training | JaR |
| ON | 30/1/19 | | Weather fine & frosty. Usual Coy training. 'D' Coy 6 Lancs Fus. played RASC in the Bde League football – result – draw. | JaR |
| ON | 31/1/19 | | Weather fine & frosty. The Batt took part in a Bde rehearsal for the presentation of colours: | JaR |

W H Clay [illegible]
Major
Cmdg 6th Battn Lancashire Fusiliers

D. D. & L., London, E.C. (A5031) Wt. W2771/M2098 750,000 5/17 Sch. 52 Forms C2118/14

VR 25

6th Lancashire Fusiliers

War Diary

February 1919

Instructions regarding War Diaries and Intelligence Summaries are contained in F. S. Regs., Part II. and the Staff Manual respectively. Title pages will be prepared in manuscript.

# WAR DIARY
*or*
# INTELLIGENCE SUMMARY.
*(Erase heading not required.)*

Army Form C. 2118.

| Place | Date | Hour | Summary of Events and Information | Remarks and references to Appendices |
|---|---|---|---|---|
| ON | 1/3/19 | | Weather light snowfall with hard frost. Battalion employed on clearing the snow from the roads. | J.T. |
| " | 2/3/19 | | Weather, fine but cold: Sharp frost during the night: The Battalion attended Divine Service in the Cinema Hall JEMELLE at 1100 hours. Capt & Adjt F. Franks rejoined from leave in U.K. Lieut W. VALLANS proceeded to U.K on leave | J.T. |
| ON | 3/3/19 | | Weather, fine but cold. Major W.H. CLAY. M.C. attended a conference at Bde H.Q. at 1200 hours. Lt Col R.F. GROSS D.S.O. visited the battalion at 1200 hours. Lieut F. RIDLER M.C. proceeded on leave to U.K. | J.T. |
| " | 4/3/19 | | Weather, fine but cold. Companies carried out the usual hours training | J.T. |
| " | 5/3/19 | | Weather Snowfall during day. Companies training as usual | J.T. |

D. D. & L., London, E.C. A(003) Wt. W1171/M2031 750,000 5/17 Sch. 52 Forms/C2118/14

Army Form C. 2118.

# WAR DIARY
*or*
# INTELLIGENCE SUMMARY.
*(Erase heading not required.)*

Instructions regarding War Diaries and Intelligence Summaries are contained in F. S. Regs., Part II. and the Staff Manual respectively. Title pages will be prepared in manuscript.

| Place | Date | Hour | Summary of Events and Information | Remarks and references to Appendices |
|---|---|---|---|---|
| ON | 6/2/19 | | Weather - fine but cold. Training as usual | RJ. |
| | 7/2/19 | | Fine but cold. Routine as usual. Lt HELDER returned from leave to U.K. | RJ |
| | 8/2/19 | | Very cold. Companies clearing snow. | RJ |
| | 9/2/19 | | Companies clearing snow of the roads. 2/Lt CHENY returned from leave to U.K. Capt White left for Adjutants course at CAMBRIDGE. | RJ |
| | 10/2/19 | | Weather fine - very hard frost. | RJ |
| | 11/2/19 | | Very fine day. Training as usual. 2/Lt Cave-Matheson returned from leave to UK | RJ |
| | 12/2/19 | | Very fine. Lieut Col Goss D.S.O. visited the Bn at 1100 hrs. | RJ |
| | 13/2/19 | | Very fine. Training as usual. Maj Clay M.C. attended a conference at Bde HQrs with the Q.M. & Adj at 1400 hrs 2/Lt Whitehead proceeded on leave to U.K. | RJ |
| | 14/2/19 | | Weather fine - a thaw commenced during the day. Training continued as usual | RJ |
| | 15/2/19 | | Thaw continued. Training as usual | RJ |
| | 16/2/19 | | The battalion attended divine service at JEMELLE at 1030 hrs Weather fine. 2/Lt STOKER & 2/Lt GIBSON returned from leave to U.K. 2/Lt A.C. GALLAWAY proceeded on leave to UK. | RJ |
| | 17/2/19 | | Weather showery. Companies cleared ~~[struck out]~~ mud from the roads. | |

A7092). Wt. W12839/M1293 750,000. 1/17. D. D & L. Ltd. Forms/C2118/14.

Army Form C. 2118.

# WAR DIARY
*or*
# INTELLIGENCE SUMMARY.
*(Erase heading not required.)*

Instructions regarding War Diaries and Intelligence Summaries are contained in F. S. Regs., Part II. and the Staff Manual respectively. Title pages will be prepared in manuscript.

| Place | Date | Hour | Summary of Events and Information | Remarks and references to Appendices |
|---|---|---|---|---|
| ON | 18/2/19 | | Weather fine. Battalion clearing roads. | [illegible] |
| " | 19/2/19 | | Weather changeable. Battalion working as yesterday | [illegible] |
| " | 20/2/19 | | Weather fine. Sunshine most of the day. 321. O.R. proceeded to U.K. for demobilization 2/Lts Abberley & Gilson proceeded as conducting officers. Col Gross D.S.O. visited the Battalion during the day | [illegible] |
| " | 21/2/19 | | Weather fine. Routine as usual. | RJ |
| " | 22/2/19 | | Weather fine Routine as usual | RJ |
| " | 23/2/19 | | Routine as usual. | RJ |
| " | 24/2/19 | | Rain most of the day. | RJ |
| " | 25/2/19 | | Very wet. | RJ |
| " | 26/2/19 | | 21 OR's proceeded to UK for demobilization. Fine weather | RJ |
| " | 27/2/19 | | Very wet day. Routine as usual. | RJ |
| " | 28/2/19 | | Very wet. | RJ |

A7092). Wt. W12839/M1293 750,000. 1/17. D. D & L., Ltd. Forms/C2118/14.

Army Form C. 2118.

Instructions regarding War Diaries and Intelligence Summaries are contained in F. S. Regs., Part II. and the Staff Manual respectively. Title pages will be prepared in manuscript.

# WAR DIARY
*or*
# INTELLIGENCE SUMMARY.
*(Erase heading not required.)*

| Place | Date | Hour | Summary of Events and Information | Remarks and references to Appendices |
|---|---|---|---|---|
| ON. | | | Present strength of battalion 232 | |
| | | | Total admitted to hospital during February 48 | |
| | | | W H Clay<br>Major<br>for Lieut Col<br>Cmdg 6 Man Fus | |

D. D. & L., London, E.C. A5093 Wt. W1171/M2031 750,000 5/17 Sch. 52 Forms C2118/14

AMS/1325.

Subject:-Acting 2nd-in-Command
9th Bn. Glouc. Regt. (P)

66th Divn.
No.8722/A.

Headquarters,
66th Division.

With reference to your No.7834(A) of the 20th January, 1919, the appointment of Captain L.B.L. SECKHAM, M.C. 6th Lancashire Fus. as Acting 2nd-in-Command, 9th Bn. Gloucestershire Regiment, (Pioneers) is approved.

(Authority M.S./C/9536 dated 2nd February, 1919).

Headquarters,
Fourth Army.
7th February, 1919.

(Sgd) HAMILTON of DALZELL, Major,
Assistant Military Secretary to G.O.C.,
Fourth Army.

-2-

O.C.,
9th Bn. Gloucester Regt.

For information.

Major,
D.A.A.G.
66th Divn.

9.2.19.

Copy to 198th Infantry Brigade.

Appendix 2

ON. le 11 janvier 1919.

Madame la Directrice de l'Ecole des Religieuses,
ON.

---

Madame,

Cela fut un reel plaisir pour les officiers et les soldats de donner cette petite fete aux enfants de ON.

Nous autres Anglais n'oublieront jamais l'heroisme de l'armee belge a Liege au debut de la guerre; heroisme qui contribua dans une si grande mesure a sauver la France de l'invasion barbare lors de la premiere attaque. Nous nous souviendrons toujours avec une profonde sympathie des terribles souffrances du peuple belge durant ces quatre annees et demies. Nous avons combattu et nous avons souffert ensemble durant cette period terrible et maintenant que la lutte est terminee, nous autres Anglais sommes en garnison pour quelque temps en Belgique, notre Alliee, ou nous avons ete partout recus a bras ouverts. C'est peu de chose que nous pouvons faire pour temoigner notre respect et notre reconnaissance a la nation belge, mais le peu que nous faisons pour faire plaisir aux enfants de nos braves Allies, n nous le faisons de tout coeur et avec joie.

Veuillez agreer Madame,

l'assurance de mes sentiments distinguees.

WHC

Lieutenant-Colonel.

Appendix 3

# HISTORY OF REGIMENTAL FLAG
# OF
# 6th(T.) Bn.LANCASHIRE FUSILIERS.

The red material is the remnant of an old ecclesiastical flag found in a partially demolished house after the capture of LE CATEAU. The gold braid was taken from this flag and the red background was then made into squares of 21 inches x 21 inches, the gold braid being used to form "Bn.H.Q. XX" on each of these squares.

Later each Battalion was ordered to fly a Regimental flag at Battalion H.Q., red being the colour alloted by Brigade to this Battalion. It was then decided to make a Regimental flag with the Coat of Arms of LE CATEAU on one side, and"Bn.H.Q. XX" on the other.

The best of these original squares was chosen, and No. 1165 Sgt.Seery, M, assisted by No.33871 Cpl.Cohen, I, made the Coat of Arms of LE CATEAU in Blue and Gold, the Blue being made from some cotton found in a house in the town of LE CATEAU, and the Gold being taken from the regulation wound stripe.

---

## DUTY ORDER.

Rank. Initials and Name. Unit.

1. You will proceed on the ...... inst., to the Concentration Camp at .................. (to be inserted by the O.C.Unit) for conducting duty with the men returning to the U.K. as Coalminers, Demobilizers or Pivotal Men, under the terms of G.H.Q.,Circular Memorandum Nos.I and 2.

2. You will then, under orders of the O.C. Concentration Camp, proceed with a party of men to the Special Embarkation Camp at ................. (to be inserted by O.C.Unit) where you will immediately report to the Camp Commandant or his representative.

3. The latter will here allot you to the Command of or for duty with a Dispersal Draft proceeding to .............. Dispersal Station (to be inserted by O.C. Embarkation Camp).

4. On arrival at ............... Dispersal Station (to be inserted by O.C. Embarkation Camp) you will report to the Dispersal Commandant.

On completion of your duty you will be granted 14 days leave to your home and be given by the Dispersal Commandant.

(a). A warrant to your home station.

(b). A warrant from your home station to .................. (The name of the Port in ENGLAND through which the officer would return if proceeding on ordinary leave will be inserted by the O.C. Unit).

The Dispersal Commandant will stamp this order with the date on which you leave the Dispersal Station.

5. On completion of your leave, i.e., on the 14th day after the date stamped on this order by the Dispersal Commandant, you will embark on the return journey and proceed at once to your Unit in the field.

6. This Duty Order will be retained on your person throughout your journey and on return will be handed over to the O.C. your Unit. It constitutes the sole authority for all stages of your journey excepting that to and from your destination on leave as covered by the warrant referred to in para. 4.

7. For further instructions as to your duties as a Conducting Officer see overleaf.

Date ............ ....................Signature.

Appendix 6

## DUTIES OF A CONDUCTING OFFICER.

1. You are responsible for and will maintain strict discipline among all men placed under your command for each stage of the journey.

2. On arrival at the concentration camp you will report to the Camp Commandant. You will make out for your own use a Nominal Roll of all men allotted to your command for the journey to the Embarkation Camp. This will be entirely distinct from the Roll on A.F.Z.9.

You will detail definite N.C.O's for duty within your party: acting N.C.O's will be made if necessary.

You will ascertain the time and place of parade for the next day's journey and communicate it to all concerned.

3. On arrival at the Embarkation Camp you will report to the Camp Commandant: parties will then be recast into Dispersal Drafts.

If you are appointed to the command of a Dispersal Draft, you will take the following action :-

(a) Under orders issued by the Camp Commandant the following documents will be withdrawn from the men of your draft and handed into your custody :-
(i) The original copy of the Dispersal Certificate (A.F.Z.10
(ii) All three copies of the Nominal Rolls (A.F.Z.9).

(b) You will check these documents with the men of your party on parade, and report any discrepancies immediately to the Camp Commandant.
You will then sort the documents as follows into envelopes which will be provided by the Camp Commandant :-
Envelope 1. The Dispersal Certificates (A.F.Z.10).
Envelope 2. Two copies of all the Nominal Rolls (A.F.Z.9).
Envelope 3. The remaining copy of the Nominal Rolls (A.F.Z.9).

(c) You will dispose of these documents as follows :-
(i) Envelopes 1 and 3 will be handed over to the Commandant of the Dispersal Station in the U.K.
(ii) Envelope 2 will be handed over to the Embarka tion Staff when your party embarks.

4. You will instruct all men of your party that the loss en route of any demobilization documents or of any articles of their arms or equipment must be reported to you at once, and that it is absolutely to their own advantage to do so.

43J.
6 sheets

Co nfidential

W A R    D I A R Y.

6th Bn Lancas Fusiliers.

Fraom 1st March 1919    to    31st March 1919.

AM 26

Army Form C. 2118.

Instructions regarding War Diaries and Intelligence Summaries are contained in F. S. Regs., Part II. and the Staff Manual respectively. Title pages will be prepared in manuscript.

# WAR DIARY
*or*
# INTELLIGENCE SUMMARY.

*(Erase heading not required.)*

| Place | Date | Hour | Summary of Events and Information | Remarks and references to Appendices |
|---|---|---|---|---|
| ON | 1/3/19 | | Very fine. Sunshine all day. Routine as usual | [illegible] |
| " | 2/3/19 | | Fine. 2 officers & 116 O.Rs. left the Battalion, cross posted to the 16th [illegible] on the Rhine. | [illegible] |
| " | 3/3/19 | | Orders received for 198 Inf Bde Group to move to FAYS on the 4th. (Appendix 1) | [illegible] |
| " | 4/3/19 | | The Battalion moved to FAYS by lorry convoy. Weather showery. | [illegible] |
| FAYS | 5/3/19 | | Very fine day. Routine as usual | [illegible] |
| " | 6/3/19 | | Wet. Routine as usual | [illegible] |
| " | 7/3/19 | | Very fine. Routine as usual | [illegible] |
| " | 8/3/19 | | Very fine. Routine as usual. [illegible] proceeded to UK on leave | |
| " | 9/3/19 | | Showery. | |
| " | 10/3/19 | | Showery. 2/Lt Whitehead [illegible] returned from leave to UK. | |

D. D. & L., London, E.C.
(A8031) Wt. W2271/M2031 750,000 5/17 Sch. 52 Forms C2118/14

Instructions regarding War Diaries and Intelligence Summaries are contained in F. S. Regs., Part II. and the Staff Manual respectively. Title pages will be prepared in manuscript.

# WAR DIARY
*or*
# INTELLIGENCE SUMMARY.
*(Erase heading not required.)*

Army Form C. 2118.

| Place | Date | Hour | Summary of Events and Information | Remarks and references to Appendices |
|---|---|---|---|---|
| FAYS. | 11/3/19 | | Weather fine. Routine as usual. Lt Col [illegible] DSO visited the Bn | OJ |
| " | 12/3/19 | | Fine but cold. Routine as usual. | OJ |
| " | 13/3/19 | | Showery. Capt Brown RAMC left for UK demobilised. 2/Lts Abbotly & Gibson returned from leave to UK | OJ |
| " | 14/3/19 | | Very fine. Routine as usual | OJ |
| " | 15/3/19 | | Showers. [illegible] RQM O'Brien left for UK on leave | OJ |
| " | 16/3/19 | | Fine but cold. Bn attended Divine Service at [illegible] | OJ |
| " | 17/3/19 | | Fine but cold. Routine as usual | OJ |
| " | 18/3/19 | | Stormy & cold. Routine as usual | OJ. |
| " | 19/3/19 | | Fine. Routine as usual | OJ |
| " | 20/3/19 | | Showers. Lieut Col [illegible] DSO visited the Battalion | OJ |
| " | 21/3/19 | | Fine day. A party from the battalion visited Waterloo | |
| " | 22/3/19 | | Snow in the afternoon. Capt Ridler MC ~~[illegible]~~ left for U.K. for demobilisation | OJ |

D. D. & L., London, E.C. (A6094) Wt. W1771/M2031 750,000 5/17 Sch. 52 Forms C2118/14

Instructions regarding War Diaries and Intelligence Summaries are contained in F. S. Regs., Part II and the Staff Manual respectively. Title pages will be prepared in manuscript.

# WAR DIARY
*or*
# INTELLIGENCE SUMMARY.
*(Erase heading not required.)*

Army Form C. 2118.

| Place | Date | Hour | Summary of Events and Information | Remarks and references to Appendices |
|---|---|---|---|---|
| FAYS | 23/3/19 | | Fine. Routine as usual | [illegible] |
| " | 24/3/19 | | Showery. Routine as usual. | [illegible] |
| " | 25/3/19 | | Cold but fine. Lieut Col Gross visited the battalion. Brig Gen. Hunter D.S.O. M.C assumed command of 60th Div. 60th Div is now called 60th Div Cadres. | [illegible] |
| " | 26/3/19 | | Fine day. A party of 5 officers & 71 O.Rs visited the grottos of HAN-SUR-LESSE | [illegible] |
| " | 27/3/19 | | Snow all day. Routine as usual | [illegible] |
| " | 28/3/19 | | Snow – 2/Lt Gibson, Vallans & Lt Mathieson & 10 O.Rs | [illegible] |
| | | | left for UK for demobilisation. | [illegible] |
| " | 29/3/19 | | Very heavy snow. | |
| " | 30/3/19 | | More snow. Routine as usual. Battalion attended Divine Service at 1030 hrs. | [illegible] |
| " | 31/3/19 | | Very cold. Lieut Col Gross D.S.O visited the battalion. | [illegible] |

D. D. & L., London, E.C. (A[illegible].) Wt. W1771/M2031 750,000 5/17 Sch. 52 Forms C2118/14

Instructions regarding War Diaries and Intelligence Summaries are contained in F. S. Regs., Part II. and the Staff Manual respectively. Title pages will be prepared in manuscript.

# WAR DIARY
*or*
# INTELLIGENCE SUMMARY.
*(Erase heading not required.)*

Army Form C. 2118.

| Place | Date | Hour | Summary of Events and Information | Remarks and references to Appendices |
|---|---|---|---|---|
| | | | Total number of men admitted to hospital during the month 3 | GA |
| | | | [illegible] Major for Lieut Col Comdg. 6th Lan Fus | |

D. D. & L., London, E.C. (A1003) Wt. W1771/M2031 750,000 5/17 Sch. 52 Forms C2118/14

CONFIDENTIAL.

# WAR DIARY

## 6th Lancs Fusiliers.

From 1st April 1919 to 30th April 1919.

---

Instructions regarding War Diaries and Intelligence Summaries are contained in F. S. Regs., Part II. and the Staff Manual respectively. Title pages will be prepared in manuscript.

# WAR DIARY
or
# INTELLIGENCE SUMMARY.
(Erase heading not required.)

Army Form C. 2118.

6th Lancs Fusiliers

| Place | Date | Hour | Summary of Events and Information | Remarks and references to Appendices |
|---|---|---|---|---|
| FAYS Belgium | 1/4/19 | | Very fine weather - Routine as usual | OJ. |
| | 2/4/19 | | Very fine day. Major W.H. Clay M.C. & Lieut Q.M. O'Brien D.C.M. returned from leave to UK. | OJ. |
| " | 3/4/19 | | Very fine day. Routine as usual. | OJ. |
| " | 4/4/19 | | Glorious day. Bn football team beat 431 Coy R.E 2 goals to one. | OJ |
| " | 5/4/19 | | Very fine day. Routine as usual. | OJ. |
| " | 6/4/19 | | Glorious weather. Bn attended Divine Service at 0930 hrs. | OJ. |
| " | 7/4/19 | | Fine day Routine as usual | CC |
| " | 8/4/19 | | Glorious day Batt team lost to RE Signals 1–4 | CC |
| " | 9/4/19 | | Dull day Routine as usual | CC. |
| " | 10/4/19 | | Fine day Routine as usual. | CC |
| | 11/4/19 | | Fine day Batt Football Team lost to 100 Batt M. G. Coy 1-2. | CC |

D. D. & L., London, E.C. (A8001) Wt. W1771/M1031 750,000 5/17 Sch. 52 Forms/C2118/14

Instructions regarding War Diaries and Intelligence Summaries are contained in F. S. Regs., Part II. and the Staff Manual respectively. Title pages will be prepared in manuscript.

# WAR DIARY
*or*
# INTELLIGENCE SUMMARY.
*(Erase heading not required.)*

Army Form C. 2118.

| Place | Date | Hour | Summary of Events and Information | Remarks and references to Appendices |
|---|---|---|---|---|
| FAYS | 21/4/19. | | Routine as usual. | RJ. |
| " | 22/4/19 | | Fine. Routine as usual. | RJ. |
| " | 23/4/19. | | Very cold. Routine as usual. | RJ. |
| " | 24/4/19 | | Routine as usual. | RJ. |
| " | 25/4/19 | | Cold with rain. Routine as usual | RJ. |
| " | 26/4/19. | | Cold. Routine as usual. | RJ |
| " | 27/4/19. | | Divine service was held at 10.45 hrs. | RJ |
| " | 28/4/19. | | Cold & wet. Capt Franks M.C. left for HUY, where he has obtained an appointment on the staff of the Liege sub-area. | RJ. |
| " | 29/4/19 | | Orders received from 66th Div Cadres for Bn Cadre to entrain at Ciney on 1/5/19 for England via Antwerp | RJ Appendix I |
| " | 30/4/19. | | Bn stores packed ready for 1/5/19. Lt Tyson left for 207 P.O.W. Coy in No 1 Area | RJ W.H. Clay Lt Col |

D. D. & L., London, E.C. (A5001) Wt. W1771/M2031 750,000 5/17 Sch. 52 Forms/C2118/14

Army Form C. 2118.

Instructions regarding War Diaries and Intelligence Summaries are contained in F. S. Regs., Part II. and the Staff Manual respectively. Title pages will be prepared in manuscript.

# WAR DIARY
# INTELLIGENCE SUMMARY.
(*Erase heading not required.*)

| Place | Date | Hour | Summary of Events and Information | Remarks and references to Appendices |
|---|---|---|---|---|
| FAYS | 12/4/19. | | Showers. Routine as usual. | RJ |
| " | 13/4/19 | | Very wet. Routine as usual. | RJ |
| " | 14/4/19. | | Dull & cold. Lt Col Gross D.S.O. visited the battalion to say goodbye. Major Clay MC assumed command of the Bn | RJ |
| " | 15/4/19. | | Very wet. Routine as usual | RJ |
| " | 16/4/19 | | Very wet Routine as usual. Capt White returned from Adj Course in UK | RJ |
| " | 17/4/19 | | Very wet. Routine as usual. | RJ |
| " | 18/4/19. | | Glorious day. Routine as usual. Capt White left for Germany, being crossposted to 15th Bn Lan Fus. | RJ |
| " | 19/4/19 | | Very fine. Routine as usual | RJ |
| " | 20/4/19. | | Routine as usual | RJ. |

D. D. & L., London, E.C.
(A8001) Wt. W1771/M2031 750,000 5/17 Sch. 52 Forms/C2118/14

www.ingramcontent.com/pod-product-compliance
Lightning Source LLC
Chambersburg PA
CBHW080849230426
43662CB00013B/2059